Object-Oriented
Programming
with Prototypes

Günther Blaschek

Object-Oriented Programming

with Prototypes

With 93 Figures

Springer-Verlag
Berlin Heidelberg New York
London Paris Tokyo
Hong Kong Barcelona
Budapest

Günther Blaschek
Johannes-Kepler-Universität Linz
Institut für Informatik
Abt. Software
Altenbergerstraße 69
A-4040 Linz, Austria
e-Mail: gue@soft.uni-linz.ac.at

ISBN 3-540-56469-1 Springer-Verlag Berlin Heidelberg New York
ISBN 0-387-56469-1 Springer-Verlag New York Berlin Heidelberg

Library of Congress Cataloging-in-Publication Data

Blaschek, Günter, 1957-   Object-oriented programming with prototypes / Günter
Blaschek   p.   cm.   Includes bibliographical references and index.
  ISBN 3-540-56469-1 (Berlin: acid-free paper).
  ISBN 0-387-56469-1 (New York: acid-free paper)   1. Object-oriented programming
(Computer science)   I. Title. QA76.64.B53   1994 005.1'1—dc20 94-39557   CIP

© Springer-Verlag Berlin Heidelberg 1994
Printed in Germany

Cover Design: Konzept & Design, Ilvesheim
Typesetting: Camera-ready by author
Exposed by Text & Grafik B. E. S., Heidelberg
33/ 5 4 3 2 1 0 - Printed on acid-free paper

Foreword

Object-oriented programming is a popular buzzword these days. What is the reason for this popularity? Is object-oriented programming the solution to the software crisis or is it just a fad? Is it a simple evolutionary step or a radical change in software methodology? What is the central idea behind object-oriented design? Are there special applications for which object-oriented programming is particularly suited? Which object-oriented language should be used?

There is no simple answer to these questions. Although object-oriented programming was invented more than twenty years ago, we still cannot claim that we know everything about this programming technique. Many new concepts have been developed during the past decade, and new applications and implications of object-oriented programming are constantly being discovered.

This book can only try to explain the nature of object-oriented programming in as much detail as possible. It should serve three purposes. First, it is intended as an introduction to the basic concepts of object-oriented programming. Second, the book describes the concept of prototypes and explains why and how they can improve the way in which object-oriented programs are developed. Third, it introduces the programming language Omega, an object-oriented language that was designed with easy, safe and efficient software development in mind.

Object-oriented *programming* has received an enormous amount of attention, but hardly anyone is aware that programming is but the tip of the iceberg. Mastery of an object-oriented programming language does not suffice for carrying out object-oriented software development. For the effective application of this technique, the production process must start with object-oriented *design*. The quality of this design is crucial to the quality of the resulting product. Good designers use a great deal of experience and intuition during the initial phases of program development. Teaching design is therefore an extremely difficult task. It is one of the particular goals of this book to provide hints and guidelines that will help the reader to get used to *object-oriented thinking*.

This book addresses professional programmers as well as students and hobbyists. Since programs are getting more and more complex and user-friendliness is an important requirement of today's software, all groups can benefit from object-oriented techniques. The reader is expected to have experience with structured and modular programming, in particular with abstract data structures and abstract data types, since these concepts constitute the foundations on which the object-oriented principles are based. Knowledge of an object-oriented language or experience with object-oriented programming is not required, although some background information could be useful for understanding the more advanced topics.

Acknowledgements

Many people, too numerous to mention them all, have directly or indirectly contributed to the Omega programming language and this book. In particular, the following persons and institutions have greatly influenced this work.

- *Prof. Peter Rechenberg* has been my teacher and mentor since 1980. He encouraged me throughout the Omega project, read the manuscript, and pointed out many philosophical aspects of object-oriented programming.
- *Hanspeter Mössenböck* read an early version of the manuscript and made many valuable suggestions. I was not able to convince him of the benefits of pure object-oriented languages, but the discussions with him directly resulted in some sections of this book.
- *Christoph Reichenberger* was always helpful when I needed someone to discuss details of Omega during the development of the language. He also carefully read the manuscript and suggested many improvements.
- *Gerhard Neuer* was (besides myself) the first Omega programmer. He implemented the garbage collector and developed essential parts of the Omega library.
- *Gustav Pomberger* supported and encouraged me throughout the whole project.
- The people at *UBILAB* (in particular *Walter Bischofberger*, *Erich Gamma*, *Bruno Schäffer* and *André Weinand*) provided insight into the secrets of the application framework ET++ and were always willing to discuss various aspects of object-oriented programming.
- *Urs Hölzle* pointed out some interesting aspects of prototypes during discussions via electronic mail.
- *Angela Lahee*, *Lucy de Lancey* and *Bob Bach* polished my English and made many improvements in the style of the book.
- The *Christian Doppler Laboratory for Software Engineering* provided the financial funding for the project.
- *Gerhard Rossbach* and several other people at *Springer Verlag* enabled this manuscript to appear as a book and patiently awaited its completion.
- *Monika Scholl* helped to check the final manuscript.

I wish to thank all these persons for their cooperation.

Günther Blaschek
Linz, Austria
September 1993

Contents

1. Reader's Guide

This chapter is intended as a guide to both object-oriented programming in general and this book in particular. The first part contains a couple of hints about how to learn object-oriented programming. The second part explains the conventions used in this book and gives a survey of its contents.

1.1   Learning Object-Oriented Programming

Only a few concepts are necessary to understand the essence of object-oriented programming. It is much harder to learn to apply these concepts to software projects. I would like to clarify from the very beginning that it can take years to become an experienced object-oriented programmer. This section is intended for the novice. Its purpose is to outline several ways in which object-oriented programming can be learned.

It is, of course, possible to learn object-oriented programming by simply doing it and acquiring experience over several years. This is the way in which most programmers start using object-oriented techniques. They often begin with an object-oriented extension of a conventional language (for example, C++) and try to apply the new language elements where this seems appropriate. This is, however, a rather painful way of learning that is characterized by trial and error. Experience shows that programmers who try to learn object-oriented programming often hesitate to use objects because they do not know enough about the underlying concepts.

I would therefore suggest starting with a sound theoretical basis. Once the workings of object-oriented programming and its consequences on program development have been understood, it becomes possible to apply this technique to any project. The concepts of object-oriented programming can be summarized in a few sentences, but there is much more to know in order to apply this technique effectively. The first part of this book (in particular, Chapter 2 *Principles of Object-Oriented Programming*) is intended as an introduction to the idea of object-oriented programming. You should read this chapter even if you already know what object-oriented programming is because this is not only the basis for object-oriented programming but also for the remainder of the book.

Studying examples is an excellent way to get used to an object-oriented programming style. Unfortunately, a textbook can only give simple examples that show how to apply selected ideas. Although these examples are important for the understanding of certain details, it is equally important to get a complete picture by studying *real* programs. The concept of object-oriented programming is already more than twenty years old, and there are millions of object-oriented programs that can serve as examples. Compilers for object-oriented languages usually come with a more or less extensive set of examples. You should spend a couple of days browsing through these programs. Since they were written by experienced programmers, you will very likely find many interesting details in them. Before you start using an application framework or a class library, you should also take a look at the internal details to understand the underlying concepts and to get an idea of how programs can be built with the library.

Example programs are also suited for experiments. One advantage of object-oriented programming is the adaptability and extensibility of programs created with this technique. You should therefore try to modify one of these programs to see how extensions can be applied. Since most existing programs are constructed on the basis of an underlying library, you will have to understand the general concepts of the library first. By changing an existing program, you are forced to familiarize yourself with the ideas behind its design. This knowledge will certainly help you when you design your own programs.

Before you start developing your first real application, you should write a small object-oriented program that performs a simple task with a simple user interface. You will very likely make a couple of mistakes before this program performs as expected. Such setbacks cannot be avoided; you should make the best of them by recording those errors you made. This will help you to avoid them in subsequent serious projects.

Using an object-oriented programming language is relatively easy, but designing an object-oriented application can get really tough for newcomers. Even if you are already an experienced programmer, you should consider yourself a newcomer. Old habits are hard to break. Programmers who have been using conventional programming languages for many years will therefore find it particularly difficult to adapt themselves to object-oriented thinking. It is easier to overcome this barrier if you can discuss your problems with someone who already has experience with object-oriented programming.

When you find yourself thinking in object-oriented terms and when you want to reimplement all your programs with object-oriented techniques, you know that you have become a real object-oriented programmer. You will then find that object-oriented programming has more applications than you could have imagined in the beginning. In fact, object-oriented techniques are intruding into almost all areas of computer science. They are being applied to databases, real-time systems, artificial intelligence, networking software, operating systems, and much more. All over the world, experts are constantly developing new ideas that may help you solve your problems. It is therefore essential to remain up-to-date with the rapid development of object-oriented programming. There are several means to keep in touch with people working in this field. The easiest is reading journals devoted especially to object-oriented programming. There are also some conferences that are worth attending. The biggest one is *OOPSLA* (*Object-Oriented Programming: Systems, Languages and Applications*), an international conference sponsored by the Association for Computing Machinery (ACM). If you live in Europe, *ECOOP* (*European Conference on Object-Oriented Programming*) may be more convenient for you.

1.2   Conventions Used in This Book

The contents of this book are structured in several ways. Of course, it consists of chapters dedicated to certain topics. Section 1.3 gives a survey of the subsequent chapters and tells you where to find what information. If you are particularly interested in certain topics, you should read this survey first. Every chapter starts with an overview of its sections. Under each section heading, you will find a couple of questions that are answered in the respective section. Subsections (with more than two numbers) are not listed in the overview. They appear, however, in the table of contents.

Code fragments are written in a sans-serif font and indented from the left border, as shown in the following example:

```
by#0  ifTrue:
   [ by>0
      ifTrue:   [ [i<=to] whileTrue: [act doWith:i; i:=i+by] ]
      ifFalse:  [ [i>=to] whileTrue: [act doWith:i; i:=i+by] ]
   ];
```

This font is also used for code fragments within paragraphs, for example, when the text explains how the variable act is used in the above example.

New terms appear in bold at the point of their introduction; other *highlighted words and phrases* are printed in italic. Illustrations and tables are numbered sequentially within each chapter. In order to look up a particular figure, consult the index at the end of the book.

References appear in the text in square brackets. They consist of the author's last name and the year of publication, e.g., [Stroustrup 1986]. In case of multiple authorship, only the first author is listed, e.g., [Goldberg 1983]. The reference section at the end of the book lists all references in alphabetical order.

Some sections are marked with small pictures to the left of the text. These icons should help you to find certain parts of the book. For example, you can search for definitions by looking for a balloon with a pair of quotes. The following summary shows which icons are used for which purposes.

 A balloon with a pair of quotes indicates a paragraph containing one or more **definitions**. The terms or phrases defined are highlighted in bold. If a term is used before it is actually defined, the first occurrence is marked with a reference icon.

 Important **code fragments** are marked with a computer symbol. This icon is only used for sections containing code that you would typically see in real programs, not for the numerous examples that are used to explain certain aspects.

Methods are marked with a triangle and a compass. In this sense, a method is a procedure that you should perform when developing an object-oriented program. It typically consists of a sequence of steps that are meant to be executed in order. Since the term "method" has a special meaning in object-oriented nomenclature, it will not be used in the sense of this paragraph elsewhere in the remaining chapters of the book.

The signpost indicates a **guideline**. It marks sections containing a set of general rules that you should keep in mind. A guideline is less formal than a method. It doesn't tell you how to solve a particular problem, but rather gives you some background information that should help you to perform your task more effectively.

Warnings are marked with a caution road sign. A section marked with this icon contains important information that can help you to avoid errors. A warning typically describes a dangerous scenario and explains what steps you should take to circumvent such problems in the first place.

The pointing hand indicates a **hint**. Sections marked with this icon contain information that may help you to make certain decisions. Hints are typically not as significant as guidelines or warnings. Some hints only apply to a specific language and others just give you some background information that could help you to understand a certain topic.

A **reference to another section** is marked with an arrow pointing to a sheet of paper with a dog's ear. A paragraph with this icon will typically also contain a sentence telling you where to look for further information. This icon is mostly used for forward references, i.e., when a term is used before it is defined. It does not mean that you should immediately go to the indicated section. Especially if you read the book sequentially, you will probably not need to look up the definition at once. However, if you prefer to look up the section referred to, this icon will help you to find the point where you interrupted your reading.

A book marks a **suggested reading**. Paragraphs with this icon will also contain a bold reference to a book or article. You will usually find this icon where a reference to important literature about a certain topic is made. If you want to know more about this topic, the bold reference is where you should start reading.

The Yin and Yang symbol marks a **comparison** or a **rating**. A section with this icon lists advantages and disadvantages of concepts, techniques, or languages. This information should show you which possibilities exist and help you to decide which one fits your purposes.

1.3   Survey

This book contains eight chapters and two appendices. Some chapters deal with
general aspects of object-oriented programming, others cover the application of
these techniques in the Omega language, and one chapter is dedicated especially
to prototypes. The chapters are arranged in an order that suggests sequential
reading. The first chapters are more general and provide the background information needed to understand the later chapters. For example, the Omega
language is introduced in Chapter 4. Having read Chapters 2 and 3, you should
be able to understand the concepts of Omega and relate them to those of other
object-oriented languages. In the succeeding chapters, code fragments in Omega
syntax illustrate how libraries are used and what object-oriented design means.
In spite of the sequential ordering, readers with experience in object-oriented
programming may skip certain chapters and concentrate on points of interest.
The following is a brief summary of the book's contents and gives recommen-
dations on who should read which chapters and in which order.

Chapter 2 (*Principles of Object-Oriented Programming*) describes the
basics of object-oriented programming. It introduces the reader to object-
oriented terminology and describes general aspects of object-oriented programming. Interesting variants found in some languages are also discussed in
this chapter. If you are already familiar with the concepts of object-oriented
programming, you may skip this chapter or read only selected sections. It is,
however, recommended that you return to Chapter 2 later.

Chapter 3 (*Prototypes*) explains the role of prototypes in the software
development process. It shows how prototypes can be used instead of classes,
what kinds of prototypes are used in existing programming languages, how state
can be represented with prototypes, and how prototypes can be simulated in
conventional class-based object-oriented languages. This chapter is meant as an
in-depth treatment of the prototype concept. Readers with basic experience in
object-oriented programming may start reading here. Since prototypes are frequently referred to in later chapters, skipping this chapter is not recommended.

Chapter 4 (*The Programming Language Omega*) contains the language
definition of Omega, a prototype-based object-oriented language. The language
is described in detail both formally and verbally. The language features are explained along with the motivation behind them; examples enhance the explanation. You should read this chapter since the notation of Omega is used in all
subsequent examples.

Chapter 5 (*Libraries and Frameworks*) discusses the significance of
libraries and shows how existing building blocks and frameworks can be used to
construct new programs. This chapter describes general properties of libraries
from the user's point of view. Since libraries and frameworks are essential tools
for efficient software development (sometimes rated even more important than
the programming language), you should read this chapter.

Chapter 6 (*The Omega Library*) introduces an example of a library. It shows the overall structure and the most essential parts of the Omega library. Since the Omega library can be thought of as an extension of the Omega language, you should read at least the first four sections of this chapter if you want to get a complete picture of the Omega language. These sections describe the central object protocol and the basic types, which can be seen as part of the language. The remaining sections show which elements are available for the construction of interactive programs. You should read them if you want to learn more about typical Omega programming style. Since the Omega framework has been loosely modeled after similar frameworks, this chapter may also serve as an explanation of the inner working of frameworks in general.

Chapter 7 (*Object-Oriented Design*) is a brief discussion of object-oriented design. The emphasis of this chapter is on object-oriented thinking. It shows the most promising approaches to effective object-oriented software development. In order to achieve this goal, two simple methods are presented that may serve as initial guidelines for the design process. Everyone should read this chapter, especially those who are new to object-oriented programming. However, even experienced object-oriented programmers may find new ideas in this chapter.

Chapter 8 (*Final Words of Advice*) discusses some selected aspects of object-oriented programming. It explains for which problem domains object-oriented programming is most appropriate and answers some frequently asked questions. The chapter concludes with a general reflection on object-oriented programming. Read at least the first and the last sections. The sections in between are important mostly for readers who actually want to use object-oriented programming in future software projects.

2. Principles of Object-Oriented Programming

This chapter explains the ideas of object-oriented programming, defines the terms used in the subsequent chapters, and discusses various general aspects of object-oriented programming. Specific programming languages are only referred to when absolutely necessary.

2.1   What Is an Object?

The term "object" is sometimes misused as a publicity stunt because of its advertising appeal. The attribute "object-oriented" is very fashionable today. Some software developers have recognized this and consequently use this tag to show that their products conform to the state of the art. However, this attribute is often misleading and sometimes even deliberately used in a wrong sense: examples are modular software products that are now advertised as object-oriented.

The purpose of this section is to give a first impression of what object-orientedness actually means. Since the method obviously relates in some way to these mysterious things called objects, we will first try to present an informal definition of this term.

In everyday language, we use the term "object" to denote things we can see or touch. This intuitive definition apparently cannot be applied to object-oriented programming, since programming relates to abstract things that can be neither seen nor touched. Webster's Dictionary gives the following five definitions (and two others which are irrelevant):

1) what is aimed at; that toward which the mind is directed in any of its states or activities; goal; aim; ultimate purpose; end.
2) a person or thing to which action, thought, or feeling is directed.
3) anything visible or tangible; a material product or substance.
4) sight; appearance; representation.
5) in philosophy, anything that can be known or perceived by the mind.

The first definition seems appropriate in the context of object-oriented programming. However, it also applies to any other programming technique, since programs are always written with a goal in mind.

The second definition declares an object as something that is acted upon. This is almost exactly the opposite of the object-oriented point of view. As we will see later, objects are not just passive items; they can also perform actions. This definition therefore characterizes conventional programming better than object-oriented programming.

In the third definition, an object is interpreted as a material thing in the real world. Applied to programming, this means that an object could be an external thing that is represented in the computer. As we will see later, this definition is not entirely wrong, but it only partially captures what we consider to be an object. The fourth definition seems to correct this picture, as it also refers to an object as a representation.

The fifth definition appears at first to be in no way related to our understanding of object because it is explicitly restricted to philosophy. However, a minor rewording can completely change the meaning of this definition and thereby make it more suitable for our purposes: "in programming, anything that can be known or perceived by the programmer's mind".

Webster's Dictionary obviously was not written as a reference for programmers; in order to get a satisfying definition, we have to twist the words and combine several definitions. Perhaps a retrospect in history can shed more light on the nature of an object.

Object-oriented programming originated with the programming language Simula [Dahl 1966]. This language was designed as a tool for simulating processes taking place in the real world. In this sense, objects were in fact real things that were modelled in the computer. Just as real "objects" (like customers in a bank or cars in a street) can perform actions, the simulated objects also had to be able to simulate the activities of their real-world counterparts. Our first intuitive interpretation and Webster's third definition seem to be quite correct in this sense. But objects can be used for more than just simulation, as we will explore in the subsequent paragraphs.

Although the notion of objects was already introduced in Simula, nobody spoke of object-oriented programming then. Some years later, researchers at the Xerox Research Center in Palo Alto defined the language Smalltalk **[Goldberg 1983]**. They found the idea of objects so convincing that they built the whole language around this concept. Smalltalk was the first programming language to be called object-oriented. Consequently, the terms defined for this language had an immense influence on today's terminology. In Smalltalk, *everything* is an object. Wherever we use the term "data" in conventional programming, we could substitute "object" in Smalltalk. But objects are more than just data. While data only represent state, objects can also perform actions. In this sense, the equation

object = state + behavior

summarizes the essence of what an object is. In conventional programming, the activities are defined as programs and procedures acting upon data. The data are entirely passive; they are the "objects" of the program (in the sense of the second definition in Webster's Dictionary). This is best illustrated by a block diagram, as shown in Figure 2-1.

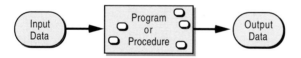

Fig. 2-1: Block diagram of a conventional program

In conventional programming, it is clearly the algorithm which is the focus of the whole program. This is indeed exemplified by many conventional problem solving strategies (e.g., stepwise refinement [Wirth 1971]). The algorithm takes input data and produces output data. In order to accomplish its task, the algorithm also uses other data internally. Data can be fairly complex and highly structured, but this is primarily seen as an additional difficulty in getting the algorithm right. The program has to deal with many sorts of data with different properties. All these differences must be taken care of in the algorithm. Needless to say, just a minor change in the data structures (such as the introduction of a new kind of data) can easily cause the whole program to break down.

In contrast, data play a central role in object-oriented programs. Different sorts of data are represented by different kinds of objects, each with its own structure and behavior. Although the objects themselves are generally quite simple, complex structures can be built by connecting objects with each other. This situation can be compared with the functioning of a car engine. The individual parts of the engine are relatively simple, but their combination and interaction results in a complex construction. There is no single algorithm that controls how the engine works. Every part must contribute in order for the whole engine to work.

Another similarity between an engine and an object-oriented program can be found in the fact that the individual parts command others to perform certain actions. For example, the engine drives a shaft, which causes the interrupter to open and close, which, in turn, sends an electric impulse to the spark plug. An interesting property of this assembly is that the individual parts are not dependent on the other parts with which they are connected. The only requirement is that two communicating parts have a common interface (shaft, cable, gear-wheel, etc.). For example, a shaft can drive mechanical breaker points or an electronic ignition. This means that the parts can be exchanged within certain limits without disabling the whole engine.

We find a similar situation in object-oriented programming. Objects have state (contact closed or open), interfaces (cable and shaft) and behavior ("send a signal to the object connected to the cable when the contact is opened"). We can think of objects as data with built-in algorithms, as depicted in Figure 2-2.

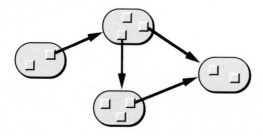

Fig. 2-2: Block diagram of an object-oriented program

Besides the fact that in object-oriented programming the algorithms are part of the objects, there is another important difference between conventional and object-oriented program structures. This difference has to do with the meaning of the arrows.

The arrows in Figure 2-1 denote the *data flow*. The algorithm actively reads the input data and produces the output data. It has to analyze the input data and must decide what to do depending on the data. This situation is similar to that of a book-keeper who deals with accounts, vouchers, bills, amounts, accounting numbers, and the like. The data processed by the book-keeper naturally determine what has to be done, but the book-keeper is completely in charge of all activities. The book-keeper actually has to decide what to do with every single piece of data.

The arrows in Figure 2-2 primarily denote the *control flow*. An object *A* commands another object *B* to carry out a certain task. In the simple case, only a plain instruction (such as "Stand up!") is needed to tell object *B* what to do. In other cases, object *B* needs further information that must be supplied by object *A*. An example of such a command is "Look up 'object' in Webster's Dictionary". In this case, object *B* must be told which word to look up and in which dictionary. We will call these additional pieces of information *arguments* in the subsequent chapters of this book. The third variation of a command requires that object *B* return the result of the operation to object *A*. An example of this case is the question "Where were you born?". Of course, such questions can also have arguments, as in "Did you see James Brown on March 12th?". The following figure summarizes these four ways of interaction between objects.

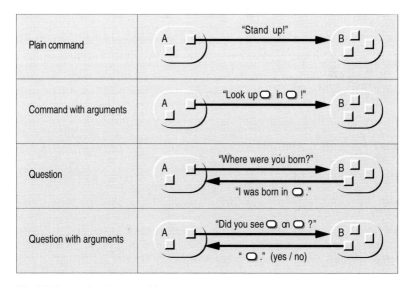

Fig. 2-3: Interactions between objects

In every dialog between two objects, one object always takes the leading part, while the other one simply performs what the commanding object requests. Such a request is called a *message* in object-oriented terminology. This is somewhat misleading because the term "message" suggests that one object merely supplies the other one with a piece of information. But since this term was introduced in Smalltalk and is widely used wherever object-oriented programming is discussed, we will also use the word message to denote such a request. According to the usual terminology, we will henceforth call the commanding object the *sender* and the other the *receiver* of a message.

In the real world, objects typically operate in parallel. For example, we would order some items from a mail-order house and go about our daily business until delivery. Such parallelism is not usual in object-oriented programming (although some languages support concurrency). Normally, the sender is suspended while the receiver is performing its task. When the receiver has finished its operation, control is returned to the sender. A message is therefore similar to a procedure call.

It is important to understand that the sender does not usually know what actions the receiver will take to accomplish its task. Such knowledge would in fact introduce an unnecessarily tight coupling between the two objects. The sender should only know how to request a particular action from the receiver, but never how the receiver will actually do it. Similarly, the receiver should never need to know the identity of the sender nor the context in which the requested task is to be performed. These strict rules guarantee that both the sender and the receiver can be replaced with other objects and that objects can be used in different environments. Information hiding is therefore a key concept of object-oriented programming that ensures reusability of objects.

Now that we know what objects are and where we can find them in the real world, it is time to demostrate how objects can be used in programs. Let's assume we have a computer with a modem that is connected to a telephone line. We want to use this modem to dial the number of a certain person, say, John Smith. Let's further assume that we already have an object that can handle such phone calls, the *phone manager*, and a string *name* containing "John Smith". The whole process would then start with some object sending the phone manager the message "Call John Smith". For the moment, it is irrelevant which object sends this initial message. We only want to see what happens as the result of the message. The following actors are involved in this play:

- *phone manager*
- *name* (a string object)
- *phone book* (contains names of persons and their phone numbers)
- *phone number* (another string object)
- *length* of the phone number (an integer object)
- *false* (a boolean object)
- *modem*

When the phone manager receives the message "Call *name*", the following dialog might take place:

- *phone manager* to the *phone book*: "Tell me the phone number of *name*".

    The phone book then looks up the *name* and returns the corresponding *phone number*. If the *name* is not registered in the phone book, an empty string is returned. In this scenario, we assume that John Smith is listed in the *phone book*, so it returns a valid number (e.g., "1234567") in response to the message.

- *phone manager* to the *phone number* (wants to know whether the number is valid): "Are you a legal phone number?"

    The *phone number* knows its *length*. All it has to do is to ask the *length* whether it is 0 or not.

    - *phone number* to its *length*: "Is your value equal to 0?"

        Since the *length* is 7, it returns *false* as the result of the query.

    The *phone number* passes the response received from its *length* (i.e., *false*) to the *phone manager*.

- *phone manager* (now knowing that the *phone number* is valid) to the *modem*: "Dial the *phone number*".

    The *modem* dials the *phone number* and returns control to the *phone manager*.

This dialog is quite typical for object-oriented programming. The phone manager doesn't know much about looking up a phone number and dialing it. It uses other objects to perform essential parts of the whole task. These objects will typically also know other objects that know how to perform certain operations. For example, the phone number asks its length to find out whether it is empty or not. The phone manager doesn't care how the phone number knows whether it is empty. It is only interested in a correct answer. Similarly, the phone book will also use many other objects to find John Smith's phone number. This part of the dialog was omitted here for the sake of brevity.

There must be certain conventions governing which messages are accepted by an object. For example, it would be useless to ask the modem object to look up a name, since the modem doesn't know anything about names. We can think of an object as an encapsulated item with a precisely defined interface. For example, the phone book would provide a set of operations for looking up names, adding new names with their associated phone numbers, determining the number of entries, removing entries, and so on. The internal structure of the phone book (i.e., how the name/number pairs are actually represented) remains hidden from the clients. Figure 2-4 shows how a phone book might look.

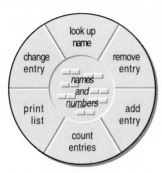

Fig. 2-4: View of a phone book object

In Figure 2-4, the services provided by a phone book object are listed around the perimeter of the object. This arrangement means that these operations can be used by clients. They constitute the interface of the object and define what messages are accepted by the object. The internal data are not accessible to clients; they can only be manipulated by means of the public operations. The structure of the internal data need not be known in order to use a phone book. For example, it is irrelevant to a client how the names and numbers are stored within a phone book. All a client needs to know is how the data can be accessed by means of the public operations. This model is similar to that of a data capsule, a module that exports only procedures and protects its internal data from unauthorized access. Objects are, however, much more powerful than modules, as we will see in the following sections.

Let us now return to the question that we asked at the beginning of this section: "What is an object?" The following enumeration summarizes the properties of objects, as far as they have already been discussed.

Objects ...
   ... are structures with *state and behavior*.
   ... *cooperate* to perform complex tasks.
   ... can communicate with each other by means of *messages*.
   ... have precise *interfaces* specifying which messages they accept.
   ... have *hidden state*.

2.2   Object-Oriented Terminology

Object-oriented programming has its own vocabulary [Wegner 1990]. We have already explained what objects are, but there are still other terms that need to be defined. This section is intended as a survey of the most important terms that are used throughout this book. Most of these terms are also used to denote other things in everyday life as well as in programming. It is therefore important to understand that they have a specific meaning in the object-oriented domain.

The definitions listed here are concise by intention. It is not the purpose of this section to explain the terms in full detail. Wherever applicable, a reference to another section is given. Since the definitions of most terms refer to other terms, circular definitions cannot be avoided. Such cross references between individual sections are marked with small arrows (➡).

2.2.1   Classes

Object-oriented programs usually operate with hundreds or thousands of objects. Many of these objects have common properties—they are of the same kind. For example, the phone book above would contain many entries, each of them with a name and a phone number (and probably also additional information such as addresses and comments). It would also be possible to have several phone books, for example, an internal directory containing all employees of a company and a separate directory containing all customers. But both phone books would have the same structure, the same interface, and the same behavior. These common properties need not be described separately for all these individual objects. Instead, we can define a **class** of objects and describe objects of this class, which ➡messages they should accept, and which ➡methods they should execute in response to these messages. The class concept is therefore an essential mechanism for the construction of object-oriented programs. Objects and classes are so closely coupled with each other that many programmers believe that object-oriented programming without classes would not be possible. We will, however, see that there are also alternate mechanisms that can be used instead of classes.

It is important to understand that objects of the same class can have different contents. For example, both "John Smith" and "James Brown" are objects of the class String, but they have different lengths and different contents. It is not always easy to decide whether two objects should be regarded as being of different classes, or whether they actually belong to the same class, but only differ in their contents. For example, the internal and the external phone book could be of the same class and only differ in that the address fields of the internal directory are always left blank, whereas all entries in the external directory have addresses associated with them. During the design of an object-oriented program, we would therefore have to ask ourselves whether the external directory is an extension of the internal directory or whether every phone directory should (at least potentially) be able to keep track of addresses. Such issues will be discussed in detail in Chapter 7 *Object-Oriented Design*.

Classes have several roles in object-oriented programming. First, we can view them as a means to identify objects with the same properties. In this sense, a class is an abstract concept that merely helps us to distinguish objects with different structure and behavior. Second, classes can also be seen as a structuring mechanism, similar to a procedure or module. This aspect is particularly important for readability and maintainability of programs because all aspects of a certain kind of objects are described in one place within a program. This locality is essential for information hiding and also helps to track down errors: If an object doesn't behave as expected, we know where to find its behavior. Third, a class is also used as a means of creating objects in many programming languages. In this sense, a class is considered an "object factory"; it "knows" how to create objects with the structure and behavior it defines.

There is a one-to-many relation between objects and their classes. Every object belongs to exactly one class, but a class may encompass many objects. If an object x is a member of class C, we say that "x is a C". We will also sometimes call x "an instance of class C". The term instance is also often used when we speak about the internal structure of objects (⇒instance variables). Please note that the terms object and instance are used differently although they evidently refer to the same thing. We use object mostly as a generic term, while we speak of instances primarily when we talk about objects of a particular class or when we want to express a relation between an object and its class ("x is an object", but "x is an instance of class C").

Another important aspect of classes is that they can be arranged hierarchically. It is possible to define a new class C1 as a specialization or extension of an already existing class C. In this case, we call C1 a ⇒subclass of C and say that C is the ⇒superclass of C1. These aspects are treated more thoroughly in Section 2.4 *Inheritance*.

2.2.2   Types

A class is similar to an abstract data type in that it defines the external interface and the behavior of its objects. There is, however, a subtle difference between classes and types. While a class is a property of *objects*, a **type** is a property of *variables* and *expressions*. In Pascal and Modula-2, we could declare VAR val:INTEGER, defining the variable val as *of the type* INTEGER. This information is important for the compiler, which needs to know what operations are intended with the variable. Wherever val appears in an expression, the compiler "knows" its type and checks whether it is used properly. Types also apply to expressions. For example, the expression FLOAT(val+1) is of the type REAL.

The type concept is only useful in *typed languages* which require variables to be explicitly associated with a particular type. If such declarations are missing from a language (as is the case in Smalltalk and Self), we speak of *untyped languages*. However, most object-oriented languages are typed. In these languages, certain compatibility rules define objects of which classes can be assigned to a variable of a certain type.

In many object-oriented languages, class names are used to identify both classes and types. For example, the name Stack can be used in C++ as a type identifier for the declaration of a variable, as in Stack * s;. In another context, the same name denotes the class, as in s=new Stack;. In the first example, Stack tells the compiler the intended use of the variable s; in the second example, it determines the structure and behavior of the object created with new.

In some object-oriented languages, classes are also called *object types*. The reader should be aware that this definition is only partially correct.

Section 2.9 *Types, Classes, and Prototypes* illustrates further aspects of types and classes. This section also explains the relation between types and ⇒prototypes.

2.3 Object References

In non-object-oriented languages, a variable x of type T is guaranteed to contain a value of type T at run time. This is no longer true in object-oriented languages because more flexible compatibility rules (see Section 2.3 *Polymorphism and Dynamic Binding*) permit the association of objects of different classes with a single variable. Since objects of different classes may also differ in size (i.e., in the amount of storage they occupy), variables cannot simply *contain* objects.

This problem is solved in object-oriented languages by means of unique *object references* that can be assigned to variables. Such a reference can be a "serial number" of the object or simply the address of the storage area occupied by the object. Figure 2-5 illustrates three different mechanisms to refer to objects.

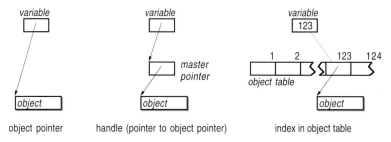

Fig. 2-5: Three possible implementations of object references

The first (and most frequently used) possibility is to store a pointer to the object in an object variable. The second method uses *handles*, which are pointers to other pointers (the *master pointers*) that finally reference the objects. The third method uses an *object table*, an array of pointers to objects. An object variable contains an object number, which is simply the index of the object in the object table.

Which of the above methods is actually used depends on the programming language and on the compiler. C++ uses object pointers, whereas many Smalltalk implementations use an object table. Master pointers are used in some Object Pascal versions.

All these techniques have one common property: An object variable never *contains* an object, but rather *refers to* an object. We therefore say that variables contain **object references**. How such references are implemented should be irrelevant for the programmer. In the subsequent sections and chapters of this book, object references will be shown in illustrations as arrows pointing from variables to objects, as if they were object pointers. You should, however, be aware that these arrows denote an abstract relation, not an implementation detail.

The fact that object variables contain references rather than objects has some important consequences:

- All references are of the same size, which in turn means that all variables are of the same size. In this way, references to objects of different classes can be assigned to the same variable. The actual size of the objects does not matter.
- An assignment x:=y does not place a copy of the object referred to by y into the variable x. Instead, only the *reference* is copied. The effect of this assignment is that both x and y refer to the same object.
- Objects do not have names. They are anonymous entities. To speak of "the object x" is therefore incorrect because the variable x might refer to a different object at a later time.
- Objects themselves can contain variables (so-called ➡instance variables). This means that relations among objects can easily be expressed by means of object references. In this way, arbitrarily complex and dynamically changing object networks can be constructed.

The semantics of object references is the source of some typical programming errors. For this reason, a separate section (Section 2.11 *Variables and References*) is devoted to the potential problems of object references.

2.2.4   Instance Variables and Class Variables

Variables can occur in several places in object-oriented programs. There can be global variables, local variables within ➡methods, and also variables within objects and classes. Variables within objects are similar to record components, whereas variables within classes can be compared with variables encapsulated in a module.

According to the usual nomenclature, variables within classes are called **class variables** and variables within objects are called **instance variables**.

These terms originate from the Smalltalk language. In Smalltalk, classes are also objects. For this reason, the term "object variable" would have been ambiguous. Thus the term *instance variable* was introduced to make it clear that these variables do not belong to the class itself, but rather to its instances. We will also sometimes refer to instance variables as **object components** or simply **components**.

The main difference between class variables and instance variables is that every single object has its own set of instance variables, whereas class variables exist only once and are shared among all instances of the class. Object variables therefore constitute an individual object's state, and class variables describe common properties of all objects of the same class. Class variables are sometimes also used for auxiliary objects that are needed by all objects of a class, but never simultaneously by more than one object.

Instance variables should be private to the object and protected against access from outside. Unfortunately, many object-oriented programming languages provide public instance variables that can be accessed and modified by clients. It must be noted that such public components violate the principle of information hiding.

2.2.5   Messages

Classes not only define the structure and the behavior of their objects, but also their interface (the set of operations provided for clients). In this sense, classes constitute abstract data types; they specify what can be done with objects and how these operations are invoked.

Objects communicate with each other by means of **messages**. A message is an abstract operation. The object is commanded to perform a certain task. In general, clients do not (and should not) know *how* the operation is performed. For example, a drawing application might tell a rectangle object rect to display itself on the screen.

There are several notations for such commands in various programming languages, but most languages use a form in which the object is specified first, followed by the name of the operation to be performed. For example, the notation rect–>display is used in C++ **[Stroustrup 1986, Ellis 1990]**, rect.display in Eiffel **[Meyer 1988]**, Object Pascal **[Schmucker 1986]** and Oberon-2 **[Mössenböck 1991, 1993]**, and rect display in Smalltalk, Self and Omega. Unless a specific programming language is discussed, the latter form will be used in the subsequent sections of this book.

The invocation of a message is called a **message send**. The object that is to perform the operation is called the **receiver** of the message.

As already explained in Section 2.1 *Object-Oriented Terminology*, messages can also take arguments and return results (see Figure 2-3). Messages returning a result (sometimes also called *function messages*) can be used within expressions. The result of such a message can then be used as the receiver of another message. For example, it is possible to ask a polygon poly to compute its enclosing rectangle and then ask the returned rectangle to compute its width. The statement w := poly boundingBox width could thus be used to compute the width of the polygon poly and assign it to the variable w.

Messages with arguments can also take different forms in various programming languages. For example, they are written like procedure calls in C++, Eiffel, Object Pascal and Oberon-2:

    phoneBook.addEntry("John Smith","1234567")

In Smalltalk, Self and Omega, such messages consist of *keywords* ending with colons, where the arguments are inserted after the colons:

    phoneBook addName: "John Smith" withNumber: "1234567"

The complete message name is "addName:withNumber:", pronounced as "add name, colon, with number, colon". The colons determine where arguments are to be inserted. Again, we will use the latter form in the remainder of this book. It has the advantage that the keywords describe the arguments that follow them.

The complete set of messages accepted by (a class of) objects is called the **protocol** of the class. The protocol of a class describes its interface; it not only defines the names of the messages but also the types of their arguments and the types of their results. We will use the following notation to specify how a message can be used:

    message without arguments and without result:
        phoneBook print
    message without arguments and with result:
        phoneBook numberOfEntries → Integer
    message with arguments and without result:
        phoneBook addName: String withNumber: String
    message with arguments and with result:
        phoneBook numberOf: String → String

We use arrows pointing to the right for the specification of the result type and insert the expected type of the argument after each keyword of a message. Messages without results are given names that express the task to be performed. They therefore usually consist of or begin with a verb. Function messages are named such that the message name expresses the result of the message. They typically consist of or begin with a noun.

The term "message" can easily be misunderstood as communication among processes executing in parallel. Although this meaning of messages appears to be quite natural, only few programming languages actually implement objects as concurrently executing processes. An example of this point of view is the Actor language [Bernat 1987].

In most object-oriented languages, messages are treated in a similar way to *procedure calls*. The main differences between a message and a procedure call are that messages always have a receiver that is responsible for execution of the operation and that the effect of a message is determined at run time by means of *dynamic binding* (see Section 2.3 *Polymorphism and Dynamic Binding*).

2.6 Methods

When an object receives a message, it reacts by executing a series of statements, an algorithm developed by the programmer. This algorithm is called a **method** in object-oriented programming.

Since all objects of a given class share the same behavior, the method to be executed for a certain message can be defined once in the class description. The method has the same name as the message to which it reacts. In some programming languages, there is no clear distinction between messages and methods; the protocol of a class is simply defined as the set of all methods implemented in the class. This is, for example, the case in Smalltalk and Self[1]. In other languages (for example, in C++ and Object Pascal), the messages are defined in an explicit class interface description, and the methods are implemented in a separate part of the source text (sometimes even in a separate compilation unit). There are also languages that allow the programmer to specify which methods should be made available as messages to clients. Examples of such languages are Eiffel and Oberon-2.

Methods are similar to procedures in conventional languages. The most important difference between a procedure and a message is that methods have an implicit parameter that represents the receiver of the message. This parameter is usually denoted by a reserved name within a method (self in Smalltalk and Object Pascal, this in C++, and Current in Eiffel). Oberon-2 is an exception to this rule; in this language, the receiver is declared as an explicit parameter that can be given an arbitrary name by the programmer. In the remainder of this book, we will use the name self to identify the receiver of a message within a method (see Section 2.5 *The Magic Word "Self"*).

Another difference between procedures and methods is that there can be (and usually are) multiple methods with the same name. Every class can have its own set of methods. It is therefore not possible to tell which method will be executed for a particular message send. At run time, the class of the receiver and the message name are used to select the proper method. This process is known as dynamic binding (see Section 2.3 *Polymorphism and Dynamic Binding*).

---

[1] Since the notion of class is unknown in Self, the protocol is defined by "slots" in the objects themselves and by slots of objects in the inheritance chain. See Section 3.2.1 *Delegation — the Self Model* for details.

2.2.7   Prototypes

Prototypes are a relatively new concept in object-oriented languages. They are, for example, used in Self and Omega *instead of classes* for the construction of objects. The structure and behavior of similar objects is not defined in a class description, but rather by the (typically interactive) construction of a prototype. Each prototype can have its own structure and set of methods, thus defining the prototype's protocol. New objects are created simply by making a copy of the prototype. Prototypes are therefore not only an abstract concept for the definition of object behavior, but also a means for instantiation of new objects.

        Section 2.9 *Types, Classes, and Prototypes* explains the relations and significant differences among classes, types, and prototypes; Chapter 3 *Prototypes* contains a detailed discussion of how prototypes are used in object-oriented programming.

2.2.8   Subclasses and Superclasses

In class-based languages, classes can be constructed by deriving a new class C1 on the basis of an already existing class C. The new class initially has all properties of the class on which it is based. New properties (instance variables, messages, and methods) can be added to C1, and certain existing properties (in particular, methods) can be changed in order to adapt the new class to specific needs. All additions and modifications only apply to the new class, but the original class C remains unchanged. Properties not defined for class C1 are automatically taken from class C. This propagation of properties is called **inheritance** in object-oriented programming (see Section 2.4 *Inheritance*).

        Inheritance not only is a means for the construction of new classes, but also defines a relation between the original class C and the new class C1 derived from C. Since C1 objects accept at least the same set of messages as C objects, they can be used wherever C objects are allowed. The most important relation in this context is the *is-a* relation: Every object of class C1 *is an* object of class C, too. This relation is transitive; i.e., when another class C1a is derived from C1, objects of this class are not only considered (special cases of) C1 objects, but also C objects.

        When several classes are derived from a single class, a tree-like hierarchy results. Figure 2-6 illustrates this hierarchy for two classes C1 and C2 derived from C and four classes C1a, C1b, C2a and C2b derived from C1 and C2.

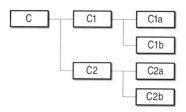

Fig. 2-6: A simple inheritance hierarchy

In such a diagram, inheritance takes place from left to right. The is-a relation can also be represented in a set diagram. Since an object of class C1a is also considered as an object of class C1 and of C, the classes can be illustrated as nested sets, as shown in Figure 2-7.

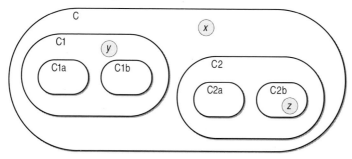

Fig. 2-7: A class hierarchy represented as a set diagram

In Figure 2-7, the gray circles labeled x, y and z denote objects of classes C, C1 and C2b, respectively. As indicated by the nested sets, object x belongs only to class C, and not to any of the other classes. Object z, however, not only belongs to class C2b, but also to C2 and to C. In set theory, we would call a set B completely contained within another set A a *subset* of A, and A would be called the *superset* of B.

In analogy to the usual set terminology, a class C1 derived from another class C is called a **subclass** of C, and C is called the **superclass** of C1. The subclass and superclass relations are transitive; i.e., a subclass C1a of C1 is also called a subclass of C1's superclass C. In this case, we would call C1a an *indirect subclass* of C, and C an *indirect superclass* of C1a. If not stated otherwise, we will subsequently always mean direct subclasses and superclasses when the terms subclass and superclass are used.

Since class names are also used to identify types, it is reasonable to extend the idea of inheritance to types as well. Wherever a hierarchy of types is discussed, we will therefore also use the terms **subtype** and **supertype**.

2.2.9   Abstract Methods and Abstract Classes

Class hierarchies can be used to describe common properties of similar yet different objects. For example, although a rectangle and a circle have different shapes, they still have many properties in common. Both rectangles and circles ...

> ... can be drawn on the screen,
> ... have a position and an extent,
> ... can be resized and moved to new positions,
> ... have a line width, fill pattern and color.

The similarity between rectangles and circles can be best expressed by arranging them in a class hierarchy such that they have a common superclass, say GraphicObject. This class will define the common properties of all things that can be drawn on the screen. All other shapes (e.g., lines, polygons, and even text) will be derived from class GraphicObject and thus inherit the instance variables, the protocol and the behavior of their superclass.

Because GraphicObject is a very general class, some operations cannot be implemented yet. For example, it is impossible to provide a general algorithm for drawing rectangles, circles, and lines. The display methods therefore must be implemented in the specific subclasses (where it is known what steps have to be taken to make the object appear on the screen). This leads to a conflict, because on the one hand we want to define the protocol of all graphic objects (including a display message), but on the other hand cannot provide proper methods for all defined messages.

The problem is solved in object-oriented programming by simply omitting methods that cannot be implemented and postponing their implementation until we really know how to implement them (i.e., in the implementation of the subclasses). When no method (or only a dummy method) exists for a given message, we speak of an **abstract method**. A class containing an abstract method is called an **abstract class**. Abstract classes are not normally used for the construction of objects. They primarily serve as an abstraction (hence the name) of several other classes. A subclass of an abstract class in which all abstract methods have finally been replaced with concrete methods (by *overriding* the abstract methods; see Section 2.3 *Polymorphism and Dynamic Binding*) is called a **concrete class**.

2.2.10   Metaclasses

In some class-based languages (in particular in Smalltalk), classes themselves are also objects. Since every object belongs to a class, class objects also belong to a class. The class of a class C is called the **metaclass** of C. Figure 2-8

illustrates the class membership relations among objects, class objects, and metaclass objects; arrows represent the *is-member-of* relation.

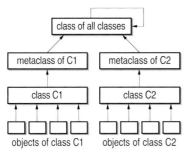

Fig. 2-8: Class membership relations between objects, classes, and metaclasses

As shown in Figure 2-8, there are usually multiple objects belonging to a given class. The class objects define the structure and behavior of the objects. Similarly, the metaclass of a class C defines the structure (i.e., the class variables) and the behavior of the class object C. Since there is only one class object for any given metaclass, the relation between classes and metaclasses is a one-to-one relation; i.e., class and metaclass objects always exist in pairs.

As metaclasses again are classes and since every class is an object, metaclasses are also objects and consequently belong to yet another class. This would lead to an infinite regression of class objects and metaclasses. This situation is avoided by means of a "class of all classes". This artificial class defines the structure and behavior of all metaclass objects (including itself).

2.2.11 Related Terms in Conventional Programming

Now that the most important terms of object-oriented programming have been defined, we will show in this section how these terms relate to the well-known terms of conventional programming. This comparison is intended to show similarities between the new terminology and the nomenclature of conventional programming techniques. Another goal of this section is to reveal the really innovative terms of object-oriented programming.

Object: There is a vague similarity between an object and a record (or structure) in conventional languages. However, objects not only contain values, but also can perform operations. There is no analogy to active objects in conventional languages.

Class: A class is similar to an *abstract data type* in conventional languages like Ada and Modula-2. However, conventional languages do not support the construction of new abstract data types from existing ones.

Type: There is no difference between types in conventional and object-oriented programming. The term *type* was simply borrowed from conventional programming.

Object reference: An object reference is similar to a *pointer*. The term *reference* is an abstraction from the actual implementation of object identification.

Instance variable: An instance variable corresponds to a *record component* (also called *record field*). The main difference between these two terms is that instance variables should (at least conceptually) be hidden from clients.

Class variable: A class variable is similar to a *global variable* in a conventional programming language. In Modula-2 and Ada, class variables can be thought of as variables encapsulated in a module or package, respectively.

Message, message send: A message send is similar to a *procedure call*. The main difference is that messages are dynamically bound (like a procedure call via a procedure variable in Modula-2 or a procedure pointer in C) and that messages are always directed to an object.

Receiver: There is no counterpart of a receiver (of a message) in conventional programming. A receiver can only be simulated with an explicit parameter of a procedure call.

Protocol: The protocol of a class is similar to a *signature* in the theory of abstract data types. Another counterpart of a protocol is an *interface description* in a modular programming language. Protocols can be found in conventional languages as definition modules in Modula-2, packages specifications in Ada, and header files in C.

Method: Methods correspond to *procedure declarations* in conventional languages. The main difference is that methods are dynamically selected at run time, whereas procedures are statically determined during compilation or linking.

Prototype: There is no term corresponding to a prototype in conventional programming. Prototypes can, however, be partially simulated with sample data structures that are copied whenever a new incarnation of such a data structure is needed.

Inheritance: Inheritance is a new concept of object-oriented programming, since it is not possible to derive new types from existing ones in conventional programming languages.

Subclass, superclass, subtype, supertype, metaclass: Since there are no inheritance relations among data types in conventional programming, these terms are unique to object-oriented programming.

2.3 Polymorphism and Dynamic Binding

In object-oriented programming, class names have two roles: They identify a class of objects (thus defining their structure and behavior) and they are used as type names in variable declarations and message specifications. According to this duality, the protocol of a class C also serves two purposes: It defines the interface of all C objects and specifies which operations are permissible with variables of the type C. For example, if class C defines the message display, all objects of the class C (and of all classes derived from C) accept the message display. This also means that the statement cv display is legal if the variable cv has been declared of type C (or of a subtype of C).

Since objects of all classes derived from C accept (at least) the messages defined in class C, it is perfectly safe to assign references to such objects to variables of type C. For example, if C1 is a subclass of C, class C1 inherits the message display from class C. Therefore, the statement cv display still has a well-defined meaning if cv currently refers to an object of class C1.

The ability of a variable to refer to objects of different classes is called **polymorphism** (Greek πολυς = many, multi-; μορφη = shape) in object-oriented programming. This feature is responsible for much of the flexibility of object-oriented programs. A piece of code containing the message send cv display will still work as expected when a reference to an object of a class other than C is assigned to the variable cv. In particular, the variable cv can refer to objects of different classes during the same execution of a program.

To allow for polymorphism, object-oriented programming languages have more flexible compatibility rules than conventional languages. According to the usual rules, the assignment x:=y is considered legal if the type Ty of the expression y is identical to the type Tx of the variable x or if Ty is a (direct or indirect) subtype of Tx. Note that the fact that expression y is of type Ty is only a *static* property of the expression. It does not mean that the evaluation of the expression will also result in a reference to an object of the class Ty. Instead, y can yield a reference to an object of a (direct or indirect) subclass of Ty. For example, y could be a variable that has been assigned a reference to such an object before. It should be clear that this does not violate the compatibility rule stated above.

It is important to understand that polymorphism is a specific feature of object-oriented programming. It is only possible because objects have "built-in" behavior; they "know" to which class they belong and how to react to messages. This is not the case in conventional programming, although some languages apparently also support assignment of different data types to a given variable. For example, consider the following Pascal code fragment:

```
VAR
    intNumber:    INTEGER;
    realNumber:   REAL;
    ...
    realNumber := intNumber
```

Although this statements looks as if an integer number were assigned to a real variable, this is *not* a polymorphic assignment. Instead, the integer value is first converted into a real number, and then the result of the conversion is assigned to the variable realNumber. The variable realNumber *always* contains a value of the data type REAL; hence it is not polymorphic.

One important application of polymorphism are *collections* — data structures containing other objects. Examples of collections are arrays, sets, lists and dictionaries (such as a phone book). Such collections are implemented as objects in pure object-oriented languages, but they can also be implemented by means of structures in hybrid languages. For example, consider the following Object Pascal code fragment:

```
VAR
    arr:    ARRAY [1..100] OF C;
    n, i:   INTEGER;
    cv:     C;
    c1v:    C1;
    c2av: C2a;
    ...
    arr[1] := cv;
    arr[2] := c1v;
    arr[3] := c2av;
    ...
    FOR i:=1 TO n DO arr[i].display;
```

Every element of the array arr represents a variable of type C. This means that each element can hold a reference to an object of class C or of any (direct or indirect) subclass of C. All three assignments in this code fragment are therefore legal. This leads to a situation in which an array contains references to objects of *different classes*. In such cases, we speak of **heterogeneous data structures**.

In the above example the FOR statement is used to display the first n elements of the array. In each successive iteration through the loop, arr[i] can refer to an object of a different class. This means that we cannot determine statically what the effect of the message arr[i].display will be. In order for this message send to work, we need a mechanism that selects the proper method at run time. This selection process is called **dynamic binding** or **late binding**.

To illustrate what dynamic binding means, let's first take a look at conventional programming languages. Some languages require that the whole program be written in a single piece of text. An example of such a language is Standard Pascal. In Standard Pascal, it is always guaranteed that the procedure to be activated by a procedure call P is contained in the same text file as the call. The result of the call can be determined *statically* by both the reader and the compiler. We therefore speak of **static binding** or **early binding** in this case because the procedure call can be bound to the statement sequence to be executed early in the construction process.

Other programming languages (for example, Ada, Modula-2, C, and many Pascal dialects) support modularization of programs. Large programs can be divided into modules (also called units or packages) in such a way that procedure calls can be separated from the procedures to be called by module boundaries. In other words, the procedure call P and the procedure P itself can be located in separate source files that are compiled separately. Most modular programming languages also allow the compilation of the procedure call at a time when the procedure itself has not yet been compiled. This means that the compiler cannot bind the call to the proper procedure since that procedure may not yet exist. The binding therefore takes place at a later time, namely when the separate modules are linked to an executable program. However, this still constitutes static binding, because the link between the procedure call and the procedure cannot be broken at run time. Whenever procedure P is called, it will activate the same statement sequence.

In object-oriented languages, not even the linker can resolve procedure calls. There must be another mechanism to find the method to be activated by a message send. We can see dynamic binding as a function that takes a message and a class as arguments and returns the method to be activated:

methodFor: MessageName withinClass: Class → Method

The methodFor:withinClass: function must be consulted *every time* when a message is sent. Since message sends are very frequent in object-oriented programs, highly efficient techniques have been developed for method lookup. We will not discuss these implementation details here, but rather describe how the lookup process works in principle.

First the class of the receiver is consulted. If a method with the desired name is found there, the selection process has already come to an end. If no matching method can be found, the process is repeated for the object's superclass, then for the superclass' superclass, and so on. In statically typed languages, a matching method will eventually be found; in dynamically typed languages, the selection process can also fail (if no matching method could be found in the whole superclass chain). These aspects will be discussed in more detail in Section 2.7 *Static and Dynamic Typing*.

2.4   Inheritance

While polymorphism and dynamic binding contribute to the flexibility of object-oriented programs, inheritance is responsible for the efficiency of the software construction process, as it allows the reuse of existing classes. In combination with polymorphism and dynamic binding, inheritance is also the reason for the adaptability of object-oriented programs.

The effect of inheritance is best explained by means of an example. Let's assume there is a class Rectangle with the following protocol.

```
Rectangle:
    width → Integer
    height → Integer
    borderWidth → Integer
    origin → Point
    width: Integer height: Integer
    moveTo: Point
    moveBy: Point
    borderWidth: Integer
    erase
    display
```

The first four messages act as queries; when a Rectangle object receives such a message, it responds by returning one of its properties. In this respect, it is irrelevant, for example, whether the object has an instance variable that holds the width, or whether it knows how to compute its width from other instance variables (e.g., the coordinates of its left and right borders). We assume that the message origin returns the top left corner of the rectangle. The result of this message is an object of type Point, of which we assume that it returns its x and y coordinates of the point when it receives the message x and y, respectively.

The next four messages (width:height:, moveTo:, moveBy:, and borderWidth:) are used to modify certain aspects of a rectangle. Note that the messages for changing and retrieving an object's attributes often occur in pairs. For example, the message borderWidth (without a colon) returns the line width that will be used when the rectangle is drawn on the screen; the message borderWidth: (with a colon) is used to modify this attribute. We will use this naming convention throughout this book, except when different message names are more appropriate, as is the case with moveTo:, moveBy: and origin. The message moveTo: interprets the argument as absolute coordinates, whereas moveBy: moves the rectangle relative to its current position. In the case of the rectangle's dimensions, we chose to use only a single message to set the dimensions of the rectangle, whereas separate messages are used to determine its width and height.

The messages erase and display are concerned with displaying the rect-angle on the screen. (For now, we will disregard window systems and assume that the rectangle can be drawn anywhere on a graphics screen). The message erase simply wipes out the entire screen area enclosed by the rectangle. The message display draws a border of a certain width within the area defined by the rectangle. The following code fragment shows how a rectangle object r can be used to draw a simple picture:

```
r width: 60 height: 20;
r moveTo: 10@10;
r borderWidth: 1;
r display;
r moveBy: (r width/2)@(r height/2);
r borderWidth: 2;
r display;
r moveBy: 20@7;
r erase;
```

We assume that vertical coordinates advance from top to bottom. As this con-vention is used in most graphics systems, we will also use it throughout this book. We furthermore assume that point objects can be constructed with the operator @. The left operand is taken as the x coordinate, and the right operand defines the y coordinate. The message r moveBy: (r width/2)@(r height/2) thus means that the rectangle r is to be moved by half its width to the right and half its height down. Figure 2-9 shows the image that is created on a gray background when the above statement sequence is executed.

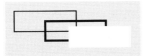

Fig. 2-9: A simple drawing with rectangles

Now that we have simple framed rectangles, we want a class that allows us to create and manipulate filled rectangles. While framed rectangles are transparent (they allow other objects to "shine through"), we want filled rectangles to be opaque. They should have the same behavior as framed rectangles, but also be allowed to the specification of their fill pattern. This means that we can define a new class FilledRectangle on the basis of Rectangle. All we have to do is to extend the interface (such that specification and determination of a rectangle's fill pattern becomes possible) and to implement the new behavior.

In general, the creation of a new class consists of two steps. First we give the new class a name and specify from which existing class it is derived. The result of this step is a class whose objects have the same interface, the same structure, and the same behavior as objects of the superclass. If we only defined the class FilledRectangle as as subclass of Rectangle, we could then create objects of this class immediately and use them wherever objects of the class Rectangle are expected.

In the second step, we define in which way the new class differs from its superclass. The following extensions and modifications are possible:

- *New messages* can be added, thus extending the *interface* of the new class. For every new message, we must also specify how objects should react when they receive the message. This means that a corresponding method must be implemented for each new message. Since messages and methods always occur in pairs, messages are defined implicitly by implementing new methods in many object-oriented programming languages.

- *New instance variables* can be added, thus extending the *structure* of objects. In many cases, objects need more "knowledge" to provide new operations. From an abstract point of view, objects of a subclass are more specialized than objects of the corresponding superclass. They not only offer more functionality, but also have more properties that must be recorded in instance variables.

- Existing *methods can be reimplemented*, thus modifying the object's *behavior*. Since such a reimplementation supersedes the inherited method that would be executed otherwise, we speak of *overriding* of methods.

The above enumeration shows *all* possible ways of modifying a subclass with respect to its superclass. It may also be useful to explain what *cannot* be changed in a subclass.

- Inherited *messages cannot be changed*. Since it should be possible to use objects of the new class wherever objects of the superclass are allowed, the newly created class must adhere to the interface of its superclass. The definitions of inherited messages (names, argument types, and result types) cannot therefore be modified[2].

- Inherited *messages cannot be removed*. Again, the reason for this restriction is the compatibility between subclass and superclass. If objects of the subclass should operate in a context that expects (at least) an object of the superclass, they must support at least the operations that are expected of objects of the superclass.

- Inherited *instance variables cannot be removed*. Some methods are typically inherited from the superclass. As these methods can (at least potentially) operate with the instance variables defined in the superclass, these instance variables must also be present in objects of subclasses.

---

[2]   Some object-oriented languages allow the redefinition of argument and result types to a limited extent. This possibility exists, for example, in Eiffel and in Omega. The rules for redefinition of a message will be discussed in Section 4.6 *Methods* in Chapter 4 on Omega.

To illustrate how inheritance and subsequent modification of a derived class works, we will now show how the class FilledRectangle can be defined and implemented on the basis of the existing class Rectangle. We begin by defining the new messages needed to set and get an object's fill pattern:

> FilledRectangle (inherits from Rectangle):
>> fillPattern → Pattern
>> fillWith: Pattern

To define the interface of the class FilledRectangle, is is not necessary to repeat the definitions of the messages inherited from Rectangle. The clause "inherits from Rectangle" is sufficient for this purpose. The fact that only the extensions are specified means that unnecessary redundancy is avoided. If the interface of the superclass is modified (for example by adding a new message), these modifications are automatically inherited by all subclasses. However, the omission of the inherited messages has the disadvantage that all superclasses must be consulted when the complete interface of a class is needed.

The second step consists of the definition of the methods for these new messages, along with the specification of the new instance variables needed for their implementation. An object of class FilledRectangle needs an additional instance variable (say, fillPat, of type Pattern) to represent the current fill pattern. The method fillPattern simply has to return the reference contained in this variable, and fillWith: has to replace fillPat with the reference passed as argument.

In the third step, we must consider which inherited methods are to be overridden. In our case, filled rectangles have a visual representation different from framed rectangles. Consequently, the method display must be overridden. All other methods can remain as they are, i.e., they can simply be inherited from class Rectangle. The following implementation shows how the method display can be implemented. The notation used here is borrowed from Omega.

```
display
[   -- first the rectangle is filled with the fill pattern,
    -- then the frame is drawn, using the overridden method
    topLeft: Point; bottomRight: Point;   -- two auxiliary points
    topLeft:=self origin;
    bottomRight:=topLeft+((self width)@(self height));
    Screen fill: topLeft@bottomRight with: fillPat;
    self (Rectangle) display
]
```

The method begins by determining the rectangle's boundaries. Two local variables topLeft and bottomRight are used temporarily to hold the coordinates of two opposite corners of the rectangle. The top left corner of the rectangle is determined by sending the message origin to self. The bottom right corner is computed by adding the dimensions of the rectangle to the top left corner. We assume here that point objects can be added with the message "+" just like numbers.

In the next step, the rectangle enclosed in these boundaries is filled with the pattern fillPat. This is usually an elementary operation supported directly by the graphics system. We assume here that an object Screen supports all these basic operations. The message fill:with: fills the screen area passed as first argument with the pattern passed as second argument. A rectangular area is constructed by means of the operator "@", which, when applied to two points, returns the rectangle between the points.

After the rectangle has been filled on the screen, the rectangle's border must be drawn. This could be done in a similar way (i.e., by calling appropriate low-level routines). However, we want to reuse as much code as possible. Since the code for displaying the border of a rectangle is already contained in the overridden display method, we only have to activate it. The message self display would activate the currently executing method, thus leading to an endless recursion. Instead, we must explicitly call the display method defined in the superclass. In Omega, such a *super call* is denoted by prefixing the message with the name of the superclass. In Smalltalk, the same message would be expressed as super display — hence the name *super call* or *super send*

In the display method shown above, we used the newly defined instance variable fillPat in the message fill:with:. The usual scope rules of object-oriented programming languages permit access to instance variables defined in class C within all methods implemented in class C. Some languages also allow access to instance variables defined in superclasses within methods of subclasses. These visibility aspects will be discussed in Section 2.6 *Information Hiding*.

The definition of FilledRectangle as a *subclass* of *class* Rectangle implicitly also defines FilledRectangle as a *subtype* of *type* Rectangle. While subclassing defines new objects, subtyping defines compatibility rules between objects and variables. In this case, a reference to an object of the class Filled-Rectangle can be assigned to a variable of the type Rectangle. For example, we could create a filled rectangle object fr, fill it with a gray pattern and assign it to the rectangle variable r:

```
fr fillWith: grayPattern;
r := fr;
```

We can now execute the statement sequence shown above for rectangles:

```
r width: 60 height: 20;
r moveTo: 10@10;
r borderWidth: 1;
r display;
```

```
r moveBy: (r width/2) @ (r height/2);
r borderWidth: 2;
r display;
r moveBy: 20@7;
r erase;
```

Now r refers to an object of class FilledRectangle. Filled rectangles accept the same messages as framed rectangles. In the case of the display message, dynamic binding now results in the activation of the new method. Figure 2-10 shows the resulting image.

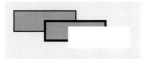

Fig. 2-10: A simple drawing with filled rectangles

Inheritance is a powerful tool for the construction of new classes. As we have seen in this simple example, the amount of code to be written can be drastically reduced by reusing methods already available in the superclass. However, inheritance must be used wisely. A sound understanding of the concept and a good deal of experience is necessary to apply this technique properly in software projects. Beginners often misinterpret the meaning of inheritance. The following mistakes, in particular, are made quite frequently:

- *Overestimation of software reuse.* For many programmers the greatest benefit of object-oriented programming lies in its reducing the amount of code to be written. In other words, they prefer implementation inheritance to interface inheritance. For example, they would derive the class Stack from class List because many operations required for stack objects (for example, extending and shortening the stack) are already implemented in class List.
- *Structure inheritance.* Sometimes new classes are based on subclasses that happen to have almost all the instance variables required for objects of the class to be developed. For example, the class Rectangle would be based on a class Point because point objects already have x and y coordinates that only need to be extended by a width and height.
- *Inheritance along a has-a relation.* New classes are often based on existing classes because objects of the new class share some properties with objects of the superclass. For example, the class Window might be derived from class Rectangle, as windows also have a rectangular shape and coordinates on the screen.

All these mistakes have one thing in common: Superclasses are chosen for the wrong reasons. This leads to unnatural inheritance relations that clients find difficult to understand and that often result in incompatibilities between related classes. It is absolutely necessary to keep the *is-a relation* in mind when looking for an appropriate superclass. In the above examples, this guideline was violated:

- A stack is not a list. Lists support more operations than stacks should provide. Because of the general operations provided by lists, it would be possible to insert new elements in the middle of a stack.
- Rectangles are not points. A point is a mathematical concept, but a rectangle is a figure that can have various visual attributes.
- Windows are not rectangles. They are not used as graphic shapes, but rather as areas that can be filled which graphic shapes.

In all three cases, a has-a relation would have been more appropriate. For example, a stack could have an instance variable of type List that holds the elements, and a window could have a rectangle describing the location and size of the window on the screen.

The implementation of a new class on top of an existing class C requires that the class C has been designed with subsequent reuse in mind. Such a design is a rather difficult task and requires much forethought. See Chapter 7 *Object-Oriented Design* for more details.

2.5   The Magic Word "Self"

Methods differ from procedures in that they are bound to objects. A method doSomething can only be activated by a message with the same name to an object that supports this message. Within the method, this object (the receiver of the message) is usually identified with a special reserved identifier. In Smalltalk, Self[3], Object Pascal and Omega, the identifier self is used for this purpose. The identifier self can be thought of as an implicit formal parameter of a method.

Methods serve several purposes. In general, they can have one or more of the following effects:

① A method can return information about the receiver's state.
② A method can modify the receiver's state.
③ A method can activate other methods of the receiver.
④ A method can send messages to other objects "known" by the receiver.

---

3   The language Self was actually named after the identifier self, as the receiver of a message plays a special role in this language.

In the first and second cases, the method must be able to access the receiver's instance variables. In the third case, it must be able to identify the receiver itself, and in the last case, the other objects must be identified. We will explore the consequences of these requirements in the subsequent sections.

Access to Instance Variables

If a method's purpose is to modify or return information about the receiver's state, we need a mechanism to access the receiver's instance variables. In most object-oriented languages, the instance variables of an object of class C can be accessed by their name within methods of class C. For example, if the location and size of Rectangle objects is stored in four integer components left, right, top, and bottom, the methods width and moveBy: can be implemented in class Rectangle in the following way:

```
width → Integer
[   -- this is an example of case ①
    ^ right – left
]

moveBy: {offset:Point}
[   -- this is an example of case ②
    left := left + offset x;
    right := right + offset x;
    top := top + offset y;
    bottom := bottom + offset y
]
```

In the first method, we used Smalltalk syntax ^x to express that the result of the expression x is to be returned as the result of the method.

Some languages (for example, Object Pascal) allow clients to access an object's instance variables as if they were record fields. For example, a client could determine the width of a rectangle r with the expression r.right–r.left. Likewise, the width of a rectangle could be incremented with r.right := r.right+1. Of course, such direct access to instance variables from outside violates the principle of information hiding. If the representation of a rectangle's state is changed in class Rectangle for some reason, the client's code is invalidated. We therefore recommend that object state be accessed only via messages.

Since the receiver of a message can be referred to by the name self within the corresponding method, the state of the receiver could also be accessed in the form self.left. The notation left is just a convenient shorthand for self.left. The explicit qualification with "self." has the advantage of making it obvious to the reader of a method that an instance variable is accessed. We will nevertheless opt for the shorter form in the subsequent examples.

Messages to the Receiver

Methods are typically very short and only perform very specific operations. They use other methods within the same class to perform part of their task. For example, the method moveTo: could be implemented in terms of the messages origin and moveBy: in the following way:

```
moveTo: {newLocation:Point}
[    -- this is an example of case ③
    self moveBy: (newLocation–self origin)
]
```

In this example, first the message origin is used to determine the current location of the rectangle. This point is subtracted from the new location, thus giving the offset by which the rectangle is to be moved. Finally, the message moveBy: is used to actually move the rectangle.

This technique is one of the reasons for the power of object-oriented programming. General operations can be implemented once in root classes — i.e., classes from which many other classes are derived. These general methods are typically independent of particular properties of the objects they operate with. For example, the moveTo: method shown above only requires that the object to be moved has some *reference point* (the location returned by the origin message) and that it supports the moveBy: message. This method would normally not be defined in every single class of graphic elements, but rather implemented just once in a common abstract superclass, say, GraphicObject. For each graphic object (be it a circle, a rectangle, a line or a polygon) the movement to a new location can be implemented with the method shown above.

When another message is sent to self within a method, dynamic binding is used to determine which method is to be executed as the result of the message. It must be emphasized that in a method of GraphicObject the identifier self can identify objects of different classes at run time. For example, consider the class hierarchy shown in Figure 2-11:

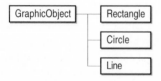

Fig. 2-11: A simple hierarchy of graphic classes

Assume that the method moveTo: is implemented in class GraphicObject. Because of the generality of the method, it need not be overridden in any of the subclasses of Image. Only the abstract methods origin and moveBy: must be implemented in most subclasses, as the locations and sizes of the various shapes will very likely be denoted by different instance variables. For example, a circle might be described by a point (the circle's center) and its radius. Consequently, the methods moveBy: and origin could be implemented as follows:

```
moveBy: {offset:Point}
[   center := center+offset
]

origin → Point
[   ^ center
]
```

If an object c of class Circle with center=20@30 receives the message moveTo:50@20, the following methods are executed:

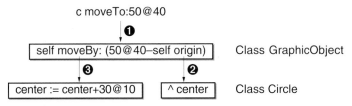

Fig. 2-12: Methods executed by messages sent to self

The message moveTo: is not found in class Circle. When it is sent to the object referenced by c, the inherited method in class GraphicObject is executed (❶). Since the identifier self still represents an object of class Circle, the messages origin and moveBy: are found in class Circle (❷, ❸). Although the method moveTo: in class GraphicObject is being executed, messages to self within this method can invoke methods defined in other classes. Since new classes can be derived from GraphicObject in the future, the effect of the execution of this method cannot be predicted.

    When writing a method of class C, one should always bear in mind that the keyword self can denote objects of subclasses of C, which may not yet exist. One should therefore never expect a particular method to be executed when sending a message to self within a method.

Messages to Other Objects

Objects of different classes normally collaborate when working on a particular task. In order to reuse as much code as possible, parts of a method's task are often *delegated* to other objects. For example, consider the message moveBy: in class Circle:

```
moveBy: {offset:Point}
[   -- this is an example of case ④
    center := center+offset
]
```

A circle is moved simply by computing the new center. The actual computation is not performed in class Circle, but rather in class Point (when the message "+" is sent to the center of the circle).

In order to send messages to other objects within a method, the other objects must somehow be "known" to the object sending the message. In most cases, the message is delegated to an object that is "owned" by the receiver. Such an ownership is found wherever an object contains a reference to another object. For example, a Circle object refers to a Point object (the circle's center). The ownership is characterized by a *has-a* relation. Where messages are concerned, the owning object is the master, and the owned object is the slave.

Messages to other objects also occur with global objects that are known to many (sometimes even all) other objects. In this case, no ownership relation exists between the sending and the receiving object. Instead, we speak of a client/server relationship. The global object provides some general services, and other objects simply use these services. In Smalltalk, class objects are global objects acting as servers. The services provided by them include the creation of new objects. As we will see later, prototypes play a similar role in Omega.

 Has-a relations, ownership, and delegation are important concepts in object-oriented programming. They can sometimes be used as an alternative to inheritance and for the implementation of dynamically changing behavior of objects. For more details on these issues, see Section 2.10 *Object Hierarchies.*

2.6 Information Hiding

The principle of information hiding has been recognized an an important means to ensure safety and integrity of software products. By information hiding we usually mean that the individual components of complex data structures should not be visible to clients. There should instead be a procedural interface defining what can be done with the data structures.

Information hiding is particularly important in object-oriented programming. Objects are often complex data structures with many components that should not be accessed by clients. There are a few reasons for such encapsulation:

- *The representation of an object is subject to changes.* It may turn out during development of a class that a different set of instance variables is better suited for the purpose of the class. If clients directly access the instance variables, they have to be modified in order to comply with the new representation.
- In contrast to records in conventional programs, *objects are not primarily used as containers* whose only purpose is to combine elementary data. Rather, the object's instance variables are used to represent the state of the object. The object itself is an *active* entity that can perform certain

operations on request. The instance variables can be considered auxiliary variables that are needed to perform these operations.

- *Objects often own other objects*. The ownership is private to the object; the relation between the object and other objects owned by it must not be disturbed by clients.
- *Objects are accessed via polymorphic references*. If an object is accessed via a variable v, the object referred to by v can change dynamically during execution of the program. We cannot be sure whether the variable v will always refer to an object with the same internal structure.

From a fundamental point of view, an object's instance variables should only be accessible from within methods in the object's class. Since the methods are part of the object, we could also say that only the object itself should be able to access its own instance variables. Such local access to the components of self is always safe, because the object "knows" its internal representation. If the representation is changed, the methods will also have to be adapted to reflect the change.

However, it is sometimes convenient to be able to access components of objects other than self. For example, consider the method "+" in class Point:

    + {other:Point} → Point
    [^ (x+other x) @ (y+other y)]

Although the argument (other) of the method "+" is known to be a Point object, we must use the messages x and y to access the other point's coordinates. Sending a message is much slower than simple access to object components. Since the addition of two points is a fairly frequent operation, we would therefore like to directly access the components x and y of the point to be added:

    + {other:Point} → Point
    [^ (x+other.x) @ (y+other.y)] [4]

Another problem arises from the fact that the structure of an object of class C is not defined exclusively in class C, but also in the superclasses of C. For example, consider the simple inheritance hierarchy shown in Figure 2-13.

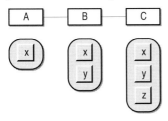

Fig. 2-13: Incremental definition of object structure

---

[4]   Note that the messages to retrieve the coordinates have the same names as the components. This is quite usual in some object-oriented programming languages.

In class A, the single component x is defined. Classes B and C inherit this component and define additional components y and z. It would be perfectly legal to access the components x and y within a method defined in class C, because the components are known to be part of a C object. However, if it later turns out that a different representation would be more appropriate in class A, the component x could be replaced with two components v and w, as illustrated in Figure 2-14.

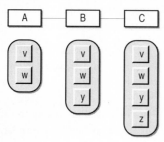

Fig. 2-14: Propagation of changes to subclasses

The "local" change to class A also affects the subclasses of A; the new components are inherited by the classes B and C. This means that all methods defined in classes B and C are invalidated if they assume the presence of the component x; all these methods have to be rewritten.

In order to avoid dependencies between classes, Smalltalk uses very restrictive access rules. An instance variable defined in class C can only be accessed from within methods implemented in class C or in subclasses of C. Clients can access instance variables only via messages. This rigid rule has the disadvantage that sometimes messages that return and modify instance variables must be provided.

Object Pascal is the other extreme. Instance variables are treated like record fields; they are accessible to everyone. This means that information hiding is not possible with objects.

In Eiffel, the visibility of components (and methods) is controlled by *export clauses*. Only exported components can be accessed by clients. Subclasses are treated differently. Methods implemented in subclasses can access all instance variables defined in all superclasses.

In Oberon-2, classes are similar to record types. They are declared within modules, where a module can contain multiple classes. Within a module, there are no access restrictions, but clients are confined to the explicitly exported components. If a subclass is implemented in the same module as its superclass, its methods have unlimited access to the components defined in the superclass. If a subclass is implemented in a separate module, only the exported components can be used. In this sense, there is no difference between clients and subclasses.

In C++, each instance variable (and method) belongs to one of three visibility categories: *Public* components are accessible to everyone, *protected* components can be accessed within the defining class and its subclasses (but not by clients), and *private* components can only be used within the defining class. In addition to these categories, C++ allows the definition of *friend classes* that are granted more rights than regular clients.

In Omega, the visibility of components (and methods) is governed similarly to C++. There are also three visibility categories (but the term *heritage* is used instead of *protected*). Omega does not support the definition of friends, but provides a means to define variables as read-only selectively for clients and heirs. Figure 2-15 shows Omega's range of visibility categories.

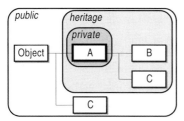

Fig. 2-15: Visibility categories for components defined in class A

An instance variable defined in class A is of course visible in methods of A. If it has the attribute *private*, it cannot be accessed from anywhere else. An instance variable with the attribute *heritage* is also visible in methods of A's heirs (in this example: B and C). *Public* instance variables can be accessed from everywhere, in particular from methods of types that are not related (with respect to inheritance) to A, such as C in this example. The following rules should give some guidance as to the circumstances under which the individual visibility categories should be used.

- *Public* instance variables should only be used for object characteristics that …
  - … are used frequently. If efficiency is not crucial, methods should be used instead to obtain the value of the instance variable.
  - … represent elementary object state (such as x and y coordinates of points). Public components should be avoided when there is no natural has-a relation in the problem domain.
  - … are not crucial for the object's integrity. For example, clients should not be allowed to modify the size of a stack explicitly.
  - … are so natural for an object that a change of the implementation is unlikely.

- The *heritage* attribute should be used in most cases. Instance variables of this category are useful for …
  - … components that are only used internally. If clients need to access them, provide a method that returns a copy of the instance variable.
  - … tightly coupled components. If there is a correspondence between two or more instance variables that has to be maintained by methods, don't make the components public.
  - … components that must be accessed by heirs in order to extend or override the object's functionality. Since it is difficult to predict which instance variables may be needed in subtypes, the heritage attribute should be used per default.
- *Private* components are useful for …
  - … components that should not be known to heirs. For example, safety-critical information (such as passwords) can be protected with this attribute. Heirs can extend the functionality, but they cannot work around the protection.
  - … auxiliary instance variables that are only used within certain methods for some particular purpose.

In general, the visibility of a component should be as narrow as possible, in order to prevent clients from unauthorized access. If in doubt, the attribute *heritage* should be used. When it turns out that clients need access to certain aspects of an object, it is usually better to introduce methods that return the required information. Public instance variables should only be used when efficiency is very important, and when the implementation of the object will not change in the future.

2.7   Static and Dynamic Typing

Some object-oriented programming languages (in particular, Smalltalk and Self) use only dynamic typing. This means that variables are only declared by their name; they are not associated with data types. For example, consider the following Smalltalk method for checking whether a point lies within the boundaries of a graphic object.

```
contains: aPoint → Boolean
    "   returns true if aPoint lies within the boundaries of the
        enclosing rectangle   "
    | extent |
    extent := self bounds.
    ^  (aPoint x >= extent left) & (aPoint x <= extent right)
    &  (aPoint y >= extent top) & (aPoint y <= extent bottom)
```

The auxiliary variable extent is declared by enclosing its name within vertical bars at the beginning of the method. The message self bounds returns the smallest rectangle that encloses the receiver. The message extent left returns the x coordinate of the enclosing rectangle. Since we know that the receiver will return an object of class Rectangle in response to the message bounds, we can be sure that the object referenced by the variable extent will accept the message left at run-time. It would, however, also be possible to assign an object of a different class to the variable extent. For example, the following fragment would be considered legal by the Smalltalk compiler:

```
| extent x |
extent := 'Hello'.
x := extent left
```

After the assignment extent := 'Hello', the variable extent refers to an object of the class String. Since strings do not understand the message left, execution of this fragment will result in a run-time error ("message not understood"). The improper use of the message left is only detected at run time when the message selection algorithm attempts to find a matching method in class String or any of its superclasses.

In order to avoid such run-time errors, most object-oriented programming languages use static typing. Variables are declared not only by giving them a name, but also by associating them with a data type. For example, the variable extent would be declared in C++ as

```
Rectangle *extent;
```

Because of this explicit declaration of extent as a variable of type (pointer to) Rectangle, the compiler can check whether the variable is used correctly. Proper usage of a variable v that has been declared as of type T means that

- Only references to "compatible" objects can be assigned to v. The term "compatibility" means in this context that the object must accept at least those messages that are defined for type T. In other words, the object must be of class T or of a (direct or indirect) subclass of T.
- Only messages defined for type T can be sent to the variable v. It must be guaranteed that (provided that v refers to a "compatible" object) the message will be accepted at run-time.

For example, the statement sequence

```
Rectangle *extent;
extent = "Hello";
x = extent->left;
```

would be illegal because the first rule is violated (Strings are not compatible with variables of type Rectangle).

In the statement sequence

```
String *extent;
extent = "Hello";
x := extent->left;
```

the second rule is violated because strings do not accept the message left. In both cases, the misuse of the variable extent can be detected by the compiler. In the first example, the compiler would reject the assignment, in the second example, the message extent->left would be marked as illegal.

Static typing enforces correct usage of variables. It ensures compatibility between the variable's *static type* (the type with which it was declared) and its *dynamic type* (the class of the object referred to by the variable at run time). The price that has to be paid for this safety is reduced flexibility. There may be many classes that support a particular message, e.g., display. If the object referred to by a variable v is to be displayed on the screen, the message v display would only be accepted by the compiler if the message display is already defined for the variable's static type. This means that there must exist a common superclass of all classes whose objects can be displayed. Even though classes in other parts of the inheritance hierarchy also may support the message display, their objects cannot be assigned to the variable v because the compatibility rules are determined by the inheritance hierarchy.

This problem is caused by different logical hierarchies. The **inheritance hierarchy** is the result of the incremental construction of classes, and the **subtype hierarchy** determines the compatibility of objects and variables. In statically typed languages, these two hierarchies are identical because subtypes and subclasses are tightly coupled. It is therefore not possible to define T2 as a subtype of T1 (because T2 extends the protocol of T1) and at the same time derive the class T2 from a different class T3 (because T2 objects have a structure and behavior similar to that of T3 objects). The difference between subtype and subclass hierarchy is irrelevant in dynamically types languages. These languages only have class hierarchies; they do not have a genuine type concept. It is therefore possible to define an abstract type hierarchy that does not correlate with the inheritance hierarchy resulting from the actual implementation.

Static typing not only ensures proper use of variables, but is also useful to define the interfaces of objects. Whenever a message with an argument is sent, an implicit assignment of the actual argument to the formal argument of the method (a local variable within the method) takes place. These assignments are also governed by the rules of static typing. For example, the message definition

```
moveBy: Point
```

guarantees that the actual argument delta of the message v moveBy:delta can only be an object of class Point (or of a subclass of Point). If the variable delta was declared with a different type, the compiler would report an error ("illegal argument"). In dynamically typed languages, the misuse of the variable delta would only be detected within the method moveBy:. Let's assume that the following Smalltalk method would be executed as the result of the moveBy: message:

```
moveBy: offset
    "move the receiver relative to its current position by offset"
    left := left + offset x.
    right := right + offset x.
    top := top + offset y.
    bottom := bottom + offset y
```

If offset refers to an object of class Color (instead of Point, as expected), the message offset x will definitely fail, since the message x doesn't make sense for colors and will therefore very likely not be implemented in class Color. This means that the program will crash because the Color object doesn't accept the message x. Many Smalltalk programmers therefore use naming conventions (e.g., aPoint) and/or explicit tests (e.g., (offset isA: Point) ifTrue: [...]) to avoid disastrous effects. As these tests have to be performed at run time, they affect the efficiency of the program.

Static typing also helps to avoid erroneous usage of expressions, even when no variables are used. In object-oriented programming, complex expressions (in which the result of one message represents the receiver of the next message) are quite frequent. For example, consider the message c bounds contains:pt, which tests whether the point pt lies in the rectangle that encloses the circle c. The message c bounds is used to determine the circle's enclosing rectangle (the so-called "bounding box"), and then the message contains:pt is sent to this rectangle. In such "chain messages", static typing can be used by the compiler to ensure their correctness. Assuming that c was declared as of type Circle, the compiler would first consult the definition of class Circle and would find that the message bounds returns (a reference to) an object of class Rectangle. Then it would find the definition of the message contains: in class Rectangle and check the actual argument's type (the static type of the variable pt) against the type of the formal argument (Point). Such extensive checks are not possible in dynamically typed languages, thus leaving the problem of ensuring integrity to the programmer.

It must also be noted that absolute safety is not possible. In particular, we need a mechanism to specify that a variable doesn't refer to an object. Usually, a special value Nil (also NIL, nil, nul, null, 0 or void) is used for this purpose. This value is implemented in different ways in various programming languages. In Eiffel, a variable always has one of two states: It either refers to an object or it is "void". In C++, a pointer variable can be assigned the value 0 (zero) which by convention does not point to any object. In Smalltalk and Omega there is a special Nil object, references to which can be assigned to *any* variable. In each of these implementations, a variable may be in a state in which it does not refer to an object of its static type (or a subtype thereof). If a message is sent to the variable, no method will be found for this message during execution of the program. Consequently, the program may crash even if static typing is being used. To avoid severe problems because of illegal Nil access, preventive steps have to be taken by the programmer, in general by explicit tests of variables (e.g., if v≠nil then ...). Some programming languages provide exception handling mechanisms that can be used to deal with such problems more conveniently.

Another frequent programming error is caused by multi-argument messages in Smalltalk. For example, assume that the width and height of a rectangle rect are to be doubled. The messages width and height can be used to determine these attributes, and the messages width: and height: can be used to change them. A straightforward solution would be the statement sequence

rect width: rect width*2.
rect height: rect height*2.

Smalltalk also provides so-called "cascaded messages" that are often used when several messages are to be sent to the same receiver, as in this example. In this case, the receiver is only specified once, and the messages are separated by semicolons:

rect
    width: rect width*2;
    height: rect height*2.

If the programmer forgets the semicolon, the compiler interprets the statement as the message width:height: to rect. If such a message is not defined in class Rectangle, the program will be aborted at run time. In Omega (which uses a similar syntax for multi-argument messages) the compiler can detect the error by means of static typing.[5]

A limitation of static typing becomes apparent when variables of different types are assigned. If the static type of the variable sub (say, T2), is a subtype of the variable super's type (say, T1), the assignment super := sub is legal. If for some reason the variable super is to be assigned to sub again, the compiler would reject the assignment because it would violate the compatibility rules. Although the variable super refers to an object of class T2, the compiler *has to* report an error, as it cannot know what the dynamic type of the variable will be during execution of the program.

Such assignments against the type hierarchy are very rare; nevertheless, they cannot always be avoided. For this reason, most object-oriented languages provide a means to tell the compiler that an assignment is safe. In C++ and Object Pascal, *type casts* are used for this purpose. The expression (T*) x

---

[5] In Self, the problem is avoided with a special syntactic rule. The first part of a multi-argument message must begin with a lower case letter, and all subsequent parts must begin with capital letters. The cascaded messaged shown here would (without the separating comma) be interpreted as two messages: first width: is sent to rect, and then height: is sent to the result of the first message.

commands the compiler to treat the variable x as if it were declared of type (pointer to) T. For example, the assignment sub = (T2*) super; would be accepted by a C++ compiler, regardless of the (static and dynamic) types of the variable super. It is, of course, the programmer's responsibility to ensure that super in fact refers to an object of class T2. If this condition is not satisfied at run time, the program may crash in an unpredictable way and could even cause serious damage. Such type casts are therefore unsafe; their use is strongly discouraged.

Other languages support better ways for assignments against the type hierarchy. For example, Oberon-2 provides *type guards* and *type tests* for this purpose. The type guard x(T) instructs the compiler to treat x as if it were declared of type T. At run time, a check is performed to see whether x really refers to an object of class T (or a subclass of T). If this is not the case, the program is aborted. In order to avoid termination of a program in unexpected (and probably critical) situations, a type test can be used to make sure that the type guard will succeed during execution of the program:

```
IF super IS T2 THEN    (* type test*)
    sub := super(T2)    (*type guard*)
ELSE
    (*error handling*)
END
```

Oberon-2 also provides a so-called *regional type guard* that also allows the programmer to discriminate between several types. Such regional type guards are used quite frequently within the Oberon system. For details, see **[Reiser 1992]**.

Omega provides a combination of Oberon's type test and type guard. It uses *conditional assignments* when the success of an assignment operation cannot be guaranteed statically. For details, see Section 4.4.2 *Dynamic Compatibility*.

2.8   Genericity

One of the most severe limitations of static typing occurs when collections of objects are to be constructed. Under such circumstances, assignments against the type hierarchy are almost inevitable. For example, consider a class DynamicArray for storing arbitrary objects with the following interface:

```
DynamicArray:
    size → Integer
    changeSize: Integer
    at: Integer put: Object
```

```
at: Integer → Object
indexOf: Object → Integer
delete: Integer
remove: Object
add: Object
...
```

Every object stored in such an array is associated with an index – an integer number ≥1. Objects are stored in the array at a certain index with the at:put: message and can be retrieved by means of the at: message. It is also possible to determine the index of an object (i.e., to search for the location of the object) with the message indexOf:. The prefix "Dynamic" means that the array can dynamically grow. Objects can be appended at the end of the array with the message add:. The message changeSize: can be used to explicitly specify how many elements the array can hold. Two messages are used to get rid of elements: delete: takes out the element at the index given as argument (thus moving all subsequent elements to the next lower index and shortening the array), and remove: takes a given element out of the array. The following message shows how the message remove: could be implemented in terms of delete:.

```
remove {element:Object}
[   index:Integer;
    index := self indexOf:element;
    index=0 ifFalse: [self delete:index]
]
```

In real class libraries, DynamicArray would be a subclass of an abstract class Collection. The superclass Collection would define a general protocol for the maintenance of collection objects, such as linear lists, arrays, and sets. Some of the messages listed in the above class definition (in particular, size, remove:, and add:) would therefore normally not be defined in class DynamicArray, but rather be inherited from its superclass.

   An object of class DynamicArray is a typical example of a *heterogeneous data structure* (see Section 2.3 *Polymorphism and Dynamic Binding*). Its elements can be objects of arbitrary (in particular: different) classes. For example, the following code fragment shows how a dynamic array with three elements can be constructed:

```
arr: DynamicArray;
pt: Point;
rect: Rectangle;
wind: Window;
```

```
arr changeSize:3;
arr at:1 put:pt;
arr at:2 put: rect;
arr at:3 put: wind;
```

After execution of this statement sequence, the array "contains" three objects of different data types. In object-oriented programming, data structures like arrays typically contain references to their elements rather than the elements themselves. When an object is put into an array, it is not duplicated. Only a reference to it is stored within the array. It is therefore not quite correct to say that "the array contains a point object." We should rather say that "the array contains a reference to a point object." We will nevertheless use the shorter form when speaking of collection objects. Figure 2-16 illustrates the effect of the above code fragment.

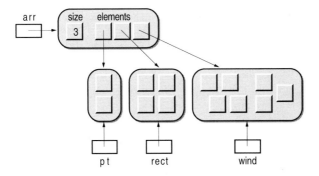

Fig. 2-16: A dynamic array with (references to) three elements

The heterogeneity of the array is indicated by the data type Object in the class definition. For example, the second argument of the message at:put: is defined as of type Object. Since Object is the most general type (at least with a single-rooted hierarchy; see Section 2.10 *Object Hierarchies*), objects of arbitrary classes can be passed as actual arguments. On the other hand, the result type Object in the definition of the message at: turns out to be a hindrance. Even though we know that the second element of the array is a rectangle, the statement rect := arr at:2 would be illegal. A type test, type guard, or a conditional assignment must be used to convince the compiler that the reference returned by the message at: is in fact of type Rectangle. A statement such as rect := Rectangle(arr at:2) must be used to retrieve the rectangle at position 2.

In many situations, collection objects are simply used to store objects of a single class. For example, we might use an object of class DynamicArray to maintain a list of all open windows in an interactive program. We would declare a variable openWindows of type DynamicArray. Whenever a new window w is opened, it is appended to the array (openWindows add:w), and when it is to be

closed, it is removed from the array (openWindows remove:w). The array only
contains windows, but the message at: only returns an object of the (static) type
Object. This unnecessary generality becomes a problem in many cases. For
example, a type cast is necessary whenever we want to treat an element of the
array as a window. This is exemplified by the following code fragment for
closing all untitled windows:

```
i: Integer;
w: Window;
i := openWindows size;
[i>0] whileTrue:
    [   w := Window(openWindows at:i);
        w title="" ifTrue: [w close];
        i := i−1
    ]
```

The type cast Window(openWindows at:i) is necessary because the message at:
returns a result of the (static) type Object. Since we want to know the title of the
window and (if the title is the empty string) close the window by means of the
messages title and close, we have to use a temporary variable w of the static type
Window. The type cast will always succeed in this situation, as we know the
context in which the array openWindows is used. However, if an object of a
different class gets inserted into the array accidentally, the type cast or the subsequent usage of the illegal object as a window will fail. Such errors are very
hard to track down, as they may be caused by methods that have been called
long ago.

Even if only window objects are put into the array, it is still cumbersome
to use type casts all the time when an element of the array is accessed. What we
need in such cases is a way to declare explicitly that we will only put windows
into the array and consequently want to get windows back whenever we retrieve
elements of the array. In yet another situation, we may want to maintain a
dynamic array of graphic objects. It would then be convenient if we could
explicitly specify that the elements of the array will always be such graphic
objects. In other words, we want to use collections for many different element
types. The compiler should help us to ensure that the collections always contain
elements of the proper classes.

The problem can be solved with **generic types** (and associated **generic
classes**). Genericity means that we can define classes with some unspecified
details. For example, a generic definition of the class DynamicArray could take
the following form:

```
DynamicArray { Element}:
    size → Integer
    changeSize: Integer
```

at: Integer put: *Element*
at: Integer → *Element*
indexOf: *Element* → Integer
delete: Integer
remove: *Element*
add: *Element*

...

This class definition is identical to that given at the beginning of this section, except that the type Object was replaced with an unspecified type Element. This type must be defined when we actually use the type DynamicArray in the declaration of a variable, as in

openWindows: DynamicArray{Window}

This declaration "generates" a new type (and corresponding class) in which all occurrences of the formal type Element have been replaced with the actual type Window. The resulting class definition is shown below:

DynamicArray:
size → Integer
changeSize: Integer
at: Integer put: *Window*
at: Integer → *Window*
indexOf: *Window* → Integer
delete: Integer
remove: *Window*
add: *Window*

...

The most important effect of this generated definition is that the compiler now has more information about the intended use of the type. In particular, this means that:

- When objects are put into the array with at:put: or add:, the compiler can verify the correctness of the actual argument's static type. For example, the message openWindows add:wind would be recognized as correct usage, but the message openWindows add:rect would be rejected, because rect is not of type Window. In this way, static compatibility rules can be used to guarantee that only windows are put into the array.
- When an element is retrieved from the array with at:, the compiler now "knows" that this element must be at least of the class Window. The result of the message at: is now of the static type Window. Again, static compatibility rules can be used to recognize the assignment wind := openWindows at: i as correct.

Generic classes are a powerful concept. They allow the construction of arbitrary object collections. There is a close correspondence between generic types and the structured types of conventional programming languages. For example, the type DynamicArray{Window} is similar to the Pascal type ARRAY [...] OF Window. An important difference between structured types and generic types is that conventional languages only provide a small set of structured types, usually arrays and sets. In object-oriented languages, genericity allows the programmer to create new types for special purposes. The following enumeration shows typical uses of generic types:

- Array: indexable collection (elements can be accessed via integer indexes)
- DynamicArray: indexable collection with flexible size
- List: ordered collection (the order of elements is important)
- Set: collection of different elements (equal elements are not duplicated)
- IdSet: collection of unique elements (identical elements are not dupli- cated)
- Bag: similar to Set, but with multiple copies of equal elements
- Dictionary: collection of key/element pairs
- Stack: elements are added and removed in "last in, first out" (LIFO) order
- Queue: elements are added and removed in "first in, first out" (FIFO) order

Class libraries often contain several variants of similar collections. The variants differ in the arrangement of their elements and the methods to access them. Some variants are typically highly optimized for special purposes.

Collections are organized hierarchically in class libraries. Usually, there is an abstract class Collection defining the common protocol for all collection classes. The diagram in Figure 2-17 shows a typical inheritance hierarchy of collection classes.

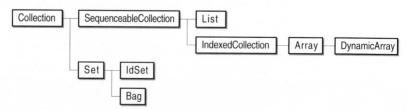

Fig. 2-17: Hierarchy of collection classes

Collection, SequenceableCollection, and IndexedCollection are abstract classes. SequenceableCollection specifies the common protocol for all collections with a defined order of elements. IndexedCollection defines the common protocol for all collections whose elements are identified with indexes.

This protocol of class Collection normally contains basic operations for adding and removing elements, as well as for membership test, combination of

collections, and iteration over all elements. The following class definition shows
a subset of Omega's Collection protocol (see Section 6.4 *Containers*):

```
Collection {Element}:
    size → Integer
    changeSize: Integer
    clear
    add: Element
    remove: Element
    addAllOf: Collection {Element}
    removeAllOf: Collection {Element}
    contains: Element → Boolean
    ...
```

The method clear removes all elements of the collection, leaving an empty
collection. The methods addAllOf: and removeAllOf: add and remove all
elements of another collection, respectively. The argument can be any collection
(for example, all elements of an array arr can be added to a set s with s
addAllOf:arr), but it must have the same element type as the receiver.

The specification of Collection does not contain messages for indexing
elements (such as at:put: and at:). These methods are specific for indexable
collections and therefore cannot be defined in the superclass.

Generic classes are not "real" classes like Rectangle and Window, as they
have incomplete definitions. They must be parameterized in order to be used.
The parameterization process can be understood as the construction of a "real"
class from a class template (similar to the construction of an object from a
class). We will in future use the term *generic class* for the incomplete class and
will speak of **generated classes** in case of the classes created from generic
classes.

The subclasses of a generic class are again generic. When class IdSet is
derived from class Set, which in turn is derived from class Collection (as shown
in Figure 2-17), parameterization results in parallel inheritance hierarchies. For
example, when IdSet is parameterized with Window, the generated class
IdSet{Window} results. The superclass of this class is Set{Window}. Figure 2-18
shows the result of the parameterization of the classes IdSet and Bag with the
element classes Window and Rectangle.

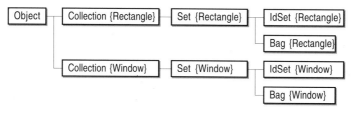

Fig. 2-18: A "family tree" of generated classes

The parameterization of generic classes is propagated through all generic super-classes. The superclass of Set{Rectangle} is Collection{Rectangle}, and the superclass of Set{Window} is Collection{Window}. All classes generated from Collection have one common superclass, Object, and the collection classes with the same element class form a separate subtree within the inheritance hierarchy. An important consequence of this hierarchy is that generated classes with different element types are not compatible with each other. This is even the case when a subtype relation exists between the element types. For example, the generated types Set{Rectangle} and Set{FilledRectangle} belong to different parts of the inheritance hierarchy, although FilledRectangle has been derived from Rectangle (see the example in Section 2.4 *Inheritance*)

Parameterization of generic classes results in many generated classes. For example, parameterization of the classes DynamicArray, List, IdSet, and Bag from Figure 2-17 with the element classes Rectangle, FilledRectangle, Window, and Point would lead to a total of 36 generated classes, as the subtree of Collection consists of nine classes, and four classes are generated for each of them. However, generation of several classes from a single generic class does not necessarily mean that the code of the generic class has to be duplicated. Dynamic binding can be used to reuse the general implementation of the generic class for all generated classes as well. If the implementation of the generic class treats objects of the pseudo-class Element as if they were of the class Object, the methods will also work for any subclass of Object (i.e., *any* class).

There is, however, one important restriction in the use of the type Element within a generic class. Since generic classes may be parameterized with arbitrary types in generated classes, the compiler cannot predict the static type of variables of type Element. Consequently, assignments of arbitrary objects to variables of type Element are not safe. For example, if the variable elem was declared of type Element, the assignment elem:=rect would be legal only within generated types with the element type Rectangle or a supertype thereof (in particular, Object). In all other cases, the assignment would be (statically!) illegal. For this reason, assignments to variables of type Element are only allowed when the source of the assignment is also of the static type Element.

Only a few object-oriented languages support genericity as described here. Genericity in this sense was first introduced in Eiffel [**Meyer 1988**]. Eiffel supports multiple parameters of generic classes and allows parameterized deri-vation of new classes (for example, the non-generic class WindowList could be derived from the generated class List{Window}).

Omega has a simpler concept of genericity. It only allows a single para-meter type and does not support derivation of new types from generated types. For more details on genericity in Omega, see Section 4.3.3 *Generic Types*.

2.9 Types, Classes, and Prototypes

Classes play an important role in object-oriented programming. Most object-oriented programming languages are built around a concept in which classes are the central mechanism for incrementally describing the structure and behavior of objects and for the construction of objects. We will use a simple example to illustrate the use of classes and to explore a different method for construction of software products.

We want to draw a circle with a cross in it. The circle shall have the radius r; its center should appear at the position x@y. We will use three objects to display this reticle:

- circ: the circle (of class Circle)
- vert: the vertical line (of class Line)
- hori: the horizontal line (of class Line)

In a class-based language, we would request the classes Circle and Line to create the objects to be displayed. In Smalltalk, there is a class object for every class. Class objects accept the message new and respond to this message by returning an object of the class. The following code fragment shows how the above task could be solved in a Smalltalk-like style.

```
circ := Circle new; circ center: x@y; circ radius:r;
vert := Line new; vert start:x@(y–r); vert end:x@(y+r);
hori := Line new; hori start:(x–r)@y; hori end:(x+r)@y;
circ display; vert display; hori display;
```

The message Circle new returns a circle with certain default attributes (for example, with its center at 0@0 and a radius of 10). The attributes are subsequently modified with appropriate messages. The same procedure is repeated for the horizontal and vertical lines. Since objects with the default properties (as delivered by new) are rarely useful, classes often provide more powerful methods for the creation and initialization of objects. For example, the class Circle would provide a message at:withRadius: that constructs a circle with the desired attributes. Similarly, the class Line would provide a method from:to: for the construction of a line with given end points. The following code fragment shows how these messages can be used to create the objects *in one step*:

```
circ := Circle at: x@y withRadius:r;
vert := Line from:x@(y–r) to:x@(y+r);
hori := Line from:(x–r)@y to:(x+r)@y;
circ display; vert display; hori display;
```

This convenient way of object construction is possible in Smalltalk because class objects have their own set of messages that can be adapted to special needs by the programmer. C++ does not have class objects; it uses so-called *con-*

structors for object generation and initialization. For every class, there is an elementary constructor that can be used to create default objects. Additional constructors (with the same name, but with different numbers and/or types of arguments[6]) can be defined by the programmer for the initialization of newly created objects. The following program fragment shows how the above task would be solved in a C++ program.

```
circ = new Circle(x,y,r);
vert = new Line(x,y−r,x,y+r);
hori = new Line(x−r,y,x+r,y);
circ−>display(); vert−>display(); hori−>display();
```

Eiffel has a mechanism similar to that of C++. A pseudo-message Create is used for the creation and initialization of objects. The notation v.Create is used to create a new object and assign a reference to the object to the variable v. The newly generated object is of the same class as the static type of the variable v.

The message Create is not a real message in the usual sense of object-oriented programming, because v.Create can even be used when v does not refer to an object (when "v is void" in Eiffel terminology). Create is therefore a message to a variable rather than a message to an object. Eiffel allows the programmer to implement his/her own Create method with different arguments in different classes. In contrast to C++, Eiffel does not support multiple constructors within a single class. The following code fragment shows how the above task would be solved in Eiffel style.

```
circ.Create(x,y,r);
vert.Create(x,y−r,x,y+r);
hori.Create(x−r,y,x+r,y);
circ.display; vert.display; hori.display;
```

Object generation in Object Pascal is similar to that of Eiffel in that the static type of a variable is used to determine the class of the object to be created. In Object Pascal, the standard procedure NEW is used to allocate storage for a new object. However, the result of this operation is an object with uninitialized instance variables. The objects must therefore be initialized explicitly by means of a message. By convention, this message has the same name as the class with the initial letter "I". The following program fragment shows how the circle with a cross can be drawn with objects in Object Pascal.

```
NEW(circ); circ.ICircle(x,y,r);
NEW(vert); vert.ILine(x,y−r,x,y+r);
NEW(hori); hori.ILine(x−r,y,x+r,y);
circ.display; vert.display; hori.display;
```

---

[6] C++ uses *function overloading* to support multiple constructors with the same name.

Every Object Pascal class has its own initialization method with a specific set of parameters. Since the initialization methods are regular methods, they are also propagated to subclasses. This means that deeply nested classes typically have many initialization methods. For example, a class FilledCircle would have a special method IFilledCircle (with the initial fill pattern as an additional parameter), but it would still provide the message ICircle (which would leave the fill pattern undefined). The programmer is responsible for invoking the proper initialization method after allocation of the object.

Another possibility for creation of new objects is the duplication of already existing objects. Some programming languages provide a general method for copying objects. For example, a copy method is defined in Smalltalk's root class, Object. Most other programming languages allow the construction of separate class hierarchies without a common root class. In these languages, a general copying mechanism can be used only if a class with such a message is available in the class library and the programmer makes sure that all classes are derived from this class.

Copying existing objects is the standard way of object creation in prototype-based languages, such as Self and Omega. In these languages, a class concept is no longer necessary. The structure and behavior of objects is defined by modelling a prototypical object. All copies of this object automatically take on the same structure, behavior, and initial content as the prototype they were created from. Whilst in class-based languages objects are created by execution of an algorithm, in prototype-based languages they are created with simple copying operations. This difference can also be described as "construction according to a plan" as opposed to "making a blueprint". Figure 2-19 illustrates object generation with classes and prototypes.

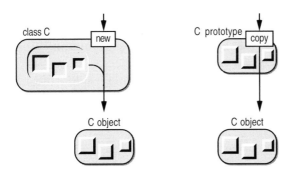

Fig. 2-19: Object generation with classes and prototypes

Classes "know" how to create (and initialize) objects. They contain a (verbal) description of their objects. This description specifies the structure and behavior of the objects as well as (an algorithm to initialize) the values of a newly created object's instance variables. Classes can therefore be seen as object templates, in the sense that they comprise a model of which new objects can be built. Classes are sometimes also called *object factories* [Cox 1986], a phrase that emphasizes the algorithmic nature of object creation.

In contrast to classes, prototypes *are* already initialized objects. They occupy storage and have instance variables with proper (i.e., meaningful) values. The only property of a prototype that needs to be described with static text is its behavior. Because the creation of a new object is performed simply by duplicating an existing object's image in memory, no algorithm is needed to describe this process. The code needed for the creation and/or initialization of an object in a class-based language is thus superfluous in prototype-based languages.

Classes are static in that they are defined by text. When the execution of a class-based program starts, no objects exist. On the other hand, prototypes are dynamic in that they constitute "living" objects. As soon as a prototype-based program starts, prototypes for all different sorts of objects that may be needed during execution of the program already exist. Consequently, prototype-based systems typically utilize a mechanism for archiving and retrieving objects on permanent storage media.

The objects created by copying a prototype have the same properties as the prototypes themselves. In particular, they have the same internal values as their original. In many cases, this is exactly what we want. For example, when we want to construct a dynamic array containing a point, a rectangle, and a window, we would start with an empty array and then add the three elements:

```
arr := DynamicArray copy;          --make a copy of the prototype
arr add:pt;
arr add: rect;
arr add: wind;
```

In this example, the name DynamicArray is used to identify the prototypical object (as opposed to the class name in class-based languages). As we will see later, a prototype's name is also used as a type identifier.

In most situations, the newly created object must be adapted to specific needs by explicitly modifying its state. The following example shows how a circle with a cross in it would be drawn in the prototype-based language Omega:

```
circ := Circle copy; circle center: x@y; circle radius:r;
vert := Line copy; vert start:x@(y–r); vert end:x@(y+r);
hori := Line copy; hori start:(x–r)@y; hori end:(x+r)@y;
circ display; vert display; hori display;
```

Note that this code fragment closely resembles the first example given at the beginning of this section. The reason for this similarity is that the fresh copy of the prototype has some (for our purpose useless) default state, similar to that of an object generated by the message new. Creation and initialization of objects is therefore generally performed in separate small steps.

Since copies made of a prototype provide the same set of operations as the prototype, they also can be copied by sending them the message copy. This means that multiple copies of similar objects can be created and subsequently adapted for special purposes. For example, we could create multiple copies of filled rectangles, each with a different fill pattern. These objects can later be used in the same way as prototypes, i.e., for creating new objects, but now with some predefined state:

```
blackRectangle := FilledRectangle copy;
blackRectangle fillWith:blackPattern;
grayRectangle := FilledRectangle copy;
grayRectangle fillWith:grayPattern;
dottedRectangle := FilledRectangle copy;
dottedRectangle fillWith:dottedPattern;

...

rect := grayRectangle copy;
rect width:50 height:20;
rect moveTo:120@150;
```

When a copy of a specific object (with known properties) is made, only those attributes that do not satisfy the current requirements need to be modified. Prototypes are therefore often initialized such that their state befits most purposes. For example, the FilledRectangle prototype would be initialized with a white fill pattern and a line width of 1.

In statically typed class-based languages, class names are used to identify the class as an object factory (as in new Circle) and as type names (as in Circle *circ). A similar duality can be found in prototype-based languages. In Omega, names with initial capital letters are used to identify both a type (in declarations as circ: Circle) and a prototype (as in Circle copy). Types and prototypes always exist in pairs. There is a prototypical object for every type, and every prototype represents a type. This subtle distinction is of course meaningless in dynamically typed languages. The table in Figure 2-20 shows some typical class-based and prototype-based programming languages with static and dynamic typing.

	typing	
	static	dynamic
class-based	C++	Smalltalk
prototype-based	Omega	Self

Fig. 2-20: Class- and prototype-based languages with static and dynamic typing

While new classes are built by formal descriptions, new prototypes are typically constructed interactively. First a new prototype is made by copying an existing one, and then the new prototype's structure, behavior, and its internal state are modified. There are different ways in which inheritance can be realized in prototype-based languages. These aspects of prototypes are discussed in detail in Chapter 3 *Prototypes*.

2.10   Object Hierarchies

Inheritance results in a hierarchical structure of classes, prototypes, and types. We will investigate possible forms of inheritance hierarchies in this section and discuss several other forms of hierarchical relations among classes and objects.

2.10.1   Single-Rooted and Multi-Rooted Class Hierarchies

In some programming languages (for example, Smalltalk), new classes must always be built on the basis of already existing classes. In other words, every class must have a superclass. There is only one exception to this rule. Since the inheritance chain cannot be infinite, there must be a class at the root of the inheritance hierarchy that doesn't have a superclass. This root class is usually called Object. Figure 2-21 shows the typical tree structure of such a **single-rooted hierarchy**.

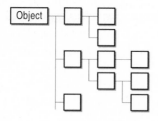

Fig. 2-21: A single-rooted class hierarchy

The principle that every class (except the root class) *must* have a superclass may look like a serious restriction at the first glance. Yet this rule is very reasonable, as it guarantees that "everything is an object". The root class Object serves two purposes:

- Since every other class inherits from Object directly or indirectly, general methods can be implemented in class Object. These methods typically implement copying, comparison, reading from and writing to external media, conversion into human-readable form, and other generally useful operations. Many of these methods can be implemented in a way that does not depend on a specific object representation. Thus, they can usually be inherited as they stand. They need not be overridden or reimplemented in subclasses.

- The protocol of class Object is spread throughout an entire program. Every object can be expected to accept at least the messages defined in class Object. This aspect of the root class is particularly important in statically typed languages, as the *type* Object can be used for variables whose dynamic type cannot be predicted. According to the polymorphic assignment rules, a variable of type Object can refer to *any* object. If a variable v has been declared as of type Object, it can still receive messages, namely all messages defined in class Object. In this way, many common operations can be performed without knowing what object the variable v refers to.

Object is an abstract class. Some methods (for example, conversion of the object into a textual representation) cannot be provided in a general way. Only dummy methods (such as returning the string "an object") can be implemented in class Object. The abstract methods must therefore be overridden in Object's subclasses. When such a message is sent to a variable of type Object, dynamic binding automatically guarantees that the correct method is executed.

Although single-rootedness is a very convenient property of a class hierarchy, Smalltalk is an exception to the rule. Most object-oriented languages allow the programmer to construct new classes from scratch without needing to inherit from a superclass. There are two reasons for this seeming flexibility. First, the inheritance of superfluous methods defined in the root class can be avoided. Second, the language designer wanted to keep the language definition as simple as possible, without the need to define the protocol of a root class.

When a class does not inherit from another class, it forms a "root" of its own, from which other classes can be derived, if desired. There will usually be many classes that are derived from a general-purpose root class (which is normally part of a class library and often called Object, CObject, or TObject), but some classes will not be part of this class tree. Figure 2-22 shows the typical structure of a **multi-rooted class hierarchy** (also called a *disconnected hierarchy*).

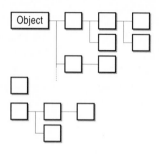

Fig. 2-22: A multi-rooted class hierarchy

Naturally, the advantages of a single-rooted class hierarchy also comprise the disadvantages of a multi-rooted class hierarchy. The following aspects should be considered when developing a class hierarchy:

- Well-designed root classes provide many (often fifty or more) generally useful methods. Classes that are not derived from such a root class cannot benefit from this functionality. Even if only some of these methods are needed, they have to be reimplemented.
- Classes that are not derived from each other or from a common root class are inherently incompatible with each other. It is not possible to declare a variable that can refer to objects of both classes. Only pointer variables and type casts can be used to work around this incompatibility, but both of these "solutions" are unsafe.
- General methods often accept objects of arbitrary classes as arguments. This is expressed by the type Object in their interfaces. If a class is not derived from Object, its objects cannot be passed as arguments to such methods. This incompatibility severely limits the utility of such objects.
- Languages that do not enforce single-rooted hierarchies implicitly encourage software developers to design their own class hierarchies. This results in a multitude of different class libraries, each with its own root class. Two such libraries are fundamentally incompatible with each other; it is in general not possible to use a class of one library in the context of the other.

As a consequence of these aspects, multi-rooted class hierarchies should be avoided, unless there is a very good reason to introduce a separate class (for example, when compatibility with type Object is *undesirable*). If the programming language does not enforce single-rooted hierarchies, a good deal of discipline is necessary to define and maintain a consistent and flexible class hierarchy.

.10.2 Single and Multiple Inheritance

Until now, we have only discussed classes inheriting from a *single* superclass. In this case, we speak of **single inheritance**. In the early days of object-oriented programming, single inheritance was the only way to derive a new class from an existing class. Single inheritance is characterized by the *extension* and *specialization* of an existing class. A class *B* can be extended by deriving a new class *C* from it and by describing the aspects in which *C* differs from *B*.

Today, object-oriented programming is primarily regarded as a tool to enhance the productivity during the software construction process. An important facet of object-oriented programming is the ability to reuse code by means of inheritance. Code that can be inherited need not be written, so it is only natural that programmers desire to inherit from as many sources as possible. If a single class can inherit from more than one class, we speak of **multiple inheritance**.

An extensive discussion of multiple inheritance is beyond the scope of this book. The purpose of this section is merely to explain when and how multiple inheritance can be used and what arguments have to be considered when using multiple inheritance.

When an object-oriented program is designed, new classes are developed. One of the tasks of object-oriented design is to find a proper place in the class hierarchy for these new classes. Although this may sound simple, it is not always easy to find a convenient superclass from which to derive a new class. Two aspects must be considered:

- *Implementation inheritance:* When working with a large class library, there is a good chance that the library contains a class that already has some properties of the new class to be developed. How much code can be reused and how easy the new class can be implemented by inheriting from an existing one depends on the choice of the superclass for the new class.
- *Interface inheritance:* Good object-oriented design is characterized by the fact that the addition of a new class does not break existing code. In other words, existing programs (or at least parts thereof) should be able to operate with objects of the new class. This is only possible if the new class is derived from an existing class, such that objects of the new class can be used where objects of existing classes are already allowed.

When looking for a superclass for a new class, the "most similar class" is often the best choice. In most cases, the selection of the superclass is not a problem, as new classes are often explicitly designed as subclasses of existing classes, in particular when the functionality of an existing class does not suffice for a specific purpose. In some cases, no similar class can be found at all, because the new class is needed for a task that is not yet covered by the class library. In such a situation, class Object is the "most similar class".

Sometimes a new class N could be derived from two classes, say, A and B. When such an ambiguity occurs during the design process, multiple inheritance can be used to unite the properties of both superclasses. However, the designer must take into account the kind of inheritance that is to be established between classes A and N as well as B and N:

- Usually class N should inherit the behavior of both classes A and B. If that is the case, multiple inheritance can be used to combine the structures (i.e., the instance variables) and the methods of both A and B. Objects of class N will therefore inherit all instance variables and all methods from both superclasses. This is not a problem when the names of all instance variables and methods are distinct; if they are not, however, a conflict occurs that must be resolved by the programmer.
- It is also possible that class N is to inherit the interface from class A, but the implementation from class B. In this case, multiple inheritance is of little use. It can be abused by inheriting from both A and B and by overriding all A methods such that the desired methods from B are executed. The problem with this strategy is that the interface of B contributes to the interface of N. If that is not desired, appropriate action must be taken to deny clients access to these methods. As we will see later, there is a better technique to implement such a variant of "multiple inheritance".

Multiple inheritance may appear as a powerful concept that helps to improve the reuse of software components. However, experience shows that multiple inheritance also increases the complexity of software products. The following list shows problems that must be considered when multiple inheritance is to be employed:

- *Conflicts.* When methods with the same name are inherited from A and B, it is not clear from which class the methods should actually be inherited. Such conflicts are inevitable when the classes A and B have a common (direct or indirect) superclass C. In this case, their interface contains several identical methods inherited from C that may or may not have been overridden in A and/or B. When methods with different implementations are inherited on more than one path, the resulting ambiguity must be resolved either by the implementer of class N or by the clients of N.
- *Duplication of instance variables.* When A and B have a common superclass C, the new class N would normally inherit the instance variables of both A and B. If objects of class C have an instance variable x, objects of classes A and B will also have an instance variable x. When N inherits from both classes, the problem arises whether x should be duplicated in N objects or not. Both possibilities can be useful in certain situations. An object-oriented language supporting multiple inheri-

tance should therefore allow the programmer to decide whether N objects shall contain one or two copies of x.

- *Complexity*. In single inheritance systems, the class hierarchy always consists of one or more trees. Trees are easy to understand, because there is only a single line of ancestors for every class. When multiple inheritance is used, the resulting class hierarchy takes the form of a directed acyclic graph (DAG). The superclasses of an individual class also form such a DAG, which makes it hard to determine statically which methods are inherited from which superclass.
- *Efficiency*. Because of the additional complexity, compilers for languages with multiple inheritance are difficult to implement. Moreover, the generated code and the run-time representation of objects must be structured in such a way that multiple inheritance becomes possible. The measures to be taken for multiple inheritance result in additional costs in both run time and memory space. This is even the case when only single inheritance is used.

Because of these difficulties, we suggest that multiple inheritance only be used when absolutely necessary. The following set of rules should give the reader some guidance concerning when to use and when to avoid multiple inheritance.

- *Is-a relation*. Inheritance establishes an is-a relation between the subclass and its superclass. When multiple inheritance is used, it must be possible to apply this relation to *all* superclasses. When N is to inherit from A and B, the statements "an N object is an A object" and "an N object is a B object" must be meaningful. Otherwise, a has-a relation should be considered for one of the superclasses. For example, a colored rectangle *is* a rectangle but *has* a color. Class ColoredRectangle should thus preferably be implemented as a subclass of Rectangle with an additional instance variable color.
- *Code reuse*. Multiple inheritance should have a positive effect on the design and implementation effort. This is only possible when a considerable amount of code can be inherited from all superclasses. When little or nothing can be inherited from a certain class, it should not be chosen as a superclass.
- *Interface inheritance*. Class N inherits the interfaces of both A and B. Consequently, all operations provided by A and B become available to clients of N as well. If unnecessary or even undesirable operations would be inherited from a class, it should not be considered as a superclass.
- *Compatibility*. Inheritance also applies to types and thus defines the compatibility between objects and variables. A consequence of multiple inheritance is that (references to) objects of class N can be assigned to variables of type A as well as to variables of type B. This means that N objects must be meaningful in both contexts. If the statement "N objects

can be used wherever objects of class X are allowed" does not hold for a superclass X, multiple inheritance is misused.

- *Object identity*. Multiple inheritance is often used to add properties to objects. For example, we might want to construct a class ForeignWorker by inheriting from both Foreigner and Worker. The problem with this approach is that when a foreign worker w is given notice of termination of employment, he is not a worker any more. The object w should therefore change its class from ForeignWorker to Foreigner. Such a "mutation" is in general not possible in object-oriented programming. Consequently, multiple inheritance should not be used to create individual objects with special properties, but only for the construction of whole classes, whose objects will belong to this class for their whole lifetime.

Another good reason not to use multiple inheritance lies in the fact that many object-oriented languages support only single inheritance. When such a language is used for the implementation of object-oriented programs, multiple inheritance must be simulated or – even better – avoided altogether. Most class libraries and application frameworks avoid multiple inheritance for the sake of simplicity. They are good examples of the fact that multiple inheritance is not really needed to implement complex software products.

The best way to develop a program without multiple inheritance is to design it with single inheritance in mind in the first place. Often simple ideas are more effective than powerful yet complex technical concepts. When multiple inheritance seems to be inevitable, it is therefore best to reconsider the basic idea behind the design. A simple solution can often be achieved by replacing an is-a relation with a has-a relation. This is, for example, the best way to implement a colored rectangle. The class ColoredRectangle would then simply be derived from class Rectangle, but extended with a new instance variable color. This approach has the advantage that has-a relations can be changed at run time. In this way, a colored rectangle can be assigned a different color, where the associated color object may even be of a different class. For example, a rectangle could be deprived of its color by assigning the instance variable color the value Nil or a special transparent color. We will see in the subsequent section that has-a relations can contribute much to the flexibility of object-oriented software.

To conclude this section, we warn the reader not to overestimate the usefulness of multiple inheritance. Even though many newer object-oriented languages support multiple inheritance, libraries and frameworks written for these languages don't generally make use of this feature. For example, the application framework ET++ [Weinand 1988, 1989] was implemented in C++ with single inheritance only.

Multiple inheritance was deliberately not included in the Omega language. We will therefore discuss single-rooted hierarchies with single inheritance only in the subsequent sections.

2.10.3   Is-a and Has-a Relations

A class C can be seen as the set of all objects belonging to class C. When object x is a member of class C, we often say that "x is a C". Inheritance extends this membership relation to superclasses. If class $C1$ is a subclass of C and "$x1$ is a $C1$", we can also say that "$x1$ is a C". This **is-a relation** is very useful to describe the compatibility between variables and objects. When $x1$ is a C, a reference to x can be assigned to a variable v of type C. After such an assignment, we will sometimes also use the colloquial form "v is a C" with the meaning that v refers to an object of class C.

Another important relation among objects is established by means of instance variables. When x has an instance variable of type T, we can say that "x has a T". Such a **has-a relation** can be used for extending the "value" of an object, in particular for implementing changing properties of objects. It is noteworthy that the word "has" does not necessarily mean ownership, although this is often the case. For example, consider an object cr of class ColoredRectangle that has another object col of class Color, as shown in Figure 2-23.

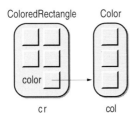

Fig. 2-23: A colored rectangle owning a color

In this example, there is a one-to-one relation between the rectangle and its color, but it is also possible that several graphic objects share the same color, as shown in Figure 2-24.

In Figure 2-24, there is a many-to-one relation between the graphic objects cr, cc, ct and the color col. This means that changes to the common color apply to all three graphic objects. For this reason, we cannot say that the colored rectangle owns its color, but we still speak of a has-a relation (because every graphic object has a color). Figure 2-24 also shows an ownership relation between the colored text object ct and the string object str. The object ct has a string, and since there is no has-a relation from another object to str, we can also say that ct owns str.

Has-a relations can be cyclic. That means, an object x can have an instance variable referring to another object y, which in turn has an instance variable referring to x. Figure 2-25 shows cyclic has-a relations among three objects.

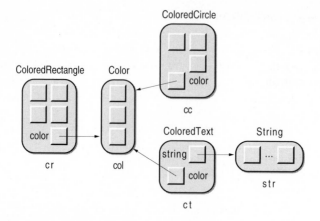

Fig. 2-24: Has-a relations among objects

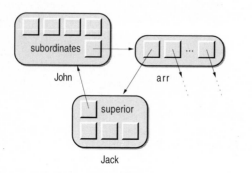

Fig. 2-25: Cyclic has-a relations

In Figure 2-25, John, the head of a department, has an array *arr* of subordinates which then has the subordinates themselves. Jack, one of John's subordinates, has a superior, which is, of course, John. This example also shows that has-a relations can be transitive. Because John has *arr* and *arr* has Jack, we can also say that "John has Jack" (in everyday speech: "John has a subordinate called Jack"). Such indirect has-a relations often occur when arrays or other kinds of containers are involved. A more direct solution would be to include numerous instance variables (one for each subordinate). The array can be seen just as a more flexible solution, as it allows an arbitrary number of subordinates to be attached without having to deal with a host of instance variables.

When a container object *c* (such as an array, a list, or a set) refers (among others) to an object *x*, we will sometimes also say that "*c* contains *x*". Such a **contains relation** also occurs in the context of windows. For example, a window can contain (a list of) different items such as buttons and editable text fields. Here, the word "contains" can also be interpreted in a geometric sense, as the window encloses the items displayed within its borders. The items contained in a window are generally known as *panes*. Panes can even be nested; for example, a window can contain two panes, each of which in turn contains a list of buttons. In such cases, the items usually also know within which pane they are being displayed; they *have* an environment, which leads to cyclic has-a relations. Figure 2-26 shows an example of a window layout and the corresponding object structure.

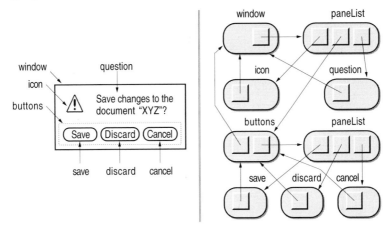

Fig. 2-26: Contains and has-a relations among parts of a window

Figure 2-26 shows only the relevant instance variables and relations among objects. The real data (for example, the button texts and the image of the icon) were omitted for the sake of simplicity. The window object contains (indirectly via the array paneList) the three panes icon, question, and buttons. Each of these panes has the object window as its environment. The button list buttons also has a pane list containing the three buttons save, discard, and cancel, which in turn have the object buttons as their environment.

The reference from the panes to their environments constitutes an **is-part-of relation**. Contains relations and is-part-of relations often occur in pairs. Such cyclic references are needed in windows when user input is to be processed. For example, a window will send an appropriate message to all its panes when its content has to be redrawn, and a pane will need to send messages to its environment in order to determine its relative position within the enclosing pane or window. These aspects will be discussed in more detail in Section 6.7 *Views, Windows and Panes*.

2.10.4 Dependencies Among Objects

Another important relation in object-oriented programs has to do with dependencies among objects. When an object x depends on another object y, it may need to update its internal state or its appearance on the screen whenever a significant change is made to *y*. For example, a change to the color *col* in Figure 2-24 may require an update of the objects *cr*, *cc* and *ct* on the screen. When the string *str* is modified, the object *ct* may need to recalculate its size and refresh the displayed image of the text on the screen.

When changes to an object *y* affect another object *x*, we say that the changes to *y* must be **propagated** to *x*. The mechanism to achieve this goal is called **change propagation**. In order for this mechanism to work, a relation must be established between the objects *x* and *y*. Since many objects can depend on *y*, the object *y* would need a list of all its dependants. But since every object could potentially have dependants, every object would need an additional list associated with it. As that would mean a considerable waste of memory, most object-oriented libraries use so-called *dictionaries* for change propagation. A dictionary is a list of ordered pairs of objects. In the case of change propagation, each pair describes the direction in which changes must be propagated. Figure 2-27 shows what the contents of a dependency dictionary might look like for the object structure from Figure 2-24.

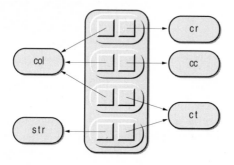

Fig. 2-27: A dependency dictionary

The first element in each pair refers to the source of a change relation, the second to the destination. The last pair thus defines a dependency between *str* and *ct*. Whenever *str* is modified, *ct* has to be updated to reflect the change. A change to an object is usually announced in methods modifying an objects state by sending the message changed to self. The corresponding method looks up the receiver in the dependency dictionary and notifies all dependants of the change. When the color *col* changes, the three colored objects *cr*, *cc* and *ct* depending on *col* get a chance to adapt themselves to the change.

There is more to change propagation than has been explained in this section. Here we have discussed *immediate change propagation*, i.e., when notifications about changes are distributed as soon as the change takes place. It is often useful to collect consecutive changes to the same object and to notify the dependants only in well-defined situations (for example, immediately before the next user input is to be processed). This strategy is called *delayed change propagation*.

.10.5 Delegation

Existing code can be reused in two different ways. The first way is to use inheritance to incorporate methods of existing classes in new classes. Inheritance does not require additional action by the programmer; as soon as a new class *C1* is derived from an existing class *C*, all methods defined in *C* automatically become available in *C1* as well.

The second method of reusing code is similar to procedure calls in conventional programming languages. When an object receives the message *m*, part of the desired operation can be performed by sending appropriate messages to other objects. When a task is passed on to another object, we speak of **delegation**.

We have already encountered delegation in Section 2.5 *The Magic Word "Self"*, when the implementation of a circle's moveBy: method was shown:

```
moveBy: {offset:Point}
[ center := center+offset ]
```

The implementation of class Circle's moveBy: method makes use of the fact that the location of a circle object is determined by its center (an object of class Point). To move a circle, it therefore suffices to calculate its new center with the Point message "+".

Text objects are another case in which delegation is useful. We use the class Text for the visual representation of character strings on the screen. Assuming that we already have a class String, we could define Text as a subclass of String and augment the new class with the additional instance variables and methods to keep track of the text's position on the screen, the typeface and font size to be used when the string is to be displayed.

However, this approach has a significant disadvantage, because it does not take type compatibility into account. Usually, all graphic classes are located in a subtree of a class library. In ET++ [Weinand 1988, 1989], the root of this subtree is formed by the class VObject (for "visual object"). In Omega, the prototype Image is used for this purpose. If we derived the class Text from String, it would not be a subclass of Image. Consequently, objects of class Text would not be compatible with variables of type Image.

To solve this compatibility problem, we have to reconsider the is-a relations between Text and other classes. In our first approach, we started with the observation that a text object *is* a string with additional visual attributes. Now we say that a text object *is* an image of a string that *has* visual attributes (most of which are inherited from class Image) and a string object containing the characters to be displayed. Figure 2-28 shows what a text object might look like with this definition. The upper part of the object contains the visual attributes inherited from class Image, and the lower part contains the additional instance variables needed to describe the contents and appearance of the text.

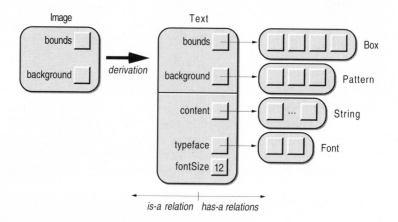

Fig. 2-28: A text object as an image of a string

In this model, a text object *is not* a string any more. Nevertheless, we would still like to be able to access the text object as if it were a string. For example, we might want to determine the text length, get at the text's characters, modify individual characters and insert other strings in the text. The following three methods show how this can be done with delegation:

```
size → Integer
[ ^ content size ]

at: {index:Integer} → Char
[ ^ content at:index ]

at: {index:Integer} put: {ch:Char}
[ content at:index put:ch ]

before: {index:Integer} insert: {str:String}
[ content before:index insert:str ]
```

All operations concerning the contents of the text are now simply delegated to the string object referred to by the instance variable content. For example, the message myText at:5 put:'s' is re-interpreted by the text object as "replace the character with the index 5 within my content with the character 's'".

Note that – since a text object cannot be assigned to variables of type String – it is not possible to use the message myText before:1 insert:anotherText to insert the entire contents of the text object anotherText at the beginning of myText. In order to make such operations possible, we need an additional method that returns the contents of a text object:

content → String
[^ content]

With this addition, the message myText before:1 insert:anotherText content can be used to insert anotherText at the beginning of myText. The same strategy could be applied to the other operations as well. For example, we could replace the fifth character of myText with the character 's' by means of the statement myText content at:5 put:'s'. However, this places the burden on the client and thus complicates the usage of text objects.

Delegation is such a powerful concept that it can even replace inheritance altogether. In the programming language Self, for example, implicit delegation is used instead of inheritance. For details on this topic, see Section 3.2.1 *Delegation – The Self Model*.

.10.6 Copy Chains

In prototype-oriented programming languages, new objects are created by copying an existing object (usually a prototype). The result of such a copy operation is an object with the same structure, behavior, and contents as the original object. A copy of an object can be copied again, resulting again in an object with the same structure, behavior, and contents. Successive copying thus leads to multiple generations of objects, as shown in Figure 2-29.

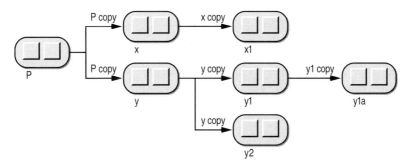

Fig. 2-29: Successive copying of objects

In this example, the object y1a was created by making a copy of y1, which in turn was created from y. In the copy chain P → y → y1 → y1a, modifications can be made to the intermediate objects in every single step. Modifications to the prototype itself can be considered as global configuration settings. Whenever a new copy is created with the message P copy, the copy will also reflect the modifications to the original.

The copy of an object is of the same class as the original object (hence the same structure and behavior). Thus, all objects depicted in Figure 2-29 are of the same class P. The "inheritance" of the class is independent of the original's static type. For example, consider the following code fragment:

```
pObj: P;
obj1: Object;
obj2: Object;
...
pObj := P copy;
obj1 := pObj;
obj2 := obj1 copy;
```

In this example, first a copy of the prototype P is created. A reference to this copy is subsequently assigned to the variable obj1 of the more general type Object. Even though the variable is of the type Object, it still refers to an object of class P. The class P is therefore preserved when another copy is created from obj1.

The ancestry defined by copy operations is not reflected in run-time data structures. In particular, it is not possible to determine at run time which other objects were created from an object, or – conversely – to find out the ancestor of a given object. In systems with automatic reclamation of unused storage, it is even possible that the ancestor does not exist any more. Copy chains therefore are merely an abstract concept; they are usually not of any interest to the programmer.

2.11   Values and References

In mathematics, variables are symbols for values. In the pair of equations $x*2=y$ and $y=x+3$, the variables x and y have the values 3 and 6, respectively. The variables have these values from the very beginning, even though it may require some calculations to determine what they are. If, in the course of further calculations, the variables x and y are used again, they will still have the values 3 and 6. The reason for this static property of variables is that *value semantics* are used throughout mathematics. Variables represent values; wherever a variable appears, it can be substituted with the value it stands for. Value semantics is also used in some declarative programming languages, for example in pure Lisp. A characteristic property of these languages is that they lack an assignment operation.

In most programming languages, *container semantics* are used for variables. A variable represents a storage area whose contents can change over time. As a result of this property, variables cannot be replaced by values, but must be *evaluated* wherever they appear. This is one of the reasons why writing computer programs is so difficult. For example, the statement x:=y/z can fail because the variable z may contain the value zero (which it did not have a microsecond earlier).

In object-oriented programming, variables are even more dynamic than in conventional programming languages. They do not contain objects, but rather refer to objects. We therefore speak of *reference semantics* in this case. The fact that "object variables" contain references to objects and not the objects themselves has several important consequences. We will use the following code fragment as the starting point for the subsequent discussion of this matter:

```
p1: Point;
p2: Point;
p3: Point;
...
p1 := 1@2;
p2 := 1@2;
```

We will observe three variables p1, p2, and p3 of type Point, where both p1 and p2 are initialized with the point object 1@2 (i.e., the x coordinate has the value 1, and the y coordinate has the value 2). Since the message "@" creates a new point object every time it is sent to an integer number, the above code fragment results in two point objects with the same contents. Nothing has been assigned to p3 yet. In many object-oriented languages, such initialized variables are automatically assigned a reference to a special object Nil. We will therefore also assume that p3 currently refers to Nil. Figures 2-30 shows the effect of the above code fragment.

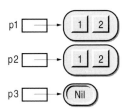

Fig. 2-30: Three point variables

The variables p1 and p2 refer to point objects with the same internal values. These objects are therefore considered *equal*. To test for equality, we use the operator "=". For example, the expression p1=p2 would return the value true, and p1=p3, the value false[7]. Note that "=" is a message. The expression p1=p3 should therefore be read as the command "Object p1, compare yourself with the argument p3 and return the value true when the other object is equal to

---

[7]   Since p1 refers to an object of class Point and p3 refers to a unique object of the special class Nil, the objects referred to by p1 and p3 are of different classes. As equality is only meaningful for objects of the same class, objects of different classes can never be equal.

you". Although equality is only defined for objects, we will also use this term informally when we say that "p1 is equal to p2". It is important to see that this is only a short form of saying "the object referred to by p1 is equal to the object referred to by p2", because the values of the variables (i.e., the references they contain) are actually *not* equal.

When we now execute the assignment p3:=p2, the content of p2 is copied to p3. Since p2 contains a reference to an object, only this reference is copied, but not the point object itself. Figure 2-31 shows the result of this assignment operation.

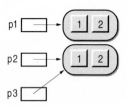

Fig. 2-31: Two variables referring to the same object

Since both variables refer to the same object, we say that the variables are *identical*. To test for identity, we use the operator "==". The expression p2==p3 therefore yields the value true. Identity is a stronger relation than equality. When x and y are identical, they are also equal, but the reverse is not necessarily true. The table in Figure 2-32 shows which relations exist among among the variables p1, p2, and p3.

	==	=
p1 • p2	false	true
p1 • p3	false	true
p2 • p3	true	true

Fig. 2-32: Relations among the variables in Figure 2-31

It is also usual to say that p3 is an *alias* of p2. This means that changes to (the object referred to by) one variable will also affect the other variable. For example, execution of the message p3 x:3 (which assigns the value 3 to the point's x coordinate) results in the structure shown in Figure 2-33.

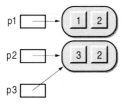

Fig. 2-33: Result of the message p3 x:3

It is important to see that the message p3 x:3 did not modify the variable p3. p3 still points to the same object, only the contents of this object have been changed. Figure 2-34 shows the relations existing among the three variables after the above modification. The changes with respect to Figure 2-32 are shown in italic.

	==	=
p1 • p2	false	*false*
p1 • p3	false	*false*
p2 • p3	true	true

Fig. 2-34: Relations among the variables in Figure 2-33

The first column of the identity/equality table has not changed because all three variables still refer to the same objects (the identity of the objects was preserved). The second column, however, contains two entries that may not be clear at first glance. As p3 was changed and p1 was not, it is not greatly surprising that p1 and p3 are not equal any more. Since p2 also refers to the changed object, the modification also affects all code fragments where p2 is used. Such collective changes are often used deliberately in object-oriented programming, but can also lead to program errors that are hard to track down. This is reflected by the change in the first line; p1 and p2 are not equal any more, although apparently neither of them has changed. On the other hand, p2 and p3 are still equal, as the identity of the objects has not changed, and since p2 and p3 are identical, they also have to be equal.

Identity of variables must also be considered when messages with arguments are sent. For example, an implicit assignment takes place when the message x m:y is executed. The actual parameter y is assigned to the formal parameter (say, z) of the method m:. During execution of the method, the variables y and z refer to the same object. Any changes made to the object referred to by z therefore also concern the variable y. This feature can be used deliberately, but it can also result in inadvertent modifications of objects.

How can two variables be decoupled so that they do not refer to the same object any more? The answer is quite simple: The object has to be copied, and a reference to the copy has to be assigned to the destination variable. However, the effect of a copy operation is not quite clear, as the object being copied can again contain references to other objects.

There are two possible ways of creating a copy of an object. The first, is to create an exact duplicate that contains the same values as the original. In Smalltalk nomenclature, such a duplicate is called a **shallow copy**. In prototype-oriented languages, the term **clone** is used for the same thing. We will subsequently assume that a message clone[8] exists for creating such copies. Figure 2-35 shows the effect of a clone operation applied to a colored rectangle (see Figure 2-23).

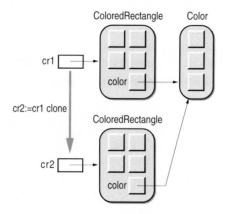

Fig. 2-35: The effect of a clone operation

Following the execution of the statement cr2 := cr1 clone, the instance variables of the resulting object have the same values as the original. Notably, the two colored rectangles share the same color. As this is undesirable in many situations, alternative copying mechanisms are needed.

Typical Smalltalk implementations also provide a method that not only copies the original object but also generates copies of all objects directly referred to by instance variables of the original. Such a copy is called a **deep copy**, and the associated message has the name deepCopy. Figure 2-36 shows the effect of this message, when applied to a colored rectangle.

---

[8]   The Smalltalk equivalent to clone is called shallowCopy.

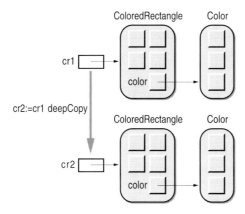

Fig. 2-36: The effect of the message deepCopy

After such a copy operation, not only the variables cr1 and cr2, but also the colors of the associated colored rectangles are decoupled. In this way, the objects referred to by cr1 and cr2 become truly independent, as the color (and all other attributes) of one object can be modified without affecting the other object.

In Smalltalk, the method deepCopy is implemented in class Object so that only *shallow* copies are made of the objects referred to by the original. That means that only objects at the first and second level are actually duplicated. If an object referred to by the original again has an instance variable that refers to yet another object, this object is *not* copied. Figure 2-37 shows the effect of the message deepCopy on a deeply nested object structure.

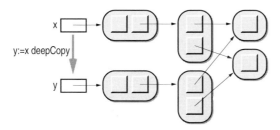

Fig. 2-37: The effect of deepCopy on a deeply nested object structure

This simplification whereby the copying process stops at the third level does not always produce the desired results. For this reason, a third method copy is used in Smalltalk as the standard method for duplicating objects. The default method copy in class Object has the same effect as shallowCopy, but can be overridden to implement a suitable copying mechanism for an individual class.

After execution of the statement y:=x clone (or y:=x shallowCopy), the variables x and y refer to distinct but equal objects. In other words, x==y returns the value false, and x=y returns the value true.

2.12   Hybrid and Pure Object-Oriented Languages

There are are two possible points of view about object-oriented programming. Some programmers see object-orientedness as a minor extension to conventional programming, while others view object-oriented programming as an entirely new programming technique. This controversy has an analogy in the concepts of object-oriented programming languages.

Some languages have both conventional and object-oriented elements. Such languages are commonly referred to as **hybrid languages**. Most of them are based on conventional programming languages; their object-oriented features were added as extensions. Examples for such languages are C++, Object Pascal, and Oberon-2.

Other languages have been built exclusively on the basis of object-oriented concepts. In these languages, all data to be processed is represented by objects, and all operations are expressed by means of message sends. To distinguish them from hybrid languages, they are called **pure object-oriented languages**. Examples of such languages are Smalltalk, Self, and Omega.

In this section, we will explore the most important differences between hybrid and pure object-oriented languages and show the advantages and disadvantages of both kinds of languages.

2.12.1   Everything Is an Object

Pure object-oriented languages can be best characterized by the sentence "Everything is an object". In this statement, the word "is" is particularly important. It suggests that an *is-a relation* exists between all sorts of data and the class Object. In fact, a common property of all pure object-oriented languages is that even elementary data (such as integers, characters, and boolean values) are treated as objects, whereas in hybrid languages they are treated differently.

In Smalltalk, all classes are derived from a general class Object, which results in a single-rooted hierarchy. The advantages of single-rootedness have already been discussed in Section 2.10.1; pure object-orientedness adds even more power to a single-rooted hierarchy, as the operations defined in class Object can also be applied to elementary data. For example, the message printString is defined in Smalltalk's class Object. As integers are also objects, they can be sent the message printString to convert them into a human-readable form. Another advantage of pure object-orientedness is that elementary data can be assigned to any variable of type Object[9], which means that elementary objects can be used wherever an arbitrary object is allowed. Furthermore, new methods can be defined for elementary classes. We already used the binary message x@y to construct a point from two integers. The method "@" could be defined in class Integer in the following way:

```
@ {yCoordinate: Integer} → Point
[   pt:Point;
    pt := Point clone;
    pt x:self;  pt y:yCoordinate;
    ^ pt
]
```

In some pure object-oriented languages, even statement sequences can be treated as objects. In Omega, so-called **block objects** can be constructed by enclosing a statement sequence in brackets[10]. For example, [n:=n−1; p:=p*2] is a block comprising two assignment statements. When such a block object appears within a method, the statements are not executed. The message do must be sent to the block in order to "evaluate" the contents of the block. Blocks are a very powerful concept; they can be used to control the execution of statement sequences. As an example, consider the following code fragment for computing the nth power of two (2^n).

```
p:=0;
n>=0 ifTrue:
[   p:=1;
    [n>0] whileTrue: [n:=n−1; p:=p*2]
]
```

In this example, three block objects are used. The message ifTrue: (defined in class Boolean) takes an argument of type Block. This block is evaluated only when the receiver of the message has the value true. In this case, the variable p retains the value 0 when n turns out to be negative. If n is zero or positive, the block is executed. After the assignment of the value 1 to p, the message while-True: is sent to the block [n>0]. When a block receives the message whileTrue:, it executes itself. If this execution yields the value true, the argument block is executed and the whole process starts again with the evaluation of the receiver. This procedure continues until the evaluation of the receiver yields the value false.

---

[9]   This compatibility is irrelevant in Smalltalk, since the concept of (static) *data type* is unknown in Smalltalk.

[10] A similar notation is used in Smalltalk. In fact, Omega's block objects were borrowed from Smalltalk.

Blocks can even be used to construct new language elements for flow control. For example, the message timesRepeat: is implemented in Omega's class Integer in the following way:

```
timesRepeat: {blockToRepeat: Block}
[ i := self; [(i := i–1)>=0] whileTrue: blockToRepeat ]
```

In this method, the counter i is initialized with the receiver's value. After that, it is repeatedly decremented by 1. As long as the resulting value is greater than or equal to zero, the block passed as argument is executed by means of the message whileTrue:.

There are many more applications of block objects. For example, Omega's exception-handling mechanism is also implemented by means of blocks. For a more detailed description of blocks, refer to Section 4.8 *Blocks and Actions*.

In hybrid languages, elementary data are treated differently. As most hybrid languages are extensions of conventional languages, compatibility with the "base language" is important. It is, for example, possible to process a Standard Pascal program with an Object Pascal compiler, as the object-oriented features were simply added without changing the elements already contained in the original language. Consequently, Object Pascal has a data type INTEGER that is incompatible with any object type[11].

Incompatibility between elementary types and object types can become quite troublesome in connection with container objects. For example, a general class List can be used for objects of any class, but not for integers or strings. To implement a list of strings, either conventional programming techniques have to be employed (which reduces the reusability of code), or the strings to be kept in the list must be stored within an object. Figure 2-38 shows how such "wrappers" can be used to circumvent the incompatibility between elementary data types and object types.

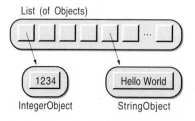

Fig. 2-38: Elementary data, wrapped in objects

If data of an elementary type E is to be processed in an object context, a class EObject has to be developed. An object of class EObject has an instance

---

[11]   Another incompatibility problem arises from the fact that Object Pascal allows multi-rooted class hierarchies. Even though most class libraries contain a root class, it is still possible to construct objects that cannot be assigned to variables of the "root type".

variable of type E and appropriate methods to access this instance variable. For example, objects of class EObject are of course cumbersome to use. Objects of class IntegerObject are not of the data type INTEGER; neither arithmetic operators nor standard functions can be applied to them. Consequently, an extra operation is required every time that the actual value of such an object is needed to perform some calculation. It is therefore not greatly surprising that this technique is rarely used in hybrid languages.

2.12.2   Uniformity Versus Efficiency

In pure object-oriented languages, all object-oriented techniques (in particular inheritance, polymorphism, and dynamic binding) can be applied to all sorts of data, regardless of whether they are elementary or not. The result is a uniform and consistent thought model that serves as the basis for the construction of all algorithms. This is very convenient for the programmer, as no mental switching between two kinds of operations is necessary.

However, there is a price to pay for such uniformity. Dynamic binding is involved whenever an operation with a simple integer number is performed, thus leading to a considerable slowdown. This is the reason why hybrid languages are generally regarded as efficient, while pure object-oriented languages are deemed slow.

The main reason why hybrid languages are more efficient lies in the fact that they do not support polymorphism with non-objects. This has two important consequences:

- The compiler can statically determine the storage requirements for conventional data. Whereas an object variable can refer to objects of different sizes, a non-object variable will always contain data of a fixed size. This means that a certain storage area can be reserved for every conventional variable at compile time. It is thus not necessary to access components of such variables via pointers, whereas in pure object-oriented languages such indirect access cannot be avoided.
- Elementary data types can be optimized. When a variable x is of the type Integer, static typing rules ensure that x will always contain an integer number at run time. The compiler can use this "knowledge" to treat the variable more efficiently. For example, special processor instructions can be used to optimize frequent operations such as the statement x:=x+1.

There is no simple solution to this problem. Compared to conventional data, additional coses cannot be avoided when objects are manipulated. In hybrid languages, these costs can be avoided simply by avoiding objects altogether, but that would be like emptying the baby out with the bath.

Several attempts have been made to avoid the run-time costs of operations with elementary objects. For example, sophisticated compilation techniques (in particular, customized compilation, message inlining, message splitting, and type prediction) are used by the Self compiler to achieve high performance [Chambers 1989, 1991; Hölzle 1991]. In Omega, elementary types are defined as monomorphic. For details, see Section 4.3.2 *Monomorphic Types*.

2.12.3 Object-Oriented Thinking

An common argument in favor of hybrid languages is that most of them are in fact extensions of conventional programming languages. For example, C++ is an object-oriented extension of C, and Object Pascal is an object-oriented extension of Pascal. A programmer can learn an object-oriented language easily when he or she already knows the underlying conventional language. C++ is a particularly impressive specimen of a hybrid language. C++ was developed several years after Smalltalk-80, yet very quickly it became the most widely used object-oriented language, because, for the army of C programmers, it was easier to switch to C++ than to Smalltalk.

Object Pascal is also an interesting example of a hybrid language, but for a different reason. Object Pascal is a rather minimal language, at least as far as object-oriented concepts are concerned. Object Pascal has only a few additional language elements to support object-oriented programming, notably:

- an object type (similar to a record type),
- methods (similar to procedures),
- messages (similar to procedure calls),
- two new predefined identifiers self and inherited,
- a new standard function Member, and
- more tolerant compatibility rules to allow for polymorphism.

These additions and modifications can easily be described in a handful of pages. An experienced Pascal programmer can grasp them in less than one hour.

This short list almost suggests that object-oriented programming is just a minor step beyond conventional programming. One could easily believe that comprehension of these few additions can convert a Pascal programmer into an object expert. However, experience tells us that this is not true at all. Learning an object-oriented language and learning to write object-oriented programs are two different things. Many C++ programmers use their C++ compiler as if it were just another version of the C compiler they had used for years. Others use objects only when it seems to be absolutely necessary – and then they often misuse them.

Learning how to write good object-oriented programs is a painful experience for many programmers. Astonishingly, this learning process is hardest for programmers who have already acquired much programming experience. When confronted with a programming problem, they often quickly come up with an idea of what the algorithm for the solution of the problem could look like, but they rarely see what kinds of data have to be processed and in which way.

In contrast, experienced object-oriented programmers intuitively know what the crucial objects are in a given problem domain. They do not think in algorithms, but rather in classes, abstractions, and relations among objects. To acquire the ability to *think object-oriented*, it is easier to start learning with a pure object-oriented language. When everything is an object and every operation is performed by means of a message, the programmer is forced to abandon conventional thought patterns. We therefore recommend starting object-oriented programming with a pure object-oriented language even if a hybrid language is to be used afterwards.

2.12.4   The Wider the Choice, the Greater the Trouble

It is a well-known fact that most problems can be solved in many different ways. When two programmers are assigned the same (sufficiently complex) task, it is very unlikely that they will develop similar programs. It is one of the most demanding challenges of computer science education to teach the "best" way to solve a problem. This is already difficult in conventional programming, but gets even more difficult when an object-oriented program is to be written in a hybrid language.

When a hybrid language is used, efficiency considerations can have a significant influence on the design of a program. For every single problem, the question "Shall I use an object here or rather stick with a more efficient conventional technique?" must be answered. For example, when a list of customers is to be processed, a conventional array or a collection class (such as Dictionary or DynamicArray) could be used. Wrong considerations can easily lead to inflexible programs when conventional data structures are used because "efficiency is crucial". It is often hard to determine which parts of a program are time-critical. Many programmers spend an enormous amount of time and energy optimizing "critical" parts of a program, and when the program is finished, it turns out that they had wasted hours only to achieve a minor performance improvement where run time is not at all important. But once a conventional data structure is being used in a certain part of a program, this design decision is often very hard to reverse. So the conventional data structure remains in the final version of the program and causes headaches and grief for those who have to maintain and extend the program.

Such problems never arise when a pure object-oriented language is used. Here the only problem is *which* class should be used for a given data structure.

But since every class serves a specific purpose, it is easy in most cases to make the right choice.

Another advantage of a pure object-oriented solution is that pure object-oriented languages often come with an extensive class library. The classes of such a library have been designed and implemented by experienced programmers. Most of them are optimized to fulfill their task in a very efficient way. For example, sets of objects are generally implemented with hash tables. Frequent operations (such as the addition and removal of new elements and membership tests) can be performed in almost constant time (i.e., the time required for these operations does not depend on the size of the set). To achieve the same result with conventional (i.e., non-object-oriented) techniques, enormous efforts have to be invested in the implementation of such a data structure. And since conventional data structures are typically tailored to a specific element type, they have to be reimplemented for every new data type that is to be dealt with in a similar manner.

Experience shows that most efficient programs are the result of a clever design and not of the usage of an efficient programming language. A "fast" programming language can, at best, improve the performance of a poorly designed program by a small factor, whereas an adequate design with the proper data structures and algorithms in the right place can yield speed improvements of orders of magnitude. It is highly recommended to avoid "dirty tricks". Most of the time they do not deliver the desired results, but result in programs that are difficult to comprehend. It is therefore best to start with a clean and homogeneous design. If parts of the resulting program turn out to be too slow, carefully directed measures can be taken at specific points within the program.

It is not easy to tell whether a hybrid or a pure object-oriented language is better suited for the solution of a given problem. A pure object-oriented design can be implemented much more easily in a pure object-oriented programming language than in a hybrid language. On the other hand, the availability of conventional data types (in particular, elementary numerical types) can help to implement certain classes of algorithms in a more efficient way. The solution of this problem was one of the goals in the design of the programming language Omega. Omega is a pure object-oriented language, yet it provides so-called *monomorphic types* which allow the generation of efficient code for operations with elementary data types.

3. Prototypes

This chapter explains the concept of prototypes in detail. The differences between classes and prototypes are discussed here together with the benefits and disadvantages of class-based and prototype-based languages. The various aspects of prototypes are explained using examples in the languages Self, Kevo, and Omega.

3.1   Constructing Objects Straight Away

Classes have been associated with objects since the beginning of object-oriented programming. They have become so common that it is generally believed that a class concept is one of the preconditions of object-oriented programming. Indeed, classes play a central role in most object-oriented languages. This is particularly the case in Smalltalk, where classes are not merely an abstract concept in the programmer's mind, but also exist at run time. For example, the Smalltalk expression obj class returns a class object representing the class of obj. In most other languages, the term "class" is often used as a synonym for "type".

The various meanings of "class" have already been elaborated in Section 2.2.1 *Classes*. The following is a brief summary of the most important aspects of classes:

- A class can be seen as the set of all objects having the same structure and behavior. In this sense, classes are a mathematical concept. For example, set theory can be used to describe the relations between subclasses and superclasses.
- Classes are a syntactical device to describe the structure and behavior of a particular sort of objects. For example, Eiffel programs consist of several source files, each of which contains a complete class description.
- Classes serve as "object factories". The information given by the programmer in form of a class description can be used to create new objects of that class.

Conventional programs consist of a static description of the algorithm(s) for the solution of a given problem. The emphasis in conventional programming is on the description of the steps to be performed when the program is executed. The data to be processed only play a minor role. This point of view is illustrated by some older programming languages (such as Basic, Fortran, and PL/I), in which the variables representing the data to be processed need not even be declared. They are merely seen as auxiliaries to temporarily hold values needed by the algorithms.

With the development of programming languages with an explicit type concept (such as Algol and Pascal), more attention was paid to the meaning and representation of data. Since then, we have been using a syntactical mechanism to describe the structure of a certain kind of data – a concrete data type. A further step in this direction were programming languages with a module concept (in particular, Modula-2 and Ada). These languages made information hiding and the construction of abstract data structures and abstract data types possible. An important consequence of this evolution is that static descriptions are used to define both the structure of the data and the operations on them. A similar notation is used in class-based languages to describe the structure and behavior of objects by means of classes.

In object-oriented programming, objects of a given class are responsible for a very specific task. To solve a complex problem, many objects of different classes must cooperate. Often a complicated network of objects must be created before the actual program can be executed. It is therefore not enough to implement just the methods that describe the object behavior required for the actual solution of the problem. Additional effort is necessary to describe what the objects look like, how they are to be created, and how they must be connected with each other. In Smalltalk (as the most prominent example of a class-based language), the object structure is described by listing the instance variables in a class definition, and class methods are used to create objects and to set up the required relations among them. Often many auxiliary methods are required for the sole purpose of initializing such an object network. A good deal of experience, imagination and forethought is necessary to describe statically what the dynamic object structure should look like at run time.

Prototypes make a more direct approach possible. Many of the static descriptions required in class-based languages can be avoided by building the necessary data structures in advance. Instead of describing the structure and contents of an object statically, the object is actually built. As soon as an object exists, its instance variables can be initialized with proper values, and object networks can be constructed by linking a number of objects together. Such a programming style is sometimes referred to as *programming by example*. The composition of the objects is typically performed interactively with an object editor or in a command language. In either case, an immediate feedback helps to avoid errors.

What remains to be done after a prototypical object has been created is to specify its behavior. But instead of defining the object behavior in the description of its class, the required methods are directly associated with the object itself. It is to be noted that this way of constructing an object comes close to our mental model of object-oriented programming: The object itself "knows" what is to be done when it receives a certain message. In class-based languages, the class "instructs" the object what to do.

 When the structure, contents, and behavior of an object can be defined directly, there is apparently no more need for a class concept. This is, however, not quite true. When copies of a prototype P are made, what result are many objects with the same structure and behavior as P. According to the aforementioned aspects of classes, the definition of a **class** as a *set of objects with the same structure and behavior* is still useful in connection with prototypes. In order to express that an object x was created by copying (or cloning) the prototype P, we will subsequently say that x *is of the class P*. Of course, class membership applies to copies of copies (etc.) of P as well.

As a consequence of the above definition of "class" in connection with prototypes, the name P of a prototype can now have three different meanings, each of which will be used subsequently in this book: P denotes ...

... the *prototype* itself (in statements, such as v := P clone),

... the *class* of the prototype (in explanations, such as "*x* is of class *P*"),

... the (static) *type* associated with the prototype (in declarations, such as v: P).

To avoid confusion, we will use the name *P* without an additional qualification only when "the prototype *P*" is meant. In all other cases, one of the two phrases "the class *P*" or "the type *P*" will be used.

3.2   Kinds of Prototypes

Object-oriented programming with prototypes has become an attractive research topic during the past decade. However, most of the work done in this area is of a rather theoretical nature. Until now, only a few object-oriented languages support prototypes. Since prototypes are a rather new concept in object-oriented programming, there is, as yet, no generally accepted definition of the term "prototype". We will therefore first give a general definition of this term and then discuss several specific prototype models.

When prototypes are mentioned in object-oriented literature [Anderson 1992; Borning 1981, 1986; Halbert 1988; LaLonde 1986, 1989; Lieberman 1986; Stein 1987; Ungar 1987, 1991; Wharton 1983], they are often associated with the notion of implicit *delegation* (see Section 2.10.5 *Delegation*). In more recent developments [Blaschek 1991, Taivalsaari 1992], a simpler definition of prototypes is used that comes closer to class-based programming. However, prototypes are always seen as a mechanism for object instantiation, and prototypes are always assumed to be self-sufficient (i.e., no additional concepts are needed to describe their structure and behavior). The following definition captures the essence of what is generally meant when the term "prototype" is used:

A **prototype** is a prefabricated object with predefined structure, contents, and behavior, from which new objects can be created by copying the prototype.

The various definitions of prototype given in object-oriented literature differ mainly in their understanding of how objects can share certain properties and how new prototypes with different behavior and/or structure are created. Before we illustrate these aspects of prototypes, let us first take a look at how the sharing and creation of a new "object species" is implemented in class-based systems.

Every single class defines the structure and behavior of a "sort" of objects. The set of available classes defines the various ways in which objects can be represented. Since an object always belongs to a specific class, only objects of existing classes can be created. To create an object with a different structure and/or behavior (that is not yet defined by one of the existing classes), a new class *N* must first be defined. We assume that there is already a class *C* with similar properties. Class N is therefore derived from class C. The new class initially inherits all properties from its superclass C. After that, it is only necessary to describe the aspects in which N differs from C. All other properties are inherited from C. It is important to see that inheritance does *not* mean copying the properties of C into N, but rather establishes a "magic" link between these two classes. An important consequence of this link is that changes to class C are automatically propagated to all its subclasses, unless these properties have been redefined there. When two additional classes P and Q are derived from C, the addition of an instance variable in C also leads to the addition of this variable in all objects of classes N, P, and Q (see Figures 2-13 and 2-14 in Section 2.6). When the implementation of a method is changed in class C, the change affects all subclasses as well, unless they contain a "private" method with the same name.

Inheritance in class-based systems means that subclasses *share* all inherited properties with their superclass. Similarly, all objects of a given class share the structure and behavior defined in the class. Figure 3-1 depicts this situation for two simple classes and their objects.

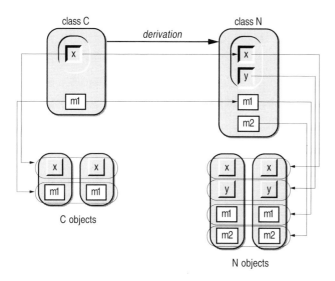

Fig. 3-1: Sharing of properties in class-based systems

The thin arrows in Figure 3-1 indicate how shared properties are propagated. For example, method $m1$ is assumed not to be redefined in class N. Classes N and C thus share the implementation of this method. Since all objects of class N have the same behavior, they also share this method.

Two separate aspects have to be considered when we speak of shared properties in connection with variables. The definition of the instance variable x in class C specifies the *presence* of x in objects of the classes C and N, but it does *not* define its *value*. The values of instance variables are always *private properties* of objects in class-based systems. To share the same value, so-called class variables are used in Smalltalk. These variables are part of the class object itself and can be used by all objects of this class. Hybrid languages do not have class objects; they therefore use conventional global variables for the implementation of shared values.

In prototype-based languages, there are no classes available to define the common properties of objects. Instead, a prototype *P* must carry all relevant properties with it. When a copy of a prototype is made, all these properties are copied into the new object. So far, this is a common feature of all prototype-based languages. There are, however, different models for the propagation of changes to the prototype (or rather, to objects in general). In Self, changes only affect an individual object; delegation is used in place of inheritance to make changes visible to other objects. In Omega, traditional Smalltalk-like inheritance is used. Kevo provides several options to enable changes to be applied either to just a single object or to a group of objects. These alternatives will be discussed in more detail in the following sections.

3.2.1   Delegation – The Self Model

The programming language *Self* [Chambers 1989, 1991; Hölzle 1991; Ungar 1987, 1991] uses delegation instead of inheritance to implement shared properties of objects. New objects can either be built by cloning an existing object or by constructing the object from scratch using special syntax. For example, the notation () stands for an empty object, and (| x. |) defines an object with a single instance variable x. Self does not have a special language element for the construction of a new prototype. In fact, there is no distinction between a prototypical object and a "regular" object. All objects have equal rights. It is possible to create an object with certain properties, make several copies of it, add a method to one of the resulting objects and then use this object as a prototype to build other objects with the new behavior.

The notion of variables is absent in Self. Instead, Self objects contain named *slots* that can be evaluated. Evaluation of a slot always returns an object. The actual effect of such an evaluation depends on the kind of the slot:

- A *constant slot* simply contains a value or a reference to another object. When a constant slot with the name x is evaluated, its content is returned.
- A *variable slot* corresponds to an instance variable; it is similar to a constant slot, but its content can be changed. Actually, a variable with the name x is represented by two slots – one slot containing a value or reference with the name x, and a slot with the name x: containing an assignment operation. The colon in the slot name indicates that an argument must be supplied when the slot is to be evaluated. Evaluation of x returns

the variable's content, and evaluation of x:y stores y in the slot with the name x.

- A *method slot* contains a method object – an object containing a sequence of statements. Evaluation of a method slot executes the statements and returns the result of this execution.

Slots are evaluated by means of messages in the context of a particular object. For example, the expression myPoint x returns the value contained in myPoint's slot with the name x, and myPoint x:12 assigns the value 12 to the x slot. Note that – since messages are used to modify variables – no assignment operation is needed in Self.

When a method within an object is executed, messages to this object (so-called *self sends* in Self nomenclature) can be written without the keyword self. For example, the expression self x: self x + self y can be written more concisely as x:x+y.

A slot can be designated as a so-called *parent slot* by appending an asterisk to its name in the slot definition. By convention, every object contains a parent slot with the name parent that contains a reference to another object whose properties are to be shared. As an example, consider the relations between the objects depicted in Figure 3-2.

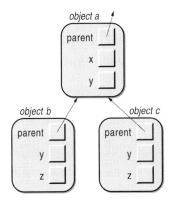

Fig. 3-2: Objects with a common parent object

When an object receives a message *m*, a slot with that name is sought in the object. If no such slot can be found, another attempt is made to find a slot named *m* in the parent object. This process can be repeated several times along a parent chain until the name is eventually found.

In the context of the object *b*, the message *z* evaluates the private slot contained in *b*. When the message *b x* is executed, the name *x* is not found in *b*. The name lookup process therefore proceeds with the search in the parent object *a* and finds an *x* slot there. In the case of *y*, a corresponding slot is found immediately in *b*, so this slot is evaluated instead of the *b* slot in the parent object. A slot in an object can thus "cover" a slot that would otherwise be found in a parent object. This is equivalent to overriding a method.

The local slots y and z are private properties of b. Since the slot x is located in a different object, we say that x is a shared slot[1] of b. In Figure 3-2, the object c could have been created by cloning the object b. Both objects have private slots y and z. No messages other than y and z are defined in b and c; they are found, if at all, in an object in their parent chain. Since both b and c refer to the same parent object, the object a represents their shared behavior.

The meaning of a local slot depends on the kind of slot it is. A variable slot corresponds to an instance variable, a constant slot resembles a read-only instance variable, and a method slot represents part of the object's behavior. A similar distinction applies to shared slots. In case of a method slot, the shared slot represents shared behavior with the same semantics as an inherited method in a class-based language. However, the lookup process is slightly different. When an object does not know how to respond to a particular message (because it does not have a local slot with that name), the message is *delegated* (forwarded) to the parent object. Shared variable slots in parent objects represent shared variables. They are thus similar to class variables in Smalltalk or global variables in hybrid languages.

The meaning of self in the Self language differs slightly from that in class-based languages. Assume, for example, that the method x in the object a sends the message y to self. When this method is executed as the result of the message a x, the message self y will evaluate the y slot of a. However, when the method x is sent to b, the initial binding of self to the object b is retained even when the message x is delegated to the object a. Consequently, the execution of self y (or simply y) during execution of a's x method will evaluate the y slot of b.

Delegation is a very powerful concept, especially when parent slots are assignable. In this way, the behavior of an object can be changed dynamically by storing a reference to a different object in the parent slot, thus changing the object's "inheritance". This is the reason why the language Self is said to support **dynamic inheritance**.

Self objects are always treated as individuals. When an object c is created by cloning an existing object b, these two objects have the same structure, contents, and behavior. According to our definition of class, the objects b and c are therefore initially of the same class. The attributes of b and c can subsequently be changed independently by adding and removing slots and by assigning new values to slots[2].

---

[1]   Note that the terms "local slot" and "shared slot" only make sense with respect to a particular object. For example, x in Figure 3-2 is a local slot of a, but a shared slot of b and c.

[2]   Note that, since inheritance is defined by parent slots, modifying a slot's content can also change the object's behavior.

The delegation scheme of Self together with the individuality of objects leads to a unique programming style. In order to change the behavior of a group of objects, it is impractical to modify the relevant properties of all object individually. Instead, **traits objects** are used to concentrate shared behavior in one object. Only an object's individual characteristics (in particular, instance variables) are stored in local slots. All properties that may be shared with other objects (behavior, constants, and shared variables) are implemented in parent objects. For example, consider the object structure depicted in Figure 3-3.

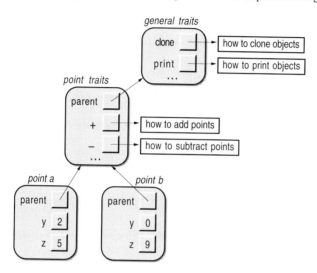

Fig. 3-3: Implementation of shared behavior with traits objects

The point objects *a* and *b* only carry their private values (i.e., their x and y coordinates) with them[3]. Since all points exhibit a common behavior, the point methods are collected in a common parent object, *point traits*. Due to delegation, any change in a method of this object automatically affects all point objects. Since the traits object for points again has a parent slot, additional (more general) methods can be "inherited" from further traits objects. The resulting hierarchy of traits objects is quite similar to the inheritance hierarchy of a class-based language. It is also to be noted that programming with traits objects leads to two categories of objects: those representing shared behavior and – at the bottom – the actual "data objects". Although Self is a classless programming language, prototypes assume the role of classes.

Prototypes and delegation are also used to implement *object pools*. The Self system includes an object called lobby containing all global objects and an object prototypes containing all prototypical objects. Similarly, an object called

---

3   To simplify matters, the assignment slots x: and y: have been omitted in Figure 3-3. The point objects shown here are "immutable", since the values of their instance variables cannot be changed.

traits contains all objects that implement reusable behavior. For example, the message traits point returns an object containing all reusable point methods. To construct a new point object, a parent slot with a reference to this traits object and two assignable slots x and y must be provided. In Self notation, a new point object can be assigned to a slot named myPoint with the following statement:

```
myPoint:    (|  parent* = traits point.
                x <- 0.
                y <- 0.
            |)
```

The asterisk marks the slot named parent as a slot to be used to resolve unknown messages. All messages not contained in myPoint (for example, "+" and "–" for addition and subtraction of points) are delegated to the object referred to by the parent slot. The equals sign after parent* defines parent as a constant slot. This means that the inheritance of myPoint cannot be changed. The slots x and y are both defined with "<- 0". This specification declares x and y as variable slots with the initial value 0.

Instead of creating a new point object from scratch, it would be more convenient to simply clone an existing point object. For this purpose, the Self system contains a prototype called prototypes containing all objects available for cloning. A new point object can therefore be created more easily with the statement myPoint: prototypes point clone.

3.2.2   Module Operations – The Kevo Model

Self's parent objects are a very powerful mechanism to implement shared properties for a group of objects. The common behavior of a particular kind of object can therefore be changed by simply adding and/or modifying methods in any one of their common parents. Such global modifications are easy to perform when the *behavior* of objects is to be changed. On the other hand, structure and contents are individual properties of every single object. Global changes to the *structure* of all objects of a particular kind (for example, the addition of a new instance variable) are therefore not so easy to apply [Stein 1988].

The programming language *Kevo* [Taivalsaari 1992] was designed specifically to overcome this restriction of delegation-based prototypes. Two mechanisms called *concatenation* and *module operations* are used in Kevo to define the structure and behavior of objects.

Every Kevo object can be thought of as carrying a complete set of all its properties with it. Since every object is completely self-contained, no parent relation is needed between objects.

When a new object *n* is created by cloning an existing object *c*, all properties of *c* are copied into *n*. Afterwards, several kinds of modification can be applied to *n* by means of **module operations**. The following table lists the possible changes to an object.

Operation	Effect
ADDS	adds a list of properties to an object.
REMOVE	removes a property from an object.
RENAME	assigns a new name to a property.
HIDE	makes a property private (i.e., invisible to clients).
SHOW	makes a property public (i.e., visible to clients).

Module operations serve to maintain of all kinds of properties. For example, the REMOVE operation can be used to get rid of a method as well as an instance variable. The operation ADDS is even capable of adding several features in one step. For example, the following statement sequence can be used to create a new object *n* from an existing object c, but with a different structure:

```
c.clone -> n;
n REMOVE y;
n ADDS
    VAR z
    10 -> z
    METHOD m2 ... ;
ENDADDS;
```

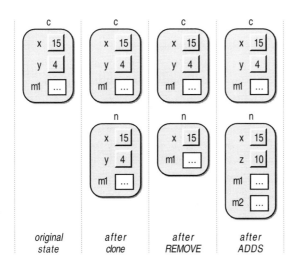

Fig. 3-3: Creation of an object with new properties in Kevo

In Kevo, the operator $->$ is used as the assignment symbol in a similar fashion as in the programming language Beta [Kristensen 1987]. The statement x$->$y is to be read as "assign a reference to x to the variable y". We assume in this example that the object c contains, among other things, a property called y. The REMOVE operation is used to get rid of this y, and the succeeding operation ADDS extends the object n with a new variable z (with an initial value of 10) and a method $m2$. Figure 3-3 illustrates the effect of the above sequence.

Note that the object n takes on a life of its own as soon as it is created. The subsequent modifications affect only this individual object, and not the object from which it originates. The same would be the case for modifications to the original object c.

To allow for collective changes of structure and behavior, module operations can also be applied to groups of objects. So-called *qualifiers* are used to specify which objects are to be modified by a module operation:

Qualifier	Affected Objects
individual	single object
clones	all clones of an object that still have exactly the same interface
descendants	all clones of an object with "the same underlying interface"
derivatives	all clones of an object

To create a new prototype with specific properties in Kevo, first a similar object is copied. After that, individual changes are applied to the object. Inheritance is thus described as equivalent to "Copying+Modification" in [Taivalsaari 1992]. After a few clones have been created from the new objects, it is up to the programmer whether further changes to one of these objects are to be applied only to this individual object or to the whole family.

In Kevo, no distinction is made between prototypes and other objects. Every single object can serve as the source of a new family.

Shared behavior is implicitly defined in Kevo by cloning objects. To keep track of similar objects, a behavior hierarchy is managed automatically by the system. Shared variables are implemented in Kevo by means of a special object called Root. Components of this object represent global variables. The objects referred to by these variables can in turn contain instance variables referring to other objects. The object hierarchy starting in Root is thus similar to a hierarchical file system, as depicted in Figure 3-4.

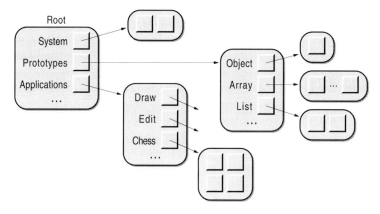

Fig. 3-4: Kevo's organization hierarchy

Combined method sends can be used to maneuver around in this object hierarchy. The name Root need not be specified, so the notation Prototypes.List can be used to get at a prototypical list object. The expression

    Prototypes.List.clone

thus creates a new list object.

3.2.3   Inheritance and Propagation – The Omega Model

Self and Kevo have in common the capacity to allow changes to individual objects without affecting other objects. A new class of objects is implicitly created by applying structural and/or behavioral modifications to an existing object. In class-based systems, all objects of the same class are always guaranteed to have the same properties and – more importantly – to retain these properties during their entire life-span. This is no longer the case when significant changes can be made to objects on an individual basis. Two objects a and b can then belong to the same class at the same time, but later have different interfaces, structure and behavior and thus belong to different classes. Such modifications are particularly severe when they affect the interface of an object, as the two objects a and b can then no longer be used in the same way.

Delegation is problematic for a similar reason. In a delegation-based language, the interface of an object is not a private property of the object. Local properties of an object constitute only part of its interface. The remaining characteristics of the object are defined in its parent(s). When a parent object is changed (which, in the worst case, may even occur while one of its methods is being executed), the interface of the object can undergo significant changes.

The consequences of the problems outlined in the above paragraphs can be summarized in one sentence:

Delegation and individual changeability of objects prohibit static typing.

For this reason, both Self and Kevo are dynamically typed languages. When static typing is not possible, one cannot statically detect whether or not it will be possible to execute a particular statement sequence. The only way out is to actually try to execute the statement sequence.

One of the goals in the design of *Omega* [Blaschek 1991] was to define a language allowing as many programming errors to be detected as early as possible. For this reason, Omega prohibits both delegation and individual changes of objects, and prefers a more traditional inheritance model.

An Omega prototype is not only used for the instantiation of new objects; it also serves as a representative for all objects cloned directly and indirectly from it. A prototype thus stands for a class of objects with common structure and behavior. To guarantee that these objects will *always* have the same properties, all relevant changes to the prototype are automatically applied (=propagated) to all clones derived from it. Only the contents of the objects are individual attributes and can thus be modified independently.

As modifications to a prototype apply to a whole group of objects, a separate mechanism is needed to create a new prototype with a different structure and/or behavior. The generation of a new prototype, derived from an existing prototype, is an interactive operation provided by the Omega environment; there is no language construct for this purpose. When a new prototype *N* is created from an existing prototype *P*, *N* initially has the same structure, contents, and behavior as *P*. After the creation of *N*, several modifications can be applied to the new prototype by the programmer:

- new instance variables can be added
- new methods can be added
- methods can be overridden
- contents of instance variables can be changed

The first three kinds of modification correspond exactly to the possible changes in a new class relative to its superclass in a class-based language. Only the last point is unique to prototype-based languages. In a class-based language, the initial contents of an object would have to be described formally by means of initialization statements.

When a clone *p* is made of a prototype *P*, *P* is said to be ***p*'s prototype**, meaning that *P* is the root of the copy chain from which *p* originated. We will also use the phrase ***p* is a *P* object** to express that *p* was created from *P* and thus belongs to the **class *P*** (= the set of all objects cloned directly or indirectly from P). Every object "knows" the prototype from which it originated. The message p prototype can be used in Omega to determine the unique object representing the class to which *p* belongs. When *N* is a prototype derived from *P*, we say that *P* is ***N*'s parent** and that *N* is a **child of *P*.** We will use the child/parent relation not only for the prototypes themselves, but also for the clones of the child *N*. When *n* is an *N* object, the statements "*n* is a child of

P" and "*P* is the parent of *n*" will therefore also be used occasionally. When we speak of derivation across multiple levels of inheritance, we will use the terms **ancestor** and **descendant** instead of parent and child. Figure 3-5 illustrates the meaning of the above definitions.

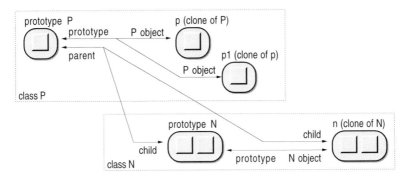

Fig. 3-5: Relations among objects and prototypes in Omega

When a new prototype *N* is created on the basis of an existing prototype *P*, what results is an object with the same contents. In this respect, creating a prototype is similar to cloning a new object. However, structure and behavior are not copied from *P* to *N* (as in Kevo), but rather inherited from *P*. As in class-based systems, a "magic link" is established between *P* and *N*. The effect of this link is that changes to *P* are automatically propagated not only to all other *P* objects, but also to the children (in fact: all descendants) of *P*. How exactly modifications to a prototype *P* affect the other objects of class *P* and descendants of *P* is explained in the following paragraphs.

- *Addition of an instance variable*: When an instance variable is added, an initial value has to be supplied by the programmer. An instance variable with this value is added to all *P* objects and to all descendants of *P*. However, the addition of an instance variable is prohibited when *P* itself or a single descendant of *P* already contains a variable with the same name.
- *Change to an instance variable's contents*: The contents of objects are private properties. Only the prototype itself is modified. However, subsequently created clones of *P* will then have the new contents. This also applies to new children of *P*, as the derivation of a new prototype also encompasses a clone operation.
- *Removal of an instance variable*: When a prototype *P* has an instance variable *v*, all other *P* objects and the descendants of *P* are also guaranteed to have an instance variable *v*. The removal of *v* from *P* is propagated to all other *P* objects and to all descendants of *P*.

- *Redeclaration of an instance variable*: As Omega is a typed language, all instance variables are associated with a static data type. It is, however, possible to change the static type of an existing variable. This is not a problem when the new type is a parent type of the original type, as the contents of this instance variable in all P objects and all descendants of P will then still be compatible with the new (more general) type. When the new type is not a parent type of the original type, the modification is still performed (and propagated to all P objects and all descendants of P), but the programmer has to supply a default value with which all incompatible contents of the variable are to be replaced.

- *Addition of a method*: The addition of an entirely new method m applies to all other P objects and to the descendants of P as well. However, things are different when an ancestor and/or a descendant of P already has a method with the name m. The addition of the method is not allowed when the existing method has a different interface (i.e., argument types and result type) from the method to be added. When the interface of the method to be added to P matches that of the already existing method(s), the addition is allowed. The new method is propagated to the entire class P and to all descendants of P, but the method is not propagated to descendants which have a method with the same name. Methods in such classes thus override the newly introduced P method.

- *Change in the implementation of a method*: A modification of a method's implementation immediately affects all other P objects and descendants of P, but the change is not propagated to classes containing a method with the same name.

- *Removal of a method*: The effect of the removal of a method depends on whether an ancestor of P contains a method with the same name or not. If such a method is present in an ancestor A, it is propagated to the class P and to all descendants of P. The formerly overridden method thus becomes effective again. When no corresponding method is implemented in any ancestor, the method is removed from class P and from all descendants of P. In either case, the propagation of the change does not affect descendants which have a method with the same name.

- *Renaming of a method*: When a method is given a new name, the method is actually removed and reintroduced with the new name. For the implications of such a change, see *Removal of a method* and *Addition of a method*.

- *Redeclaration of a method*: Methods can be redeclared with different argument and/or result types. In either case, the change is propagated to all other P objects and to all descendants of P. When a descendant already contains a method with the same name, only its interface is affected by the redeclaration. Accordingly, the current implementation of the method will very likely not match the new interface. Manual corrections to the imple-

mentations of methods are therefore necessary after a method redeclaration.

It is important to see that structural and behavioral changes to a prototype P
always affect *all* other P objects as well. It is therefore guaranteed that all
objects cloned directly or indirectly from P have the same structure and
behavior. The name P not only identifies the prototype P, but also statically
determines the interface of all P objects. Hence, the name of the prototype can
also be used as a *type name* (see Section 3.1). When a variable p is declared of
type P, the usual compatibility rules determine that p may refer to P objects
and to descendants of P. Modifications to a child N of P are always relative to
the structure of its parent P. For this reason, all objects referred to by p are
guaranteed to have at least the same set of instance variables and the same set of
methods of P.

Static type information not only helps to avoid programming errors, but
can also be used by the compiler to generate more efficient code. Note, in
particular, that no run-time search for methods is required.

An Omega prototype P can have not only local instance variables, but
also so-called *shared variables*. In contrast to a regular instance variable, a
shared variable does not exist in every single P object, but only once. It can be
thought of as being associated with the prototypical object itself.

.2.4   Comparison of Prototype Models

Although Self, Kevo and Omega are all prototype-oriented languages, their
basic concepts are entirely different. The table in Figure 3-6 summarizes the
most important differences among these languages.

	Self	Kevo	Omega
behavior sharing mechanism	delegation	concatenation and module operations	inheritance and propagation
state sharing mechanism	delegation	separate container objects	shared variables of prototypes
prototype generation	cloning and modification	cloning and modification	interactive operation
individual changeability	yes	yes	no
dynamic inheritance	yes	no	no
static typing	no	no	yes

Fig. 3-6: Concepts of Self, Kevo, and Omega

Among the languages discussed, Self is outstanding because of its dynamic nature. The delegation mechanism together with assignable parent slots provides enormous flexibility. Kevo is more restricted in that it neither supports delegation nor dynamic inheritance. Kevo's strength lies in the many different ways in which modifications can be applied to individual objects or groups of objects. Finally, the Omega approach is rather traditional. Conventional inheritance in the sense of Smalltalk and C++ is used to implement shared behavior, while delegation and changes to objects on an individual basis are not supported. On the other hand, Omega is the only prototype-oriented language using static typing.

Language concepts have a considerable influence on the way in which a programmer solves a given problem [Rechenberg 1990]. This is particularly true in the case of object-oriented programming languages. Even the three prototype-oriented languages discussed here differ significantly in many aspects. As it would be impractical to cover all possible facets of prototype-oriented programming in this book, we will subsequently concentrate on the Omega model.

3.3 One-of-a-Kind Prototypes

Classes are a wonderful concept for the collective description of an entire group of objects. It is, however, too much of a good thing to define a class that will only have one object. Those in favor of hybrid languages argue that such a situation constitutes a misuse of object-oriented programming, and that conventional data structures and procedures should be used instead of an object with a unique behavior.

There are, however, situations in which polymorphism and dynamic binding are desirable. For example, the application framework ET++ uses such unique objects for portability reasons. A global variable gWindowSystem[4] of type WindowSystem is used for all system-dependent window operations. WindowSystem is an abstract class. It defines an abstract interface for all window-specific operations and serves as the root of several concrete classes that actually implement the abstract operations in terms of the underlying hardware and operating system. When ET++ is initialized, a variable config determines which window system is to be used. The following code fragment shows a typical initialization sequence.

```
WindowSystem *gWindowSystem;
FontManager *gFontManager;
InkManager *gInkManager;
```

---

[4]   The names of global variables always have an initial "g". This useful convention was
      adopted from the application framework MacApp [Schmucker 1986].

```
Font *gsysFont;
Ink *gHighlightInk;
...
Init (int config)
{
    switch (config) {
    case SunWindows:
        gWindowSystem = new SunWindowSystem;
        break;
    case X11:
        gWindowSystem = new XWindowSystem;
        break;
    case NeWS:
        gWindowSystem = new NeWSWindowSystem;
        break;
    case SunServer:
        gWindowSystem = new SunServerWindowSystem;
        break;
    }

    gFontManager = gWindowSystem->MakeFontManager();
    gInkManager = gWindowSystem->MakeInkManager();

    gSysFont = gFontManager->MakeFont(Times, 12, Plain);
    gHighlightInk = gInkManager->MakeHighlightInk();
}
```

According to the value of the config parameter, one of four different window system objects is assigned to gWindowSystem. This is the only place in the entire program where such an explicit distinction is necessary. All further operations with the currently installed window system are performed via dynamically bound messages. For example, the object referred to by gWindowSystem is requested to return the appropriate font manager and ink manager[5] for the current window system. These objects are then in turn requested to return the default font and the highlight color to be used for selections. Not only WindowSystem, but also FontManager and InkManager are so-called *one-of-a-kind* classes. Only Font and Ink in the above example are traditional classes in the sense that they will generally have many objects.

One-of-a-kind classes are also used in the Smalltalk system. For example, Boolean is an abstract class with two subclasses, True and False, each of which has exactly one object, namely true and false, respectively. The actual objects do not have an internal state. They only have a certain behavior, as defined in the corresponding class. Consider, for example, the following implementations of the methods & (and) and ifTrue: in the classes True and False:

---

[5]   In ET++, *ink* is an abstraction for both colors and patterns.

class True:

& aBoolean
"Since the receiver is known to be true, answer the argument"
^ aBoolean

ifTrue: aBlock
"Since the receiver is true, answer the result of
  evaluating the argument"
^ aBlock value

class False:

& aBoolean
"Since the receiver is known to be false, answer the value false."
^ false

ifTrue: aBlock
"Since the receiver is false, do nothing and answer nil."
^ nil

When the message (**x&y**) ifTrue: [*do something*] is executed, dynamic binding is used to determine whether the block is to be evaluated or not. This definition of the behavior of boolean values by means of classes is a very impressive example of the power of dynamic binding.

The two examples above show how one-of-a-kind classes can be used in a natural way. However, such classes result in unnecessarily complex run-time data structures. Figure 3-8 shows which objects are involved in the Smalltalk implementation of boolean values.

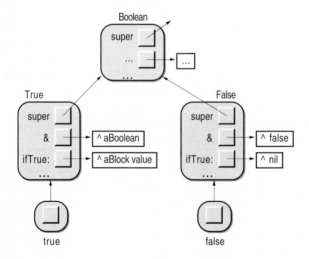

Fig. 3-8: Boolean classes and objects in Smalltalk

Although only two objects are actually needed, *three* classes are required to define these objects' behavior. The classes True and False define the specific behavior of their respective objects, and the class Boolean defines the common methods for both classes. The reason for this multitude of objects lies in the fact that objects cannot have their own behavior in class-based languages; they always need a class that defines what is to be done when a message is received. This situation is not unique to Smalltalk. The division between the classes which define behavior and the objects which actually show behavior also appears in hybrid languages, albeit that the distinction is more of a conceptual nature, as no class objects exist at run time.

Since objects have built-in behavior in prototype-based languages, one-of-a-kind classes (or, rather, one-of-a-kind *objects*) can be implemented more naturally with prototypes. In Self, only two self-sufficient objects true and false are needed to achieve the same effect as outlined above in Smalltalk.

In Omega, several one-of-a-kind prototypes are used. For example, the mouse attached to the computer is represented by a prototype called Mouse. Since prototypes are globally accessible, the messages Mouse globalPosition and Mouse buttonDown can be used from anywhere to determine the current location of the mouse pointer on the screen and whether the mouse button is currently being pressed.

Another example of a one-of-a-kind prototype is the object Workspace that represents the entirety of objects. The workspace object "knows" how many objects exist, how much space is left for allocation of new objects, and how to iterate over all currently existing objects.

Since one-of-a-kind objects are expected to exist only once, special provisions have to be made to prohibit the instantiation of additional objects of the same kind. In Omega, this is done by overriding the clone method. By convention, the clone method of a one-of-a-kind prototype always returns the prototype itself.

An interesting aspect of one-of-a-kind prototypes is that they can be used to simulate conventional *modules* or *packages* in the sense of Modula-2 and Ada. The prototype provides a set of services through its interface. Its instance variables constitute encapsulated data, and its methods assume the role of conventional procedures.

One-of-a-kind prototypes can even be used in the sense of a main program. In contrast to most hybrid languages, the notion of "program" or "application" is missing from the Omega language. To implement the equivalent of a program, a new prototype (say, MyApplication) is derived from Application. In this way, the new prototype automatically inherits most of the typical behavior of an interactive application. Only some methods must be overridden in order to implement the particular behavior of the new application. Finally, the application can be invoked with the message MyApplication run.

The steps that have to be taken to create a new application are discussed in Section 6.9 *Applications*.

3.4   Persistent Prototypes

In class-based languages, the structure, behavior and contents of objects are described statically by means of declarations and executable statements. When a new class is created, the programmer starts with a formal definition of the objects to be. The objects themselves only come into being when the program is executed. Some of these objects are rather short-lived; they are created on demand and become superfluous once they have fulfilled their assigned task. Examples of such objects are so-called *command objects* in interactive applications. When the user requests an operation (for example by selecting a menu command), a command object representing the operation to be performed is created. After the command has been interpreted, the corresponding object is no longer needed and can be disposed of[6].

Other objects have a longer life-span. Some of them are created during the initialization phase of an application and stay alive as long as the application is running. Examples of such objects are application objects, window objects and objects representing global state (such as a window list); objects of this kind only have a meaning as long as the application is running. They can be discarded when the application terminates, as they will be created anew when the same application is invoked the next time.

As classes are static descriptions of objects and serve as object factories at run time, it is always possible to create new objects from scratch when they are needed. A typical property of most class-based languages is that no objects at all exist immediately after the invocation of an application.

When working with a prototype-oriented language, we face an entirely different situation. To create a new object, an existing object is always needed to clone the new object from. Therefore, when a prototype-oriented application starts, at least one object is needed for every single type. This means that a mechanism is needed to make prototypes survive across invocations of applications.

The desire for long-lived objects is not unique to prototype-oriented languages. Such so-called **persistent objects** are also needed when data generated by the user are to be stored on external media for later use. The mechanisms for archiving and retrieving objects are commonly referred to as **passivation** and **activation**. An object is called "active" when it exists in the

---

6   When the application allows the user to undo an operation, the command object is kept
       around a little bit longer. When the next command is an undo command, the effect of the
       previous command is reverted by sending the message undo to the command object.
       However, undoable command objects will typically also be discarded after a short while
       (typically when undoing the command is not reasonable any more).

computer's memory and can "actively" take part in the execution of an application. It is called "passive" when it has been converted into some external format (usually a sequence of characters) and resides in a file or database.

One of the problems of activation and passivation is that the "passivated" objects will in general not retain their identity. Passivation does not discard the objects in memory but rather just creates external copies of them. During activation, new objects are created and their contents are initialized with the externally stored information. The problem becomes evident when the activation takes place during the same execution of the program when the original objects still exist.

For this reason, the currently available prototype-oriented languages use a different approach to make prototypes survive. As programming with prototypes means that "living" objects are constantly being dealt with, prototype-oriented languages are typically embedded in an interactive environment. To preserve all existing prototypes across session boundaries, a *snapshot* is made of the whole system (the so-called **workspace**). The resulting external representation is then called an **image** of the workspace. The advantage of the snapshot technique is that only an entire workspace can be saved and subsequently reloaded. The identity of the objects and the relations among them are thus preserved.

3.5 The Prototype Corruption Problem

Prototypes are extremely useful for the creation of new objects, but there is also a potential problem in their use. Consider, for example, the following simple code fragment:

```
welcomeMessage := String;
welcomeMessage add: "Hello Fred! ";
...
goodByeMessage := String copy;
goodByeMessage add: "Good Bye, Fred! ";
```

A simple but nevertheless frequent error was made here: Instead of copying the String prototype, the prototype itself (or rather, a reference to it) was assigned to the variable welcomeMessage. After that, the greeting "Hello Fred! " was appended to the object referred to by welcomeMessage. In this way, the String prototype was inadvertently modified. When the prototype is subsequently copied, the resulting string will not – as expected – be empty (which is the default state of the String prototype) but rather contain the message "Hello Fred! ". Consequently, the variable goodByeMessage finally contains the string "Hello Fred! Good Bye, Fred! ", which is definitely not what the programmer intended.

When a modification to a prototype has an adverse effect on objects subsequently created after the prototype, we speak of **prototype corruption**. The inadequateness of a prototype's contents can vary to a large degree. In less serious cases, the ensuing behavior of the program will simply be surprising (as in the above example). In severe cases though (for example, when the prototype contains a nil reference rather than the expected reference to a legal object), the program may even crash.

The prototype corruption problem is not relevant in class-based languages, since new objects are always constructed by executing a plan. As long as the plan remains the same, intact objects with the same initial contents will always be generated.

One problem with corrupted prototypes is that the corruption can remain undetected for a while. A prototype-oriented system will usually contain many prototypes for different purposes. During execution of a program, usually only a subset of these prototypes will be used. It is therefore possible that a currently redundant prototype is being corrupted in the course of a program execution. But prototypes can live for a long time. In particular, the corruption of a prototype can survive several programming sessions through passivation and activation. It is therefore important to detect corrupted prototypes as early as possible and to restore their desired state.

Once a corruption has been detected, it can easily be corrected by assigning proper values to the prototype's instance variables. However, the corruption can have been caused by a programming error. The problem can therefore appear again when a particular method is executed. Consequently, it does not suffice to remove the symptoms. Rather, the cause of the corruption must first be detected before the disease can be cured.

Corruption can even be a problem with objects other than prototypes. For example, a modified copy of a prototype can be used for the creation of new objects. Also, an object associated with a prototype can be in an invalid state. For example, a prototype representing a graphical object could have an instance variable that refers to a color object. If that object is copied along with the prototype, the ensuing objects will also be in an unwanted state, even though the prototype itself may be in a proper condition.

Although it is often quite easy to mend a corrupted prototype, it would be even better to avoid the need in the first place. But how can prototype corruption be circumvented? One possibility would be to forbid modifications to the state of prototypes. However, that would degrade the performance of an entire program, as run-time checks would be required whenever an attempt to change the contents of an instance variable were made.

Another possibility is to restore the state of critical prototypes in certain intervals (such as immediately after an image has been loaded into memory). But this is only a temporary solution, since the prototypes may again be corrupted during a session.

Some prototypes are used exclusively for the generation of new objects. Hence, a simple preventive measure is to check for references to prototypes in other objects, since such references are often the reason for an inadvertent modification of a prototype. In Omega, a special operation exists for this purpose. Execution of the message Workspace referencedPTs returns a set containing all prototypes to which references from other objects exist. When a prototype P is found to which no references should normally exist, the message Workspace allReferencesTo:P can be used to figure out which objects refer to P. In this way, some potential problems can be detected before a prototype actually gets corrupted. Once an illegitimate reference to a prototype has been found, it must be discovered just how this reference was established. If the reason was an error in a method, the faulty reference can be reintroduced by executing that method one further time.

The lesson to be learned from this discussion is that the convenient instance creation mechanism in prototype-oriented languages is not without cost. Since prototypes – unlike classes – not only define structure and behavior but also the initial contents of objects, the state of prototypes must be considered as part of a program and therefore treated with the same care as declarations and methods. In fact, more attention must be paid to the contents of objects, since these properties can change dynamically during execution, whereas declarations and methods cannot. To enable the programmer to interactively inspect and edit the contents of objects, suitable mechanisms must be provided by a programming environment supporting prototypes.

.6   Prototypes and Prototyping

Computer programs are complex technical products. An enormous effort is required to create a useful program that meets the requirements of the user. Nowadays programs are expected to provide a clear and comprehensible (preferably graphical) user interface. But how good a user interface actually is, often becomes evident only when the program is finished and put into the hands of its users. It can then turn out that essential parts of the program are more of a hindrance than a help to the user. Many of these problems can be avoided when prototyping is used in the early stages of a software project.

Prototyping is a software engineering discipline that is gaining more and more importance [Bischofberger 1992; Boar 1984; Connell 1989; Floyd 1984; Pomberger 1991]. Its goal is to create a tentative program (or parts of a program) that can be used for experiments before the development of the actual program starts. Such preliminary versions are called *prototypes*. In order to avoid confusion with prototypes in the sense of this book, we will call them *system prototypes* (as opposed to *prototypical objects*) in the remainder of this section. In software engineering, three different kinds of system prototypes are usually distinguished [Floyd 1984]:

- *Explorative prototypes* are used to verify the completeness of a requirements definition. As the user interface (especially the dynamic behavior)
  of a program is hard to describe with static text, a simple version of the
  program is built. Such a system prototype can then be used to check
  whether the verbal specification of the program to be was correctly
  understood. As the name implies, they allow the prospective users to
  explore the functionality and user interface of the program and thus
  provide an opportunity to discuss certain aspects before the relevant parts
  are actually implemented.
- *Experimental prototypes* are used during development of a program in
  order to try alternative designs. Before a crucial design decision is made,
  several variants are partially implemented. Experiments with these implementations can provide further insight and thus lead to an adequate system
  architecture.
- *Evolutionary prototypes* are used during design and implementation of a
  system. First a program with only a fraction of the desired functionality is
  built. This program is then augmented successively, until all desired
  functional parts have been added. An evolutionary prototype can thus be
  seen as an intermediate step in the software construction process.

System prototypes are supposed to reduce the costs of program development by
detecting misunderstandings at an early stage. Less adaptation is necessary
when the adequacy of the program has already been verified during the requirements definition phase. For example, user interface prototypes are used to
evaluate and verify those parts of the program specification that define how the
anticipated users will work with the program. In general, system prototypes
need not be fully functional. They need only bear a reasonably close resemblance to the real application to be developed. An important requirement
therefore is that such system prototypes can be produced much faster and more
cheaply than the final application. This goal can only be achieved when
appropriate tools are used to implement the system prototypes. Such tools
commonly allow the designer to interactively define the user interface (typically
screen layouts) of a program. The prototyping tool can then be used either to
simulate the behavior of the program or to generate a source text that can
subsequently be compiled and executed. Object-oriented programming can be of
much help during development of a system prototype, as it allows the designer
to incrementally add functionality to the system prototype [Pree 1990].

In contrast to system prototypes, prototypical objects do not represent a
preliminary stage in the course of a program's development. Instead, they are
finished objects constituting the first in a series of similar objects. Compared to
the ease with which a copy can be made of an existing prototypical object, the
development of the initial exemplar is an extremely difficult and expensive task.
Prototypical objects are therefore more like prototypes in other technical disci-
plines, such as the prototypes constructed before serial production of a new

article starts. Prototypical objects thus play an entirely different role to system prototypes.

There is, however, one application of prototypical objects in the process of the construction of a system prototype. Several typical objects representing user interface elements (such as windows, buttons, and menus) can be assembled with little effort by means of prototypical objects. When the proper tools are used, the user interface of a program can even be defined without writing a single line of code. The availability of such tools can thus make prototypical objects an ideal mechanism for prototyping.

3.7   Prototypes in Class-Based Languages

Object-oriented programming requires an object-oriented language, since conventional programming languages do not support polymorphism, dynamic binding, and inheritance. But how about object-oriented programming with prototypes? Are prototype-oriented languages required to implement prototypes in the sense of this book or is it also possible to simulate prototypes in class-based languages?

This question is easy to answer when we try to identify the essence of a prototype. At the beginning of Section 3.2 *Kinds of Prototypes*, a prototype was defined as "a prefabricated object with predefined structure, contents, and behavior, from which new objects can be created by copying the prototype". As classes already define the structure and behavior of their objects, a prototype can be implemented in a class-based language simply by creating an exemplary and properly initialized object of every class. An additional requirement is that a mechanism must be available to make copies of the thus-created objects. A single-rooted class hierarchy is very helpful in trying to achieve this goal. Thus, a copy method implemented in the root class is applicable to all objects, and hence also to the prototypes.

When prototypes are to be used throughout an entire program for the creation of new instances, the prototypical objects must be created at the very beginning, i.e., during the initialization phase of the program. The following program fragment shows how prototypes of the classes Button and Alert could be created in a C++ program:

```
gButtonPT = new Button;
gAlertPT = new Alert;
gAlertPT->SetSize(200,60);
gAlertPT->CenterOnScreen();
gAlertPT->AddButton(gButtonPT->Copy()->Label("OK"));
```

In this example, we introduced the convention that a variable representing the prototype of a class *C* should always have the name g*C*PT, where the initial letter "g" indicates that the variable is global.

The above example shows that the creation of a prototype also involves an initialization of the object with certain default values. For example, the alert prototype is by default 200 pixels wide and 60 pixels high; it is centered on the screen and has a single button labelled "OK".

To create a new object of a particular class, a copy of the corresponding prototype must be made. The following code fragment shows how the alert prototype defined above can be used to create a specific alert:

```
deleteAlert = gAlertPT–>Copy();
deleteAlert–>SetMessage("Do you really want to delete this file?");
deleteAlert–>AddButton(gButtonPT–>Copy()–>Label("Cancel"));
```

As shown here, one advantage is that new objects with a standard behavior can easily be generated. Of course, the same effect could be achieved in C++ by providing a special constructor that generates a standard object. However, a prototype has the advantage that it can be prepared outside the class and customized in a way that was not anticipated when the class was implemented. In this way, every application can define its own set of prototypes without the need to implement new subclasses with a different constructor. When by convention all new objects are created by cloning a prototype, it is also very easy to introduce new behavior in existing parts of a program (e.g., in parts of the class library). For example, a new class ColoredButton could be derived from Button and an object of this class assigned to gButtonPT.

Prototypes can also be used to implement dynamic type checking in languages that do not provide this feature. To achieve this goal, two additional methods must be implemented in every class. The first method, Prototype, should return the class' prototype object and the second method, Parent, should return the prototype object of the base class. These methods are simple one-liners, as shown below for the class Alert, from which we assume that it was derived from the class View.

```
virtual Object *Alert::Prototype() { return gAlertPT; }
virtual Object *Alert::Parent() {return gViewPT; }
```

With these methods, type checking can be implemented in the root class Object in the following way:

```
bool Object::IsA(Object *ptToLookFor)
{
    Object *pt;
    pt = this–>Prototype(); // start with the receiver's prototype
```

```
        while (pt != ptToLookFor) {
            if (pt == gObjectPT) return false;  // reached the root without success
            pt = pt->Parent();
        }
        return true;  // ptToLookFor was found on the way towards the root
    }
```

To check whether the object referred to by the variable myObj is of class Alert or of a subclass of Alert, the statement if (myObj->IsA(gAlertPT)) {...} can be used. It must, however, be noted that all these mechanisms only work when the class hierarchy has a root class.

Prototypes can also be used to create objects of a class for which only the class name is known at run time. For this purpose, all prototypes must be registered along with the name of their respective class. They can, for example, be stored in a global dictionary, say gPrototypeDictionary. This registration should be performed immediately after the prototype has been created in the initialization part of the program. Once the dictionary has been set up, the message

gPrototypeDictionary->Lookup(new String("Alert"))

can be used to retrieve the prototype of the class Alert. Of course, the dictionary is more meaningful when the class name is specified by a variable rather than a constant. To get a new object for a class specified by its name, the following function NewObject can be used:

```
    Object *NewObject(String *className)
    {
        Object *pt;
        pt = gPrototypeDictionary->Lookup(className);
        if (pt) return pt->Copy();
        return nil;  // no prototype with the given name has been registered
    }
```

A typical application of such a mechanism to generate objects by their class name is the activation of previously passivated objects. Upon passivation, the objects can be written to a disk file in legible form that includes the object's class name. For example, a Rectangle object containing two Point objects (one for the top left corner, and one for the bottom right corner) could be represented by the string

Rectangle(Point(0,0),Point(200,60))

To activate the object again, first the class name (className) has to be read from the file (denoted by the Stream object s). Then, the function NewObject can be used to generate an object of the class denoted by className, and finally the object generated is requested to read its instance variables from the stream:

```
s >> className;
obj = NewObject(className);
obj -> ReadFrom(s);
```

Within the Rectangle method ReadFrom, the same mechanism is used recursively to read the two instance variables[7].

As demonstrated in this section, prototypes are useful even in class-based programming languages, despite the fact that extra measures have to be taken to implement them. In particular, the prototypical objects must be created explicitly at the beginning of the program, as they do not exist permanently. The next chapter will show how these issues are dealt with in a *real* prototype-oriented programming language.

---

[7] The technique described here is only the basic mechanism for activation and passivation. More sophisticated algorithms are necessary to avoid multiple passivation of identical objects and to correctly process recursive data structures.

4. The Programming Language Omega

This chapter introduces the prototype-oriented programming language Omega. The syntax and semantics of the language elements are defined semi-formally and explained with numerous examples. The description is nevertheless incomplete; some details that are not relevant for the understanding of the rest of the book have been omitted.

4.1   Concepts and Conventions

Thousands of programming languages are available today, and new ones are constantly being developed. Now that object-oriented programming has become so popular, almost every language developed recently supports some kind of object-orientedness. In 1989, eighty-eight object-oriented programming languages were surveyed in an article [Saunders 1989]. It can safely be assumed that since then the number of object-oriented languages has increased quite substantially.

When there are already so many object-oriented languages available today, a good reason is needed to justify the development of yet another language. In the case of Omega, dissatisfaction with other languages and a certain amount of curiosity provided the initial motivation to design a new language. The Omega project started in 1990 as an attempt to incorporate object-oriented prototypes into a type-safe language. The definition of Omega was guided by the following goals:

- *Simplicity*: The language should be based on only a few principles. It should be easy to learn and convenient to use.
- *Generality*: It should be possible to use the language for all sorts of problems. In other words, Omega should become a general-purpose language.
- *Safety*: The language should use static typing and incorporate automatic storage reclamation.
- *Efficiency*: It should be possible to generate efficient machine code and to optimize operations with elementary data types.

Some of Omega's key concepts have already been introduced in Section 3.2.3. Here is a brief summary of Omega's most important features:

- *Pure object-orientedness*: Everything in Omega is an object. Reference semantics is used for variables and dynamic binding is used for all methods.
- *Prototypes*: Omega uses prototypes instead of classes to specify the structure, behavior, and initial contents of objects.
- *Type-safety*: Static typing is used throughout the language. Conditional assignments are provided for those cases where the static typing rules are too rigid.
- *Access rights*: The visibility of instance variables and methods can be specified in a flexible way by the programmer. Variables can be defined as read-only, and methods can be protected against overriding.
- *Genericity*: Generic types can be used to implement general-purpose prototypes that can be parameterized with other types.

- *Monomorphic types*: Elementary data types are classes and as such inherit from Object, yet their definition as monomorphic enables the compiler to perform certain optimizations.
- *Block concept*: Statement sequences are treated as objects. Flow control is not part of the language, but rather implemented in terms of messages. New control flow structures can be invented by the programmer.
- *Run-time checks*: Extensive checks against numerical errors, storage overflow, and violations of index bounds are performed at run time.
- *Exception handling*: Run-time errors result in exceptions for which handlers can be provided by the programmer.
- *Garbage collection*: Omega does not provide a language element or method for explicit disposal of objects; the storage used by unreferenced objects is automatically reclaimed by a garbage collector.
- *Programming environment*: Prototypes (and other objects as well) can be manipulated interactively in a convenient programming environment.
- *Workspace concept*. All objects (along with all relevant information) are kept in a single encapsulated workspace.

In the remainder of this chapter, the individual language elements of Omega will be described in detail in a semi-formal style. The syntax of the language elements is described with rules written in EBNF (Extended Backus-Naur Form). The following EBNF elements are used in the subsequent sections to describe the Omega language:

> Character = "h" .

Single characters are enclosed in quotes. Here, Character represents the lower case letter h. This means that the character h must be present wherever Character appears within a rule.

> String = "eat" .

When more than one character is enclosed within quotes, these characters form a string that must be specified in precisely the given form. In this example, String represents the word eat.

> Sequence = Character String .

Elements that must be present in a specific order are listed consecutively. In this example, Sequence represents the word heat, i.e., the concatenation of h and eat.

> Alternative = "h" | "m" .

Vertical bars separate alternatives. Here, Alternative represents either h or m. For example, the sequence Alternative String represents either heat or meat.

> Precedence = ("h" | "m") String .

Parentheses can be used to bind symbols together. Normally, concatenation binds adjacent symbols more strongly than a vertical bar. This precedence rule can be broken by enclosing an alternative in parentheses. For example, Precedence stands for either heat or meat, but the same rule without the parentheses (i.e., "h" | "m" String) represents either the letter h or the word meat.

| Option   = [Character] .

Elements that can be omitted are listed within brackets. Here, Option represents either the letter h or nothing. For example, the sequence Option String stands for one of the words heat or eat.

| Repetition   = "s" { "ing" } .

Repetition of elements is described by listing the elements to be repeated within braces. The enclosed elements can be repeated an arbitrary number of times (including none). Here, Repetition represents the words s, sing, singing, singinging, and so forth.

The variant of EBNF used here is borrowed from N. Wirth's description of Modula-2 [Wirth 1985]. Every language element is described by a named rule. The rule names for character sets and symbols begin with a lower case letter, and the names for syntax rules begin with a capital letter. In order to distinguish EBNF rules clearly from code fragments, they are marked with vertical bars at the left margin.

In the following sections, only the syntax of the individual language elements is described formally in EBNF. Each rule is then augmented with verbal explanations of context conditions associated with it. Where appropriate, simple examples are used to demonstrate the correct use of the various language elements.

4.2   Lexical Elements

This section describes the elementary building blocks of Omega. In the first part, the character set used in the formulation of Omega programs is defined, and the second part explains how symbols can be constructed with these characters.

4.2.1   Character Set

A subset of the ASCII character set is used to formulate Omega methods and expressions to be executed interactively. The following rules define abbreviations for certain classes of characters used in the subsequent descriptions of the symbols.

decimalDigit	=	"0"	"1"	"2"	"3"	"4"	"5"	"6"	"7"	"8"	"9" .
hexDigit	=	decimalDigit	"a"	"b"	"c"	"d"	"e"	"f" .
letter	=	"a"	"b"	"c"	"d"	"e"	"f"	"g"	"h"	"i"
			"j"	"k"	"l"	"m"	"n"	"o"	"p"	"q"	"r"
			"s"	"t"	"u"	"v"	"w"	"x"	"y"	"z" .
capitalLetter	=	"A"	"B"	"C"	"D"	"E"	"F"	"G"	"H"	"I"
			"J"	"K"	"L"	"M"	"N"	"O"	"P"	"Q"	"R"
			"S"	"T"	"U"	"V"	"W"	"X"	"Y"	"Z" .
separatorChar	=	"'"	"''"	"(" | ")"	"["	"]"	"{"	"}"	";"	","	"." .
opChar	=	"+"	"−"	"*"	"/"	"\"	"="	"<"	">"	"&"	"|"
			"#"	"@"	"$"	"%"	"~"	"^"	":"	"?"	"!" .

The usual ten digits are used to write decimal numbers. In addition, the letters a to f are used to denote the hexadecimal values 10 to 15, respectively. Omega is a case sensitive language. That means that capital letters are distinguished from their lower case forms. National letters such as "ä" and "ñ" are not considered as letters. The characters listed as separators constitute syntactic elements of Omega, and opChar lists the characters of which operators can be constructed.

.2.2   Symbols

A *symbol* is an atomic element of a programming language. The symbols of Omega can be divided in two categories:

- A set of *elementary symbols* is used for assignment operators and for the separation and grouping of other symbols. They have a fixed appearance and must always be written as subsequently shown.
- *Compound symbols* are used to formulate names, operators and constants. They are constructed by concatenating letters, digits, and special characters.

Elementary Symbols

assignmentOp	=	":="	":?=" .
parenthesis	=	"(" | ")" .
bracket	=	"["	"]" .
brace	=	"{"	"}" .
separator	=	";"	","	"." .

Two different assignment operators are used in Omega. Their meaning is described in Section 4.7 *Expressions*. Parentheses, brackets and braces are used in the formulation of expressions, statement sequences and for the specification of generic types, respectively. Separators are used to explicitly separate successive language elements from each other.

Note: • The above rules have only been used to enumerate the elementary symbols of Omega. The rule names will not appear in subsequent rules. Instead, the literal form of the symbols will be used.

Identifiers

identifier	= letter { letter	capitalLetter	digit } .
ptIdentifier	= capitalLetter { letter	capitalLetter	digit } .
declaredIdent	= identifier ":" .
initIdent	= identifier "::=" .

Identifiers consist of an arbitrary sequence of letters and digits, where the first character must be a letter. There is no limit to the length of an identifier. There are two kinds of identifiers: Those beginning with a lower case letter are used as names of *variables* and *messages*, whereas the names of *prototypes* always begin with a capital letter. When used in a declaration, a ptIdentifier denotes the type associated with a prototype, otherwise it stands for the prototypical object itself.

Variables to be declared within a method must be immediately followed by either a single colon or the initialization symbol "::=".

The following names are predefined in Omega and can therefore not be used as identifiers:

• self
• Same
• Parameter

Examples:

      i numerator heaven7 anObject   *identifiers*
      T Object Point3D BitMatrix   *prototype identifiers*

Note that identifiers are case sensitive; anObject and anobject are thus different identifiers. It is considered good programming style to use descriptive identifiers in order to make lengthy commentary unnecessary. Short names (such as i and n) should only be used for auxiliary variables within methods; they should never be part of an object's interface. Capitalization should be used to indicate word boundaries in identifiers consisting of more than one word, as in BitMatrix.

Keywords

keyword	= identifier ":" .

A keyword is (part of) a *keyword message*. It has the same form as an identifier (note that keywords always begin with a lower case letter), but ends with a colon. As the colon is part of the keyword, it must *immediately* follow the preceding letter or digit.

Examples:
  x: t42: isA: contains: changeSize: rockAroundTheClock:

Integer Literals

integer	= decimalInteger
	| base hexDigit { hexDigit } .
decimalInteger	= decimalDigit { decimalDigit } .
base	= decimalInteger "r" .

There are two forms of integer literals. A sequence of decimal digits constitutes a decimal integer number. In order to express numbers using a base other than ten, the number must be prefixed with a decimal integer followed by the letter "r" (for "radix"). The base must be in the range 2 through 16. For bases greater than ten, the letters "a" through "f" represent the values 10 through 15.

Integer literals of either form are always of class Integer. They are represented as two's complement 32-bit numbers. The values of integers are thus restricted to the range -2147483648 through 2147483647 (-2^{31} through $+2^{31}-1$) [1].

Note: • Integer literals are always unsigned. To express negative integers, the unary operator "~" (defined as sign inversion in class Integer) must be used. For example, 123~ denotes the value -123.

Examples:
  0 10 000000000 2147483647
  2r1010 (=10) 8r33 (=27) 16r1a (=26) 16rffff (=65535)

Real Literals

real	= decimalInteger "." decimalDigit { decimalDigit }
	[exponent] .
exponent	= "e" ["+" | "–"] digit { digit } .

Real literals are always written in decimal form. They are represented as decimal integers that are followed by a decimal point and a series of fractional

---
[1]   The class LongInteger can be used to represent arbitrarily large integer numbers.

digits. They may have a trailing exponent consisting of a decimal integer with an optional sign that is preceded with the letter "e". The value of a real literal of the form xey is computed as $x \cdot 10^y$.

Real literals are always of class Real. They are represented as 32-bit floating point numbers in IEEE format. Their absolute value is therefore restricted to approximately 3.0e38, and their mantissa cannot be expected to have more that 6 significant digits[2].

Notes: • Like integer literals, real literals are always unsigned. To express negative real numbers, the unary operator "~" (defined as sign inversion in class Real) must be used. For example, 123.0~ denotes the value -123.0.

• Real literals must have at least one digit before and after the decimal point. 5., .5, and 1.e6 are therefore not legal real literals.

Examples:
    0.0   3.14159   0.001   1.0e3 (=1000.0)   2.1e-6 (=0.0000021)

Character Literals

| character | = "'" (printableChar1 | "'" "'") "'" .

| printableChar1   = *any printable character except* "'" .

Character literals are printable characters enclosed by single quotes. To represent the single quote character, it must be duplicated. In other words, four successive quotes must be used to represent the character "'".

Character literals are always of class Char. They are represented as extended ASCII values in the range 0 through 255. This means that non-standard ASCII characters are allowed in character literals, depending on the character set used on a particular computer. For example, 'Ω' is a legal character literal on Macintosh computers.

Note: • Non-printable characters (in particular, those with ASCII values less than 32) cannot be represented with character literals. Instead, the message asChar of Integer must be used. For example, 13 asChar yields the carriage return character.

Examples:
    ' ' *(space)*   '''' *(single quote)*   'A'   '@'

String Literals

| string   = """ { printableChar2 | """ """ } """ .

| printableChar2   = *any printable character except* """ .

---

2   The class LongReal can be used to represent larger floating point numbers.

String literals are sequences of printable characters enclosed by double quotes. To represent the double quote character, it must be duplicated. For example, four successive double quotes must be used to represent a string literal containing the single character """. The length of string literals is not limited. However, a string literal cannot extend over more than one line.

String literals are always of class StringConstant (a subclass of String). They can be seen as sequences of character literals. This means that non-standard ASCII characters are allowed in string literals. For example, "•Omega•" is a legal string literal on Macintosh computers.

Notes:
- Non-printable characters (in particular, those with ASCII values less than 32) cannot be part of string literals. Instead, concatenation must be used to construct strings containing such characters. For example, the message 9 asChar+"Hello" yields a string starting with a tabulator character.

- Objects of class StringConstant are immutable. Attempts to modify a StringConstant object result in an exception. To get a string whose contents can be changed, the message asString must be used to convert a StringConstant object into an object of class String. For example, the expression "Hello" asString constructs a new modifiable String with the initial contents "Hello".

- StringConstant objects are unique throughout the entire Omega system; no two StringConstant objects with the same contents can exist at any given time. When the string literal "Hello" (i.e., a reference to the StringConstant object with the contents "Hello") was assigned to the variable welcome, the expression welcome=="Hello" will return the value true.

Examples:
>   "Welcome to the machine"   "I wouldn't say ""no"""
>   "" *(the empty string)*   " " *(a string consisting of a single space character)*

Operators

operator	=	opChar { opChar } .
opChar	=	"+" | "–" | "*" | "/" | "\" | "=" | "<" | ">" | "&" | "|"
		| "#" | "@" | "$" | "%" | "~" | "^" | ":" | "?" | "!" .

Operators are used as "identifiers" for unary and binary messages. They consist of one or more special characters of the ASCII subset defined by opChar. The length of operators is not restricted. It is nevertheless a good idea to use only short operators whose meaning can intuitively be understood by the reader. Long and cryptic sequences of special characters are awkward to type and hard to remember.

Notes: • ":", ":=", "::=" and ":?=" are used for other purposes and can therefore not be used as operators. It is, however, possible to construct operators containing one of these symbols (such as ":=:").

• Since comments start with two successive minus signs (see below), operators cannot have "--" as their first two characters.

Examples:

        + = == << <-> #&@%$?

Comments

Comments are written in the same form as in Ada. They begin with two successive minus signs and include all characters until the end of the line.

Note: • Two minus signs as part of an operator and within a string do not begin a comment.

Examples:

        --

        -- the line above is an empty comment
        ----
        self invalidate; -- the pane must be redrawn

Whitespace

Spaces, carriage return characters and tabulators (commonly referred to as *whitespace*) can be used to nicely format Omega methods. Such whitespace characters are only allowed *between* symbols, but not *within* symbols[3]. Since symbols are formed always of the longest character sequence possible, whitespace characters are sometimes necessary to separate symbols. The following examples illustrate situations in which whitespace characters (or their absence) give a different meaning to a program.

• "whitespace" is a single identifier, but "white space" denotes the message space sent to white.
• "x!!" denotes the unary message "!!" sent to x, but "x! !" means the message "!" sent to x and thereafter sent once more to the result of the first message.
• "<--" is an operator, but "< --" is an operator followed by a comment delimiter (the rest of the line is ignored).

---

[3]   Character and string literals are the only symbols that can contain space characters.

.3 Types and Prototypes

The terms *type* and *prototype* have already been defined previously. Particularly noteworthy are Omega's prototype concepts, introduced in Section 3.2.3. The purpose of this section is to explain how types are defined using prototypes and to elucidate the actual make-up of a prototype. Furthermore, the standard types of the language and special kinds of types are discussed.

Types and prototypes always exist in pairs. Whenever a new prototypical object is created, a new type is defined and vice versa. Prototypes are generated interactively in the Omega programming environment with a menu command. The creation of a new prototype N is similar to the cloning of an existing prototype P, except that the new prototype must be given a unique name. The prototype P automatically becomes the parent of N. It is, however, possible to change N's inheritance later. The structure of N initially equals that of P, and N inherits all methods from P. The prototype N can therefore immediately be used in the same way as P. Subsequently, additional components and methods can be added to N, and existing methods can be overridden by adding methods with the same interface as inherited methods.

It is important to see that there is no significant difference between a prototype and its clones. Both can be used in the same way, and their contents can be modified independently of one other. When structural or behavioral changes are applied to either a prototype or one of its (direct or indirect) clones, these changes are automatically propagated to all other objects of the same class. However, the prototype is the only object of a class that has a unique name. All other objects are anonymous. The only way to refer to such an object by a name is to assign it to a variable, say x. But as the contents of variables can change, x may at some later instant refer to a different object. In contrast, the name of a prototype always denotes the same object; it is, for instance, impossible to write something like P:=x.

When a prototype is no longer needed, it can be explicitly deleted by means of a menu command. The deletion of a prototype P has several severe consequences that may violate the integrity of the Omega workspace. The following operations are automatically performed when a prototype is deleted:

- Since the prototype P also represents the type P, existing instance variables of the (static) type P within other objects cannot retain this type any longer. They are therefore redeclared to the deleted prototype's parent type.
- The prototype P also represents a class of objects. This means that all other objects of class P have to be removed as well. Variables referring to one of these objects (or to the prototype itself) are automatically initialized with Nil.

- The prototype may serve as the parent of other prototypes. Children of the deleted prototype are therefore modified such that they now immediately inherit from *P*'s parent.

As the deletion of a prototype is a potentially dangerous operation, it is suggested that prototypes be removed only when it is absolutely sure that the operations listed above will not have an adverse effect on other important objects.

4.3.1   Standard and System Types

The programmer can always create new types for special purposes. During development of a program, hundreds of prototypes can come to existence. There is, however, a small set of types without which no Omega program could be written. These types are called **standard types**, as they are considered parts of the Omega language. One reason for the existence of standard types is that expressions can contain literals. In particular, the types Integer, Real, Char, StringConstant, Block and Action are defined as standard types for this reason. As these types are derived from other types, their (immediate and indirect) parent types Object, Container, ByteArray and String are also standard types.

A second group of types is required primarily for the benefit of the compiler and/or the programming environment. These types are called **system types** in Omega terminology. This category consists of the types Boolean, Nil, Collection, Array, Pointer, Wrapper and Workspace.

Figure 4-1 shows the inheritance hierarchy of Omega's standard and system types.

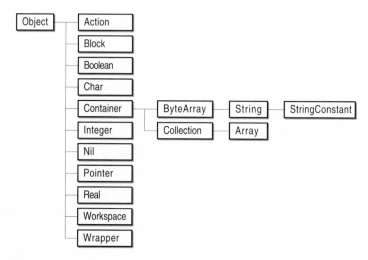

Fig. 4-1: Inheritance hierarchy of Omega's standard and system types

As standard and system types are considered part of the Omega language, their prototypes cannot be removed. For a similar reason, the structure of some of these prototypes can only be changed within limits. For example, it is not possible to add, redeclare, and remove components for most of them. Likewise, certain methods of these prototypes are also protected against changes made by the programmer. It is, however, possible to add new methods to all standard and system prototypes. In particular, new behavior can be added to *all* objects by adding methods to Object.

.3.2 Monomorphic Types

One of the problems with pure object-oriented languages is that they use dynamic binding for *all* messages, even for simple arithmetic operations. However, studies of typical Smalltalk programs have shown that dynamic binding would not be needed in most cases. For example, variables referring to Boolean objects at one instant almost always continue to refer to Boolean objects throughout their life. Polymorphism is thus only rarely needed in the case of elementary data types.

This observation lead to the definition of **monomorphic types** in Omega. Whereas a variable of a polymorphic type P can be assigned children of P as well, variables of a monomorphic type M can only refer to objects of class M. This fact can be used by the compiler to avoid expensive message lookups, as the class of the objects referred to by monomorphic variables can be determined statically. That means that efficient inline code can be generated for operations with monomorphic values.The following types are defined as monomorphic in Omega:

- Action
- Block
- Boolean
- Char
- Integer
- Pointer
- Real

All of Omega's monomorphic types are immediate children of Object. A further restriction of monomorphic types is that no new types can be derived from them. They are – and always remain – leaves in the inheritance tree.

Although monomorphic objects are treated in a special way, they are still objects. In particular, there is a prototype for each of these types, and the prototypes inherit from Object. Consequently, methods defined for Object automatically also apply to elementary objects, such as Integer and Boolean. For example, the message 123 asString yields the string "123", and true typeName returns the string "Boolean".

Practical experience with Omega has shown that monomorphism doesn't impose a real restriction on the way in which programs are written. The small loss of flexibility is negligible, but the gain in efficiency is quite notable.

4.3.3 Generic Prototypes

When a new prototype is created from an existing one, it can be defined as generic by specifying a default parameter type (usually Object). For example, the Array prototype is generic with the default prototype Object. With this definition, the Array prototype and its clones[4] can be used to store arbitrary objects. When only objects of a specific class are to be stored in an array, a variant of the generic prototype (a so-called *generated prototype*) can be created by appending the desired parameter type within braces to the type name of the generic prototype. For example, the notion Array{Window} defines a variant of the Array prototype that can only hold Window objects and children of Window. Such parameter specifications can be nested. For example, the notion Array{Array{Button}} can be used to create an array of arrays (i.e., a matrix or two-dimensional array) of buttons. As Omega is a pure object-oriented language, elementary data are also represented as objects. It is therefore also possible to specify monomorphic types as actual parameters of generic types. For example, Array{Integer} is a legal variant of the Array prototype.

Within methods of a generic type, the pseudo type Parameter (see Section 4.3.4 *Pseudo Types*) denotes both the current parameter type and the prototypical object of that type. This also applies to a generic prototype's interface specification. For example, the methods add: and at: are specified as follows:

add: Parameter
at: Integer → Parameter

According to this definition, the prototype Array{Window} and its clones only accept windows as arguments of the message add:. Due to Omega's static typing, the correct usage of such generated objects can be checked statically by the compiler. Similarly, the message at: is guaranteed to return objects of class Window. The pseudo type name Parameter can thus be thought of as being substituted with a real type when an actual type of a generic prototype's parameter is specified. Note that several parameterizations (even with types as yet unknown) are possible. It is therefore not possible to statically predict the actual types of variables of type Parameter. The implications of this uncertainty are discussed in Section 4.3.4 *Pseudo Types*.

---

[4]   The prototype itself should never be used to store objects, as it serves as the source of clone operations. Adding objects to the Array prototype itself is thus considered as prototype corruption.

The default parameter of a generic prototype defines minimum requirements for subsequent parameterizations. When a type D is specified as the default parameter of a generic prototype G, a parameterization of the form $G\{T\}$ is legal only when $T=D$ or when T is a descendant of D. This restriction is particularly useful when certain operations are to be performed with objects of type Parameter within a generic prototype, for example, when the parameter objects are expected to accept a message that is known to be defined for a prototype S (and therefore also for all its children). To guarantee that all parameter objects will support the operation associated with this message, the type S can be specified as the default parameter type. However, such restrictions are not needed in most cases. For this reason, Object is commonly used as a generic prototype's default parameter type.

In most conventional programming languages supporting genericity, a generic type G serves only as a template, from which real types can be constructed by means of parameterization. It is therefore not possible to use G as a type without specifying a parameter type. In contrast, a generic prototype in Omega is already a real object. The specification of the type name G alone is equivalent to $G\{D\}$, where D is the prototype's default parameter type. For example, the notations Array and Array{Object} are synonymous and denote the same object.

Generated prototypes are not created explicitly by the programmer, but rather as by-products of other operations. For example, when the compiler comes across a type specification of the form $G\{T\}$, it creates a new variant of the generic prototype G, if that variant doesn't already exist. The creation of a new variant of a generic prototype is similar to cloning: First, a copy of the generic prototype is made, and then the prototype T is defined as the new object's parameter. This assignment can be thought of as storing a reference to T in an invisible instance variable of the newly generated prototype[5]. When another object is created by making a copy of $T\{G\}$, the parameter type is thus passed on to the new object. In fact, every object of a generic or generated class "knows" the type of its parameter. For example, the message parmTypeName can be used to determine the type name of such an object's parameter.

The creation of a new generated prototype may result in the creation of a couple of additional generated prototypes. For example, consider the simplified inheritance hierarchy of Omega's collection types shown in Figure 4-2.

---

5   This is only a thought model; in the Omega implementation, no such instance variables are wasted to store a prototype's parameter type. Instead, so-called *maps* [Chambers 1989] are used to keep track of all properties common to a class of objects.

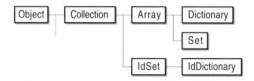

Fig. 4-2: Simplified inheritance hierarchy of Omega's collection types

All types (except, of course, Object) depicted in Figure 4-2 are generic with the default parameter type Object. When a new variant of, say, Set is created (e.g., Set{File}), a parent object is needed for the newly generated prototype. Thus, the prototype Array{File} is also created, unless it already exists. This indirect generation process is continued until either the desired parent object already exists or a non-generic prototype has been encountered. The inheritance hierarchy after the generation of Set{File} and IdDictionary{TextFile} is shown in Figure 2-5.

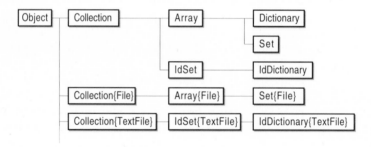

Fig. 4-3: Inheritance hierarchy of generated types

Note that there is no parent/child relation among the three variants of Collection. Although a File is an Object and a TextFile is a File, a Collection of Files is *not* a collection of Objects. The reason for this is that the types Collection (or, to be more precise, Collection{Object}) and Collection{File} have different interfaces. For example, consider the specifications of the methods add: and at:

add: Parameter
at: Integer → Parameter

In the case of Collection{File}, the add: method expects an argument of type File, whereas Collection{Object} allows arbitrary objects to be added. For this reason, an object of class Collection{File} cannot be assigned to a variable objColl of type Collection{Object}, as the message objColl add: would then allow the addition of arbitrary objects to a collection that is supposed to hold only files. The inheritance hierarchy of generated types thus consists of separate "type families" (see Section 2.8 *Genericity*).

.3.4   Pseudo Types

The two type identifiers Same and Parameter do not denote specific prototypes, but rather serve as fill-ins for other prototypes.

The identifier Same can be used to identify the type of the current receiver[6]. It can be specified ...

... in declarations of variables within methods,

... as return type of messages, and

... as prototype identifier,

but not ...

... in declarations of instance variables,

... as type of a formal parameter of a method, and

... as actual parameter of generic prototypes.

Even though a method belongs to a specific prototype, the meaning of Same can be different in successive invocations of the same method. For example, consider the following method isPrototype of Object:[7]

```
isPrototype → Boolean
[    myPrototype:Same;
     myPrototype := self prototype;
     self==myPrototype
]
```

In this implementation, the type Same is used to declare the variable myPrototype that is subsequently assigned the receiver's prototype (which is of the *same* class as the receiver). When the message isPrototype is sent to an object of class Object, the pseudo type Same has therefore the same meaning as Object. The method isPrototype is implemented only once in Object. All other prototypes simply inherit this implementation. When the message isPrototype is sent to an object of another class (e.g., Window), the same method is executed. But now, the receiver is of the class Window, so Same now denotes the type Window.

The pseudo type Same is particularly useful as the result type of a message. Examples of such messages are clone and copy, both defined in Object with the following interface specifications:

```
clone → Same
copy → Same
```

The type Same is a *static* indication that the result of the message will always be of the same class as the receiver. This knowledge can be used to statically ensure correct usage of these messages. For example, the assignments marked

---

[6]   The meaning of Omega's Same is similar to that of Eiffel's like Current [Meyer 1988].

[7]   In contrast to the notation introduced earlier, the symbol "^" is not needed in Omega to specify the result of a method. Instead, the last expression within a method determines the value to be returned to the caller. For details, refer to Section 4.6 *Methods*.

with "✔" in the following code fragment are all considered legal, whereas the assignments marked with "✗" violate Omega's compatibility rules:

```
o:  Object;
w:  Window;
z:  ZoomWindow;        -- a child of Window
r:  Rectangle;
...
w := w copy;      ✔
o := w copy;      ✔
w := z copy;      ✔
r := r clone;     ✔
w := w copy;      ✔
w := o copy;      ✗
w := r clone;     ✗
z := w copy;      ✗
```

From the client's point of view, the pseudo type Same in an interface specification of a message can be thought of as a fill-in for the static type of the receiver of that message – whatever that may be.

The pseudo type Same was introduced in Omega primarily to guarantee static type-safety with copy operations. In languages without a similar construct (such as C++), only the most general type Object can be specified as the result type of copying operations. The result of a copy message would then always be of the static type Object; simple statements such as w := w copy would therefore not be possible, as the compiler would not be able to detect that the result of the copy message is in fact compatible with the variable w. Consequently, explicit type casts must be used to persuade the compiler to accept such assignments. As Omega is a prototype-oriented language, the messages copy and clone are used rather frequently in Omega programs. It would therefore be unacceptable to force the programmer to use a type cast whenever he or she wants to create a new object.

The pseudo type Same is not only used as the result type of copy operations, but also for methods that are not expected to return a meaningful result. By convention, such methods always return self, and consequently the corresponding messages are defined with the result type Same.

The specification of Same as the result type of a message constitutes an obligation for the corresponding method to make sure that an object of the proper type is returned when the method is executed. In order to statically guarantee that the result of such a method will be of the same class as the receiver, the expression to be returned must be of the static type Same. The following recursive rule defines what expressions are considered as of type Same:

- self is an expression of type Same.
- Same is an expression of type Same (see below).
- A variable v declared as v:Same is an expression of type Same.
- When e is an expression of type Same and m is a message with the result type Same, then the message expression e m is also of type Same.

For example, the following implementation of the method copy conforms to these rules:

```
copy → Same
[ self clone copyParts ]
```

The message copyParts commands the receiver (here: the object created as the result of self clone) to create copies of all relevant objects referred to by its instance variables. As copyParts is not expected to return a meaningful result, it is defined with the result type Same.

As Same is a *static* type identifier, a variable of that type may refer to an object that is actually a child of the receiver's prototype. Anyway, an object of type Same can be expected to accept at least the messages defined for the prototype containing the currently executing method. That is, at least the messages defined in Object are applicable to expressions of type Same. Within a method of type Collection, an expression of type Same is also guaranteed to accept the messages add: and remove:.

Like every other prototype identifier, the name Same can also be used within an expression to denote a prototypical object. However, that prototype cannot be identified statically. Instead, the value of Same is determined at run time as the current receiver's prototype.

The second pseudo prototype is Parameter (see Section 4.3.3 *Generic Types*). Use of the identifier Parameter is allowed only in connection with generic prototypes. It can appear ...

... in declarations of variables within methods,
... as return type of messages,
... as prototype identifier,
... in declarations of instance variables,
... as type of a formal parameter of a method, and
... as actual parameter of generic prototypes.

In other words, the type Parameter can be used within a generic prototype like any other type. The restrictions listed above for Same do not apply to Parameter.

As was the case with Same, the meaning of Parameter cannot be determined statically. It is only guaranteed that Parameter denotes at least the generic prototype's default parameter type. Since no further assertions can be made statically, only the messages defined for the default parameter type can be applied to expressions of type Parameter. As the most general type Object is typically used as a generic prototype's default parameter type, only the basic set of messages defined in Object can be sent to Parameter objects.

It is also possible to use the name Parameter as the actual parameter type of another generic type. For example, the message asIdSet is implemented in Collection as follows:

asIdSet → IdSet{Parameter}
[IdSet{Parameter} copy addAllOf:self]

asIdSet first makes a copy of the IdSet[8] prototype with the same actual parameter. As collection prototypes do not contain any elements by default, the result of the copy message is an empty set. Then, the message addAllOf: is used to add all elements of the receiver to the set. When applied to an Array object arr, the result of the message arr asIdset is a set with the same elements as arr, but without the duplicate elements[9].

The following recursive rules define which expressions are considered as of type Parameter:

- Parameter is an expression of type Parameter (see below).
- A variable or formal method argument v declared as v:Parameter is an expression of type Parameter.
- When e is an expression of type Same and m is a message with the result type Parameter, then the message expression e m is also of type Parameter.
- When e is an expression of type Parameter and m is a message with the result type Same, then the message expression e m is also of type Parameter.
- When e is an expression of type G{Parameter} and m is a message with the result type Parameter, then the message expression e m is also of type Parameter.

The above rules apply only within methods of a generic prototype. For clients of such a generic object, the type Parameter is only relevant when it appears in the specification of a generic prototype's message. In that case, the pseudo type is always substituted with the actual parameter type. For example, the interfaces of the Array messages add: and at: are transformed into the following form when an object of type Array{Window} is used:

add: Window
at: Integer → Window

As the actual types represented by Same and Parameter cannot be predicted statically, special compatibility rules have to be observed with them. These rules are explained in detail in the following section.

---

[8]   IdSet is an abbreviation of "Identity Set". Such a set may contain equal, but not identical elements.

[9]   To compute the number of duplicates in arr, the message arr size – arr asIdSet size can be used.

.4 Compatibility Rules

The term "compatibility" has two different meanings in Omega:

- *Dynamic compatibility* defines the classes whose objects a variable d of a given type D may refer to at run time. When the dynamic compatibility rules are fulfilled, messages sent to d are guaranteed to be understood by the object referred to by d[10].
- *Static compatibility* uses only declarations of variables and method interfaces to define whether an expression s may be assigned to a variable d. As the run-time class of an expression's value cannot be determined statically, the static rules are more restrictive than the dynamic ones. When the static compatibility rules are met, it is guaranteed that the dynamic rules will be satisfied at run time.

In the following Section 4.4.1, first the static compatibility rules of Omega are listed. Section 4.4.2 discusses dynamic compatibility and shows how variables can be guaranteed to refer to proper objects at run time.

4.1 Static Compatibility

In statically typed languages, compatibility rules are intended to ensure proper use of variables and expressions. In a pure object-oriented language, all operations with objects are performed via messages. In order to make sure that the message x m will always succeed, it must be guaranteed that the variable x can only refer to objects that will accept the message m at run time. In order to achieve this goal, Omega's compatibility rules govern (references to) which objects may be assigned to which variables. These rules naturally apply to explicit assignments of the form x:=y, but there are also two less obvious forms of assignments that take place when messages are called and when they return a result. The following are the three forms of explicit and implicit assignments that are governed by Omega's compatibility rules[11]:

- In an explicit assignment of the form d:=s, the static type S of s must be compatible with the static type D of d.
- When a message with arguments is sent (e.g., x m:s), an implicit assignment of s to the method's formal argument d takes place. The static type S of the actual argument s must be compatible with the formal argument's type D.

---

[10] That statement is not quite true, as variables may contain references to Nil. In that case, they will not accept all possible messages. This aspect of compatibility is discussed in Section 4.4.1.

[11] In this enumeration and in the subsequent discussion of compatibility, s denotes the *source* and d denotes the *destination* of an assignment. The types of s and d are assumed to be S and D, respectively.

- When a method returns a result, the static type S of the expression to be returned must be compatible with the type D specified as the corresponding message's result type, as the sender of the message expects to get an object of class D as the result of the message.

It is important to see that compatibility is *not* symmetric. When the assignment d:=s is legal, the assignment in the opposite direction (s:=d) is not necessarily legal, too. Note that the first type in the phrase "S is compatible with D" always denotes the *source* type, and the second always denotes the *destination* type of an assignment. It can be read as "an expression of type S can be assigned to a variable of type D".

A source type S is said to be **statically compatible** with a destination type D when one of the following compatibility rules is satisfied. Each rule is listed under a separate heading and defined in a single sentence. After that, the consequences of that particular rule are explained in more detail.

Reflexivity

"Every type T is compatible with itself".

This may seem obvious, but it is worthwhile to note that this is the essential compatibility rule governing assignments to variables of monomorphic types and of the pseudo types Parameter and Same. Most other rules apply to polymorphic variables only.

Polymorphism

"Descendants of a polymorphic type D are compatible with D".

This is the compatibility rule used in most statically-type object-oriented languages. This rule implies that variables of type Object may refer to objects of *all* classes (even monomorphic ones).

Nil

"Nil is compatible with every polymorphic type D".

This rule actually breaks the condition that only objects with at least the same capabilities as defined in type D can be assigned to variables of type D. Nil is an immediate descendant of Object (see Figure 4-1). According to the above rule, it would only be possible to assign Nil to variables of type Nil and to variables of type Object. Yet, Nil can be assigned to variables of any other polymorphic type.

Nil is a special one-of-a-kind prototype that essentially stands for "no object". In most hybrid languages, a special value (for example, zero in C++) can be assigned to variables in order to express that the variable does not refer to any object at all. In Omega, Nil is a *real* object. Since the prototype Nil inherits from Object, at least these messages defined in Object can be safely sent to a

variable that refers to Nil. The following messages, in particular, have a well-defined behavior when sent to Nil:
- The comparison operators "=", "==", "#", and "##" can be used to compare Nil with other objects.
- The message asString returns the string constant "Nil".
- The messages clone and copy return Nil.
- The message isNil returns true. For every other object, isNil returns false.

The intention of the polymorphic compatibility rule is to ensure that messages to a variable d (of type D) will always be accepted by the object referred to by d at run time, because descendants of D inherit the messages defined in D. This assurance is no longer given when d refers to Nil. For example, d could be of type Array and contain a reference to Nil. The message add: would then be statically legal, but since add: is not defined for type Object and therefore not inherited by Nil, no corresponding method will be found when the message add: is sent to d. In that case, an exception will be raised. For more details on exceptions, see Section 4.9.4 *Exception Handling*.

Note that variables of the types Parameter and Same are "moving targets". Within a generic type G with the default parameter type Object, the pseudo type Parameter can (depending on the actual parameterization) denote a polymorphic as well as a monomorphic type. An assignment of Nil to a variable of the type Parameter is therefore only legal when G's default parameter type is a type other than Object. For the same reason, Nil cannot be assigned to a variable of type Same within a method of Object. As a method m implemented in Object is inherited by all monomorphic prototypes, the type Same can denote a monomorphic type when the message m is sent to a monomorphic object.

Same

"Same is compatible with the type containing the current method and its ancestors".

When a prototype D contains a method m, expressions of the pseudo type Same (in particular, self) can be assigned to variables of type D and of ancestors of D. Such assignments are safe because the method m can only be executed as the result of a message to an object of class D or to a descendant of D (which inherits the method m). This rule also means that expressions of type Same can be assigned to variables of type Object.

This rule also applies to uses of Same within methods of monomorphic types. Since the receiver of a message defined in a monomorphic type D is always known to be an object of class D, the type Same has the same meaning as D within methods of D.

Parameter

"Parameter is compatible with the current prototype's default parameter type and its ancestors".

Within a method of a generic type G with the default parameter type D, expressions of the pseudo type Parameter can be assigned to variables of the type D or any of its ancestors. Such assignments are safe because the actual parameter must either be D or an descendant of D. An object of type Parameter is therefore known to accept at least the messages defined for D. This rule also implies that expressions of type Parameter can be assigned to variables of type Object.

4.4.2   Dynamic Compatibility

In certain cases, the static compatibility rules are too rigid. For example, a reference to an object of class Window may for some reason have been assigned to a variable v of type Object. Static typing restricts the use of v to those messages that have been defined in Object. Although v actually refers to a Window object, no window-specific operations can be performed with this object via the variable v. In such a case we say that the view of the object has been narrowed by assigning it to a variable of a more general type.

The problem with the static polymorphic compatibility rules is that they are "one-way rules". Once the view of an object of class C has been narrowed by assigning it to a variable v of a type other than C, further assignments to other variables cannot widen the view of the object any more. Note that it is not possible to assign the variable v to a variable of type C, as the validity of such an assignment cannot be guaranteed statically. It is therefore necessary to dynamically check whether the assignment would conform to the compatibility rules. If this is the case, we speak of *dynamic compatibility*.

 An object s of class C and a variable d of type D are said to be **dynamically compatible** when ...
   ... $C=D$, or
   ... D is polymorphic and C is a descendant of D.

Obviously, the class C can only be resolved at run time. It is less obvious that the check performed in step 2 may require to dynamically determine the type D as well. This is necessary when the variable d was declared statically with a pseudo type:
   • When d was declared with the type Same, the type D is determined by the current receiver's class.
   • When d was declared with the type Parameter, the type D is determined by the current receiver's parameter type.

In Omega, so-called **conditional assignments** are used to perform assignments according to the rules of dynamic compatibility (i.e., to widen views of objects). A conditional assignment takes the form $d:?=s$, where the respective static types S and D of the expression s and the variable d need not be statically compatible with each other. Such a conditional assignment is executed in four steps:

1. The expression s is evaluated. The result is an object of a class C. Note that the class C is a dynamic property of s; when s is denoted by a variable of the static type S, C can be any subclass of S.
2. The dynamic compatibility of the class C with d's type D is checked.
3. If the check in step 2 succeeds, s is assigned to d; otherwise, the variable d is left unchanged.
4. The result of step 2 is converted into a boolean value (true for success, false for failure) that is finally returned as the result of the entire operation.

Steps 2 and 3 of this procedure are inseparable. No other operations can be performed while these two steps are being executed. This indivisibility guarantees that no interference can endanger the correctness of a conditional assignment.

A conditional assignment can be seen as an attempt to assign an expression to a variable. The assignment is executed only if does not violate the rules for typesafety. In contrast to similar concepts in other programming languages, failure does not lead to an exception. Another difference is that the result of a conditional assignment is checked *after* the attempt has been made. The following examples demonstrate some typical uses of conditional assignments.

Class Discrimination

It is sometimes necessary to dynamically ascertain the type of a certain object. For example, we may want to check whether an event in an interactive application was caused by a click of a mouse button, and, if so, whether the click occurred within the menu bar. Event is a general type with several children, one of which is MouseClick. The following code fragment shows how a conditional assignment can be used to treat an incoming event as a mouse click:

```
ev:Event;  click:MouseClick;
...
(click:?=ev) ifTrue: [
    click inMenuBar ifTrue: [ currentMenuBar handle:click ]
];
```

Test for Equality

The message "=" is defined with an argument of type Object in Object. In this way, it is possible to test two objects of arbitrary classes for equality. In order to implement a specific test in a descendant of Object, the default implementation of "=" must be overridden. For example, two Point objects are considered equal if they have the same x and y components. Unfortunately, the overriding method must adhere to the interface defined in Object. The argument can therefore be an object of any class. The following implementation of the method "=" in Point shows how a conditional assignment can be used to check whether the argument really is a Point object, and, if that is the case, whether its x and y components are equal to those of the receiver.

```
= {other:Object}  → Boolean
[   pt:Same;
    (pt:?=other) and: [(x=pt.x)&(y=pt.y)]
]
```

In this method, the variable pt is declared of type Same. The conditional assignment therefore verifies whether the argument is at least of the same class as the receiver. Only when this is the case are the coordinates then compared[12]. Note that even an argument of class Point might fail the test. When a new prototype Point3D is derived from Point without overriding the method "=", the message Point3D=Point will return false because Same is substituted with Point3D during the conditional assignment, and Point is not compatible with Point3D.

Assertion

Message interfaces are usually designed to serve a general purpose. These interfaces may later turn out to be too lenient in specific cases. For example, Omega's event handler objects usually exist within a certain context, an "environment". An object of class EventHandler can be installed in a certain context by sending it the message environment:. A pane is a special sort of event handler that must be installed in a view object[13]. A conditional assignment can be used in Pane's method environment: to make sure that this condition is met:

```
environment: {context:EventHandler}  → Same
[   aView:View;
    "A pane's environment must be a View" assertion: aView:?=context;
    install self into aView
]
```

---

[12]   The message and: performs a short-circuit operation; the second condition will not be tested
        if the first condition yields the value false.

[13]   Event handlers, panes, and views are central user interface elements of the Omega library.
        They are described in Chapter 6.

The message **assertion:** takes a boolean argument. The value of this argument must be **true**. If that is not the case, an exception is generated (see Section 4.9.4 *Exception Handling*). In this example, the argument **context** must pass the conditional assignment to the View variable aView.

4.3 Type and Prototype Identifiers

The following rule describes how types and prototypes are identified in Omega programs:

Type   = ptIdentifier ["{" Type "}"]
           | "Same"
           | "Parameter" .

The simplest type identifier is a name with an initial capital letter or one of the predefined pseudo types Same and Parameter. When the type denoted by an identifier is generic, an additional specification of the desired parameter type may follow. When the parameter specification is omitted for a generic type G with the default parameter D, the meaning is the same as if $G\{D\}$ had been specified. When a parameter P is specified, it must be a child of the default parameter D or the default parameter D itself. Note that the parameter type is recursively denoted by the symbol Type.

Examples:
Integer Boolean Array Same Parameter
Action{Integer} Set{Parameter} Array{Array{String}}

.5 Variables

There are three different kinds of variables in Omega:

- *Instance variables* are local to objects. The instance variables of an object are used to hold the object's state. New instance variables can be added to a prototype P interactively. The addition of an instance variable v to P also affects all other P objects and all descendants of P (see Section 3.2.3 *Inheritance—The Omega Model*). The variables v of these objects will initially have the same value, but these can be changed for every object individually afterwards. Instance variables exist for as long as the objects to which they belong, or until they are interactively removed by the programmer.
- *Shared variables* belong to an entire group of objects. Like an instance variable, a shared variable v is defined interactively for a prototype P, but it is allocated only once. All objects of class P and all descendants of

P share the same variable. In this respect, shared variables are similar to Smalltalk's class variables. When P is a generic prototype, the variable is also shared among generated prototypes and their descendants. Shared variables are independent of objects. A shared variables exists until it or the prototype for which it has been defined is interactively removed by the programmer.

- *Temporary variables* are declared within methods and blocks. They come into being when the execution of the method or block in which they have been declared starts and cease when the method or block terminates. Unlike instance variables and shared variables, temporary variables are not associated with objects and thus do not represent state. Instead, they are used to hold intermediate values during the execution of an algorithm.

In this section, only the first two "classes" of variables are discussed. The term "variable" therefore is only used for instance variables and shared variables here. Temporary variables are explained in Section 4.7 *Expressions*.

The screen snapshot in Figure 4-4 shows how a new variable is defined for a new prototype P in the Omega programming environment.

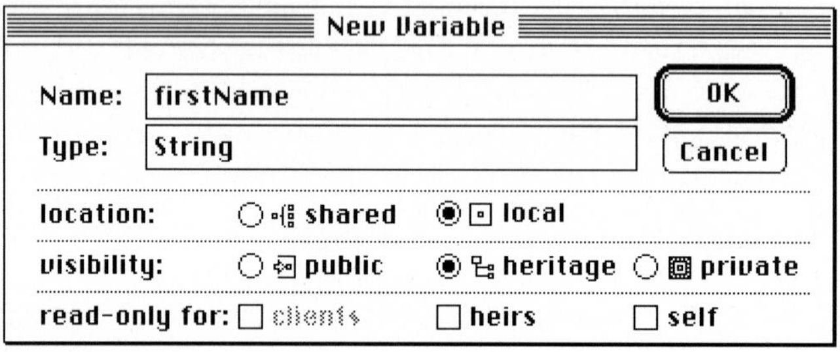

Fig. 4-4: Interactive declaration of a new variable

As depicted in Figure 4-4, the following attributes must be specified when a new variable is declared for a prototype P:

- The variable's *name* must follow the rule for identifier, as specified in Section 4.2.2 *Symbols*. When a new variable is introduced in the prototype P, its name must be distinct from all other (shared or instance) variables of P, its ancestors and its children.
- The name of the variable's *type* must follow the rule for Type as specified in Section 4.4.3 *Type and Prototype Identifiers*. However, the standard types Block and Action, the pseudo type Same and generated types parameterized with Parameter (such as Set{Parameter}) are not allowed for variables. Furthermore, shared variables cannot be of the pseudo type Parameter, as they exist only once for all variants of a generic prototype.

- The *location* of the variable must be specified as either "shared" or "local" (for instance variables).
- The *visibility* of the variable must be "public", "heritage" or "private". Private variables defined in prototype *P* can only be accessed from within methods of *P*, heritage variables can also be used within methods of *P*'s children, and public variables may be accessed from everywhere. The visibility of a variable is independent of its location. Both local and shared variables can have each of the visibility attributes described here.
- The variable's *modifiability* can be specified for each group of objects that has access to the variable. In the case of a public variable, clients can be prevented from modifying the variable by specifying it as read-only for clients. The modifiability of a variable is a hierarchic attribute. The table in Figure 4-5 shows the possible combinations of the access rights for all visibility attributes.

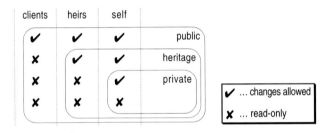

Fig. 4-5: Modifiability of variables, depending on their visibility

When a variable defined in a prototype *P* is read-only for methods of *P*, it is also read-only for methods within children and clients of *P*. On the other hand, when clients are granted write access to a variable, heirs and self cannot be denied such access. In other words, foreigners cannot have more rights than members of the "inner circle".

It is important to understand that a read-only variable does not mean that the object referred to by it cannot be changed, as such changes can happen indirectly as the result of a message to the variable. It is, however, guaranteed that the reference contained in a read-only variable cannot be redirected to a different object.

 A variable that is read-only for all categories may be considered as a *constant*. For example, true and false are immutable shared variables of Object. They are defined with the attribute "heritage", which is essentially the same as "public", since every other object is a descendant of the Object prototype.

Variables defined within a prototype *P* can be accessed within methods of *P* and its descendants simply using their name. In the case of an instance variable *iv*, the name *iv* always stands for a component of self. When an instance variable *iv* of another object *obj* is to be accessed, the notation *obj.iv*

has to be used. For example, the following method add: of Point accesses the instance variables of both self and the argument other.

```
add: {other:Point} → Same
[   x:=x+other.x;
    y:=y+other.y;
    self
]
```

The same notation is used to access public shared variables of a prototype. For example, the prototype Real has a public shared read-only variable pi that can be used from anywhere with Real.pi.

4.6   Methods

Like variables, methods are also defined interactively. The screen snapshot depicted in Figure 4-6 shows how a new method asString is defined in the Omega programming environment.

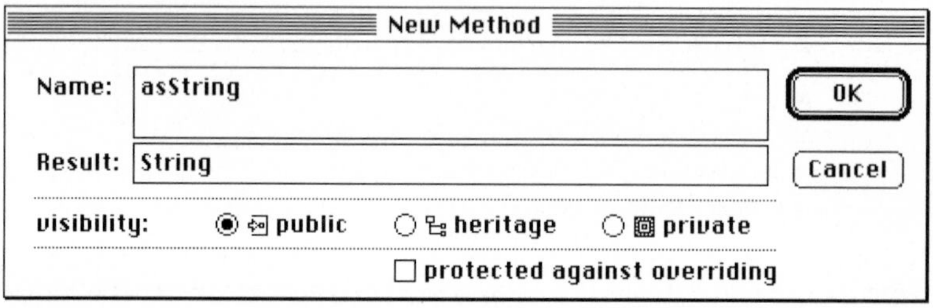

Fig. 4-6: Interactive declaration of a new method

The interface of a method consists of two parts. The first part defines its *name* and the *types of its arguments*, if any. The second part defines its *result type*. Both components define how the method can be used by clients, i.e., how a message to invoke the method must be formulated. The following rules describe the form of the first part of such a message definition.

```
MessageDef     = UnaryDef
               |  BinaryDef
               |  KeywordDef .

UnaryDef       = identifier | operator .

BinaryDef      = operator Type .

KeywordDef     = keyword Type { keyword Type } .
```

Three different kinds of messages are possible in Omega:

- *Unary messages* take no arguments. They can be identified by either an operator or an identifier. For example, the identifiers asString, clone, and parent and the unary operator "!"[14] are defined for Object, and the operator "~" is used for negation and sign inversion in Boolean and Integer, respectively.
- *Binary messages* take a single argument and are denoted by operators. For example, "== Object" and "= Object" of Object are used to check whether the receiver is identical or equal to the argument of the message. In Integer, the binary messages "+ Integer" and "− Integer" are used for arithmetic operations, and "@ Integer" is used to construct a Point object with the receiver as x coordinate and the argument as y coordinate. The Char message "* Integer" is used to construct a string consisting of as many copies of the receiver as the argument specifies. For example, the message 'X'*5 yields the string "XXXXX".
- *Keyword messages* take one or more arguments. A keyword message is defined by listing all its parts with the expected argument type after every keyword. For example, the Object message "isA:Object" checks whether the receiver is dynamically compatible with the argument, and "printOn:Printer" outputs the object in an adequate form on the printer specified as argument. In Array, the message "at:Integer" returns the object at a given index, and "at:Integer put:Parameter" replaces the object at the index given as first argument with the object specified after put:.

Operators can denote unary as well as binary messages. The kind of message is determined by the presence or absence of a type after the operator. Once an operator has been introduced as a unary message in a prototype *P*, the same operator can no longer be used for a binary message in ancestors and descendants of *P* and vice versa.

The result type of a message can be any of the types defined in Section 4.4.3 *Type and Prototype Identifiers*. The formal argument type specified with a binary or keyword message is restricted in that Same and generic types parameterized with Same are not allowed. The following example explains the reason for this restriction.

Same would be convenient as argument type of the identity and equality tests "= =" and "=" in Object. The intention of such a definition would be to specify that an object *c* of class *C* can only be compared with another *C* object or with children of *C*. However, *c* can be assigned to a variable *obj* of type Object. After such an assignment, variables of *any* type would be statically allowed as arguments of the messages "==" and "=". This means that the *C*

---

[14] The exclamation mark commands the receiving object to present itself to the user in an appropriate way. For example, the message "Hello"! displays the message "Hello" on the screen, and Beep! gives an audible alarm.

method "=" would be confronted with an argument that doesn't comply with the specification of that method.

The specification of a message *m* within a class *C* constitutes a contract between the clients of *C* and the implementer of the corresponding method. The argument types limit the ways in which clients can use the message and serve as a guarantee for the implementer that only objects of specific classes will be passed as arguments. The result type constitutes an obligation for the implementer to write the method in such a way that only objects of specific classes will be returned to the sender of the message. The client can rely on this specification.

When a method of *C* is overridden in a descendant *D* of *C*, the interface of the method must comply with the specification defined in *C*. It is, however, possible to make slight modifications to the interface, provided that the static typing rules are not violated. In particular, this means that ...

... argument types can be made more general, and

... result types can be made more specific.

The first rule means that the more specific *D* objects can accept more general arguments, when they are able to handle them. As the message specification in the *sub*type now accepts a *super*type of the original argument type, such a variation of a message specification is called ***contra*variance**. The following example shows why such an interface modification does not violate the static typing rules.

Assume that PictureViewer objects are able to display Picture objects in a window. The message "show:Picture" is used to tell a PictureViewer object what picture is to be displayed. After the development of the PictureViewer prototype, an additional effort is made to display graphical representations of all sorts of objects. The result is the new prototype ObjectViewer, a child of PictureViewer. To tell an ObjectViewer object which object is to be displayed, the specification of the message show: is now changed to "show:Object". In this way, ObjectViewer announces that it is capable of displaying arbitrary objects as well as Picture objects. When a variable ov is declared of type ObjectViewer, it is legal to pass, for example, an array, a complex number or a file object as an argument of show:. When ov is assigned to a variable pv of type PictureViewer, users of pv are bound by the original specification and can therefore only pass Picture objects as arguments of show:, which is perfectly safe because they simply do not use the additional capabilities of the ObjectViewer object referred to by pv.

Similarly, the second rule means that the more specific *D* objects can promise to return more specific results in response to particular messages. As the message specification in the *sub*type now returns a *sub*type of the original result type, such a variation of a message specification is called ***co*variance**[15].

---

[15] The specification of Same as the result type of a message is a special case of covariance, in which the result type always "follows" the type of the receiver.

The proof of why covariance in the case of result types is just as safe as contra-variance in the case of argument types is left here to the reader.

Like variables, methods can have the visibility attributes "public", "heritage", and "private" (see Figure 4-6). A private message m can only be used in other methods within the same prototype that contains the method m. Heritage messages can also be used by methods in descendants, and public messages are available to clients as well. The following guidelines give some hints as to which visibility attributes should be used under which circumstances.

- Most messages will have the attribute *public*. These are the messages that determine how an object can be used. Every operation that may be useful for clients should be made available by a public message, provided there is no danger of misuse.
- Messages with the attribute *heritage* are generally used to hide poten-tially dangerous operations from clients. It is considered good program-ming practice to avoid large methods. Instead of implementing a method m with hundreds of lines of code, it is better to develop several smaller methods that are used within m by means of *self sends*. As the "sub-methods" are only used internally, they need not be part of the official interface. When they are defined as heritage, descendants still have the chance to reuse or to selectively override these methods in order to apply a partial modification to the public method m.
- Messages with the attribute *private* are reserved for internal use. This attribute is particularly useful for safety-critical operations that should only be executed under certain conditions. For example, some low-level operations of File (which may disturb a file's integrity when called at the wrong moment) are defined as private.

To prevent heirs from overriding a method, the corresponding message can be defined as "protected". This attribute is automatically assigned to private methods, but can also be used for public and heritage messages. For example, the identity test "==" is defined as protected in Object. The message "=" is used in many places where a specific behavior is expected. The protection of this message ensures that the system integrity cannot be endangered by overriding methods that change the expected default behavior. The message " #" is protected against overriding for a different reason: Inequality of objects is simply defined as the negation of equality. The method "#" thus simply calls "=" and negates the result of this message. It would be unnecessary to override this implementation. The definition of "#" as protected encourages (in fact, forces) the implementer of a new prototype P to define equality and inequality of P objects with other objects by re-implementing the method "=" only.

The interactive definition of a message for a prototype P just extends the interface of P. But the interface is only one side of the coin; it is also necessary to specify which algorithm is to be executed when the message is received at run time. This is done by writing a method for the message. The following rules define the general appearance of a method.

Method	= [MethArguments] "[" Sequence "]" .
MethArguments	= "{" ArgumentDecl { ";" ArgumentDecl } "}" .
ArgumentDecl	= declaredIdent Type .
Sequence	= Expression { ";" Expression } .

When a message has arguments, the corresponding method must begin with braces containing the declarations of the arguments. Every argument is declared by giving it a name (that must immediately be followed with a colon; see the rules for identifiers in Section 4.2.2 *Symbols*) and associating it with a type. The identifiers (without the colon) must be unique; that is, they must be different from each other and also from shared and instance variables defined in *P* and its ancestors. When a message has more than one argument, the argument declarations must be separated with semicolons. The number of arguments in MethArguments must be the same as the number of parameter types in the message specification (MessageDef, defined at the beginning of this section). The argument types must correspond one-to-one with those in the message specification.

Within a method, the arguments are treated as *temporary read-only variables*. That means, arguments can only be input parameters of a method. There are no output, reference or VAR parameters as in Ada, C++ and Modula-2. To pass a single value to the caller, the method can return that value as its result (see below). To return multiple values to the caller, either a compound object containing all these values must be used or the values must be stored in an object passed as argument by the caller.

The body of a method consists of a sequence of expressions enclosed in brackets. When the method is activated at run time, all these expressions are evaluated successively. The value of the last expression constitutes the result of the method that is returned to the sender of the corresponding message. The values of all preceding expressions are ignored. However, this does not mean that all expressions except the last one are superfluous, as the evaluation of an expression can have several side effects, such as sending messages to other objects and changing the state of the receiver. As the last expression determines the result of the method, its (static) type must be statically compatible with the result type of the corresponding message.

The execution of a method can be terminated prematurely by sending the special message return to an object. In that case, the receiver of return is returned as the result of the method, and all remaining expressions are ignored. The receiver of return must be statically compatible with the result type of the corresponding message. The message return constitutes a special case; it is predefined in Object and treated in a special way by the compiler. For this reason, return is defined as *protected*.

 It is considered good style to include one or two *comments* between the parameter declaration and the method body. These comments should address the user of the method and explain its purpose. The way in which the method accomplishes its task should only be explained when this is necessary to understand how the method cooperates with other objects and/or methods. The Omega programming environment provides a menu command that extracts the definitions and comments of an object's methods and thus generates a simple textual documentation of the object's interface.

Examples:

Object's method "copy → Same":
    -- returns a copy of the receiver by first cloning the receiver and then
    -- sending the message copyParts to that clone. You should never need
    -- to override the message copy. To implement a different copying scheme,
    -- re-implement the method copyParts instead.
    [self clone copyParts]

Object's method "asString → String":
    -- the default implementation of this method returns a string
    -- consisting of the article "a[n]" and the receiver's type name
    [self typeName withArticle]

Object's method "# Object → Boolean":
    {other:Object}
    -- returns true if the receiver is not equal to the argument
    [(self=other)~]

Object's method "printOn: Printer → Same":
    {printer:Printer}
    -- sends a graphical representation of the object to the printer
    [self asImage printOn:printer; self]

Char's method "isLetter → Boolean":
    -- returns true when the receiver is a letter of the English alphabet
    [ch::=self upperCase;
      (ch>='A')&(ch<='Z')   ]

Integer's method " @ Integer → Point":
    {yCoord: Integer}
    -- returns a Point object with the receiver as x coordinate
    -- and the argument as y coordinate
    [Point clone x:self y:yCoord]

Integer's method "isPrime → Boolean":
    -- returns true if the receiver is a prime number
    -- values<2 (including negative ones) are considered non-prime
  [self<=1 ifTrue:[false return];
      self odd ifFalse:[(self=2) return]; *--2 is the only even prime number*
      div::=3; *--successively divide the receiver by all odd numbers ...*
      [div*div<=self] whileTrue: *--...up to the square root of self*
        [self\div=0 ifTrue:[false return]; div:=div+2];
      true   ] *--no divisor found; hence, the receiver must be prime*

Note that Omega's method syntax deviates from the notation we used in previous examples. From now on, all subsequent listings of methods will have the form used in the above examples.

4.7   Expressions

Expressions are the syntactical vehicle to describe how objects are to be computed. It is important to keep these two aspects apart. Expressions are not objects; they just describe how objects are to be computed at run time. An expression must be *evaluated* in order to deliver an object. This object is then said to be the expression's value.

In this section, expressions are described in terms of their syntax and their static and dynamic semantics. The static semantics define the compatibility rules that must be obeyed when an expression is formulated and the static type of the expression; the dynamic semantics describe the effect of the evaluation of the expression.

An expression can take one of the following forms:

Expression	=	ElementaryExpr
	|	MessageExpr
	|	CascadedExpr .

An expression can be an elementary expression (usually just a literal or a variable), an expression denoting message or a cascaded expression (an expression consisting of a series of concatenated messages).

Elementary expressions are explained in the following Section 4.7.1. Message expressions and cascaded message expressions are defined in Section 4.7.2. Section 4.7.3 finally describes the priorities of messages and operators.

4.7.1   Elementary Expressions

> ElementaryExpr   =   Literal
> | Prototype
> | "self"
> | Declaration
> | Variable
> | Assignment
> | "(" Sequence ")"
> | Block
> | Action .

An elementary expression can take nine different forms. The first seven are described in separate subsections below; the last two are discussed in Section 4.8 *Blocks and Actions*.

Literals

> Literal   =   integer I real I character I string .

The simplest form of an elementary expression is a literal, denoted by an integer number, a real number, a character or a string literal (see Section 4.2.2 *Symbols*). The type of such a literal is Integer, Real, Character or StringConstant, respectively. The result of the evaluation of a literal expression is statically determined by the value of the literal.

Prototypes

> Prototype   =   Type .

Prototypical objects are denoted by *type names*. Prototypes are globally visible; the only static restriction is that the pseudo prototype identifier Parameter can only be used within methods of a generic prototype.

In most cases, the prototype identified by a type can be determined statically; the evaluation of such prototypes is similar to that of literals. However, the evaluation of a prototype must be performed at run time in the following three cases:

- The pseudo prototype Same evaluates as the receiver's prototype. The value of Same can be determined statically only within a method of a monomorphic prototype.
- The pseudo prototype Parameter denotes the prototype representing the parameter of the current receiver.
- A prototype of the form $G\{$Parameter$\}$ evaluates as the prototype representing the variant of G with the same actual parameter as the receiver. Note that the evaluation of such an expression may require the con-

struction of a new generated prototype at run time (see Section 4.3.3 *Generic Types*).

self

The predefined identifier self denotes the current receiver of the method being executed. It is always of type Same within a method of a polymorphic prototype *P*. That is, self can evaluate as a child of *P* at run time. When used within a method of a monomorphic prototype *M*, self is considered as of type *M*.

Declarations

Declaration	= declaredIdent Type [":=" Expression]
	| initIdent Expression .

Declarations are special expressions in which new temporary variables are introduced with a *unique* name *x*. In contrast to most other block-structured programming languages, Omega does not allow multiple uses of the same variable name in different levels of nested scopes. This rule helps to avoid programming errors caused by name conflicts.

A declaration associates the new variable *x* with a type. When the declaration is evaluated at run time, the variable is assigned an initial value. A declaration can take three different forms:

- A *complete declaration* of the form *x:T:=e* specifies both the static type *T* of the new variable *x* and an expression *e* with whose value the variable is initialized when the declaration is evaluated. The type of expression *e* must be statically compatible with *T*.
  For example, the expression (w: Window := GrowWindow copy) open is a legal use of a complete declaration. The variable w is declared as a Window variable, but at run time it is assigned a GrowWindow object. The resulting expression is of type Window, but its evaluation yields the GrowWindow object that was assigned to w. This object is subsequently sent the message open.
- A *declaration with an implicit type* takes the form *x::=e*. The variable is declared with the static type of the expression *e* and initialized with the result of *e* when the declaration is evaluated. This form is particularly useful for the declaration and initialization of monomorphic variables. Instead of a complete declaration x:Integer:=1, the shorter form x::=1 can be used.
- A *declaration with implicit initialization* takes the form *x:T*. The variable is declared as of type *T*; the initial value of the variable is determined by the type *T*, as shown by the table in Figure 4-7.

static type	initial value
polymorphic type	Nil
Integer	0
Real	0.0
Boolean	false
Char	Char.nul
Pointer	Pointer.nil

Fig. 4-7: Initial values of implicitly initialized variables[16]

A newly defined temporary variable *x* can be used immediately *after* its declaration. Note that, since the initialization expression is part of the declaration, the variable cannot yet be used immediately within that expression. For example, the declaration x::=x+1 would be illegal for obvious reasons.

In all forms of declarations, the static type of the entire declaration is the type of the new variable, and evaluation of the declaration yields the value that was assigned to the variable.

Temporary variables cannot be declared of the types **Block** and **Action**. The reason for this restriction is explained in Section 4.8 *Blocks and Actions*.

Variables

| Variable   = [ElementaryExpr "."] identifier .

Variables are denoted by identifiers. The type of the identifier *x* is the static type with which the variable *x* was declared. When *x* is evaluated, the object currently referred to by *x* is returned. A variable *x* must be known at the point where it appears in an expression. An identifier *x* within a method *m* of a prototype *P* can denote ...

... a *local or shared variable* defined in *P* or an ancestor of *P*. When *x* is defined in an ancestor of *P*, it must have one of the visibility attributes *public* or *heritage*. When *x* identifies a shared variable, it represents a specific variable that is known statically. When *x* is local, it denotes an instance variable of the current receiver. The evaluation of a local variable thus involves an implicit evaluation of **self**.

... a *formal argument* of the method *m*. Evaluation of *x* yields the object passed as the corresponding actual argument by the sender of the message *m*.

---

[16] Char.nul is a public shared read-only variable of Char containing the ASCII character with the ordinal number 0. Pointer.nil is an implementation-defined value that does not represent a legal storage address.

... an *argument of an action object* (see Section 4.8).

... a *temporary variable* declared previously within the method *m*.

A variable identifier *x* can be preceded with an elementary expression *ee* and a period. This form is used for external access to instance variables and shared variables of objects other than self.

When *ee* is of the type *E*, the identifier *x* must be the name of a local or shared variable defined in the prototype *E* or one of its ancestors. When *ee.x* is used in a method of the prototype *P*, the variable must be visible within *P*. According to the visibility rules defined in Section 4.5 *Variables*, a variable *x* defined in a prototype *D* is visible within a method of *P* if one of the following conditions is met:

- *x* has the visibility attribute *public*.
- *P* is identical to *D*.
- *x* has the visibility attribute *heritage* and *P* is a descendant of *D*.

When *x* denotes a shared variable, the result of the evaluation of the preceding elementary expression *ee* is ignored, as the variable is defined uniquely by its name and the static type of *ee*. However, when *x* denotes an instance variable, the result of the evaluation of *ee* is needed to locate the object to which the instance variable *x* belongs. Note that such an evaluation may fail when *ee* is of a polymorphic type, as the expression may be evaluated as Nil. In this case, a "Nil access" exception is generated (see Section 4.9.4 *Exception Handling*).

The notation self.*x* has the same meaning as the simple identifier *x*. In fact, *x* may be regarded as an abbreviation of the explicit form self.*x* in the case of instance variables and shared variables of the receiver.

Assignments

Assignment   = Variable (":=" | ":?=") Expression .

Two kinds of assignments can be used to give a variable a new value. The symbols ":=" and ":?=" are used to distinguish conditional and unconditional assignments. As the static and dynamic semantics of these two forms are quite different, they are described separately.

In an *unconditional assignment* of the form *x:=e*, the expression *e* must be statically compatible with the variable *x*. The evaluation of an unconditional assignment is performed in two steps. First the expression *e* is evaluated, and then the result of that evaluation is assigned to the variable *x*. The type and the value of the entire assignment are the static type and the value of *e*.

In a *conditional assignment* of the form *x:?=e*, the static compatibility between *e* and *x* is irrelevant. The evaluation of a conditional assignment is performed in three or four steps (see Section 4.4.2 *Dynamic Compatibility*). First the expression *e* is evaluated. Second, the dynamic compatibility of the result of the evaluation with the static type of *x* is tested. If that test succeeds, the result of *e* is assigned to *x* in the third step, otherwise this step is skipped.

In the last step, the result of the second step (true for success, false for failure) is returned as the result of the entire assignment. A conditional assignment is always of type Boolean.

A common precondition of both kinds of assignments is that the variable *x* must not be read-only. In particular, assignments to formal arguments of messages and actions are not allowed.

Note that the expression *e* on the right hand side of an assignment may again consist of an assignment. According to the rules stated above, a chain assignment of the form *x*:=*y*:=*z* is executed from right to left. It is equivalent to *x*:=(*y*:=*z*).

Expression Sequences

A sequence of *expressions enclosed in parentheses* is to be considered as a single expression. The type of such a sequence is the type of the last expression within the sequence. An expression sequence is evaluated by evaluating all its expressions in order of appearance. The value of the sequence is determined by the value of the last expression. The results of the preceding expressions are ignored. For example, the expression sequence (x::=1; x:=x+1; x+1) is of type Integer; it returns the value 3 and leaves the value 2 in the variable x.

Parentheses are generally used to enforce a particular order of execution. For example, the expression 2+1~ yields the value 1 (2 plus –1) because the unary message "~" has priority over the binary message "+", whereas the expression (2+1)~ yields the value –3. The order in which messages are executed is discussed in detail in Section 4.7.3 *Precedence of Messages*.

.7.2 Message Expressions

MessageExpr	=	UnaryExpr
			BinaryExpr
			KeywordExpr .

In analogy to the three kind of methods, a message expression can be a unary, binary, or keyword expression. The syntax of these message expressions is defined in the following three subsections. Since almost the same rules apply to all kinds of messages, the common static and dynamic semantics of message expressions are mentioned at the end.

Unary Expressions

| UnaryExpr | = ElementaryExpr UnaryMsg |
| | | UnaryExpr UnaryMsg . |

| UnaryMsg | = [Parent] (identifier | operator) . |

A unary message expression begins with the specification of the receiver, which must be an elementary expression or a unary expression[17]. An arbitrary number of unary messages can be sent successively. The unary message expression $x\ y\ z$ is equivalent to $(x\ y)\ z$; that is, unary messages are executed from left to right.

A unary message is denoted by either an identifier or an operator. For example, "100 random ~ !" is a legal unary expression. First the message random is sent to 100. The result is a random number in the range 1 through 100. The message "~" then inverts the sign of the random number, and "!" displays the negative random number on the screen.

Binary Expressions

| BinaryExpr | = BinaryOperand BinaryMsg |
| | | BinaryExpr BinaryMsg . |

| BinaryOperand | = ElementaryExpr | UnaryExpr . |

| BinaryMsg | = [Parent] operator BinaryOperand . |

The receiver of a binary message expression must be an elementary expression, a unary expression or a binary expression. An arbitrary number of binary messages can be sent in succession, where every binary message consists of an operator and an argument (which must – like the receiver – be an elementary or a unary expression). The binary message expression x+y*z is equivalent to (x+y)*z; that is, binary messages are executed strictly from left to right.

Note that it is syntactically impossible to detect whether, for example, "x $ y" denotes the binary message $ with the argument y or two unary messages $ and y. The meaning of this expression depends on whether the message $ is defined as unary or as binary for the static type of x.

Keyword Expressions

| KeywordExpr | = KeywordOperand KeywordMsg . |

| KeywordOperand | = ElementaryExpr | UnaryExpr | BinaryExpr . |

---

[17] Note that every expression can be written as an elementary expression by enclosing it in parentheses.

```
KeywordMsg        = [ Parent ]
                    keyword  KeywordOperand
                    { keyword  KeywordOperand } .
```

The receiver of a keyword message expression must be an elementary expression, a unary expression or a binary expression. Only a single keyword message can be sent to the receiver. A keyword message consists of an arbitrary sequence of keywords, each followed by an argument.

Note that x y:a z:b denotes the *single* keyword message y:z: with the arguments a and b. When y: and z: are meant to be separate messages, parentheses – as in (x y:a) z:b – or cascaded messages (as explained later in this section) must be used.

Semantics of Message Expressions

When a message m is sent to an expression e of the static type E, a method with the name m must be defined in the prototype E or at least one of its ancestors. When a message has arguments, the types of the expressions specified as actual arguments must be statically compatible with the formal argument types of the message, as defined in the prototype containing the corresponding method. The static type of a message expression is the return type of the message. When the message's return type is specified by a pseudo type, the following rules apply:

- When the message has the return type Same, the message expression is of the same type as the receiver of the message.
- When the receiver's type is a generic type G with the default parameter type P or a generated type $G\{P\}$:
  - When the message has the return type Parameter, the message expression is of the type P.
  - When the message has a return type of the form $R\{$Parameter$\}$, the message expression is of the type $R\{P\}$.

The evaluation of a message expression is performed in several steps:

- The receiver is evaluated.
- The actual arguments (if any) are evaluated from left to right.
- The receiver is searched for a method with the same name as the message. Due to Omega's static typing rules, a corresponding method will usually be found in the receiver or one of its ancestors. Only when the receiver is Nil, may the message lookup fail and result in a "Nil access" exception.
- Memory is allocated to the method's arguments and temporary variables.
- The values of the actual arguments are assigned to the formal arguments.
- The expression sequence contained in the method's body is evaluated.

- The result of the message expression is determined by the result of the last expression within the method body or an expression that was sent the message return within the method.

In the second step, the arguments are evaluated from left to right, independently of each other, such that the evaluation of an argument does not affect the results of previous arguments. For example, consider the following expression sequence:

```
x::=1;
anObject m:x n:(x:=x+1)
```

In this example, the evaluation of the first argument x returns the value 1. During evaluation of the second argument (x:=x+1), the value 2 is assigned to x. Since the first argument has already been evaluated, its value is not affected by the subsequent assignment to x. Similarly, the receiver is evaluated independently of the arguments. For example, the result of the sequence (x:=2; x*(x:=x+1)) is 6, but the evaluation of (x:=2; (x:=x+1)*x) yields the value 9.

Parent Messages

As indicated by the rules for UnaryMsg, BinaryMsg and KeywordMsg, a message can be preceded by a parent specification:

> Parent   =   "(" ptIdentifier ")" .

A parent specification for a message contained in a method m of the prototype $P2$ with the (immediate) parent $P1$ consists of the name $P1$ within parentheses. A message with a parent specification (a so-called **parent message**) can only be sent to self. The static and dynamic semantics of a parent message of the form *self (P1) m* are similar to that of the message *self m*. The following enumeration lists the differences between these two forms:

- In *self m*, a method with the name m must be present in $P2$ or in one of its ancestors; in *self (P1) m*, a method m must be present in $P1$ or in an ancestor of $P1$. Consequently, only inherited and overridden methods can be identified with this form.
- The method executed as the result of *self m* is determined at run time by dynamic binding, but static binding is used to determine the parent method in *self (P1) m*.

The identifier within the parentheses must be the name of the immediate ancestor. The explicit specification of the ancestor makes it clear for the reader where the method lookup starts in the case of a parent message. However, it is not possible to use parent messages to explicitly invoke a method in one of the parent's ancestors. For example, assume that $P1$ is the parent of $P2$ and $P0$ is the parent of $P1$. A message of the form *self (P0) m* would be correct in a

method of *P1*, but illegal in a method of *P2*. However, the evaluation of the
parent message *self (P1) m* in *P2* will result in the invocation of *P0*'s method
m when *P1* doesn't contain a method with the name *m*.

Parent messages are useful in cases where an inherited method should not
be overridden entirely, but rather extended with additional operations. For
example, the following code fragment shows how the implementation of the
method asString in IdSet reuses the overridden implementation of Collection.

IdSet's method "asString → String":

    -- returns all elements of the set, enclosed within braces

```
[   str::=self (Collection) asString;
    str at:1 put:'{';
    str at:str size put:'}'   ]
```

The Collection implementation of asString constructs a string containing textual
representations of all elements of a collection, separated with commas and
enclosed within parentheses (e.g., "(1,2,3)"). The IdSet implementation of
asString first invokes the overridden method and lets it do the dirty work.
Afterwards, the parentheses are replaced with braces.

Another typical use of parent messages is to be found within the
copyParts messages of many prototypes that have more instance variables than
their parents. The message copyParts is called within copy to give a newly
cloned object the opportunity to copy certain objects referred to by instance
variables. For example, copyParts is implemented in Pane as follows:

Pane's method "copyParts → Same":

    -- copies all View instance variables and the receiver's background

```
[   self (View) copyParts;
    background:=background copy;
    self   ]
```

First, the overridden copyParts method is invoked. In this way, all objects
referred to by inherited instance variables are copied. Afterwards, only the new
object referred to by background need be copied.

Parent messages are also used to treat user input differently from the
parent. The following example illustrates how mouse clicks in the zoom area of
a ZoomWindow are implemented on the basis of GrowWindow's handling of
them:

ZoomWindow's method "doClick:MouseClick → Boolean":

    -- copies all View instance variables and the receiver's background

    {click:MouseClick}

```
[   click inZoomBox ifTrue:[(self handleZoom:click) return];
    self (GrowWindow) doClick:click   ]
```

In this example, an initial check is made to discover whether the mouse click appeared within the window's zoom box. If that is the case, the click is handled by a separate message handleZoom:, if not, the click is simply passed to the overridden method of GrowWindow.

Cascaded Messages

CascadedExpr	=	MessageExpr { "," Message }.
Message	=	UnaryMsg I BinaryMsg I KeywordMsg .

Cascaded messages are a convenient means of sending a message to the result of a previous message by separating the messages with commas. The effect of a cascaded message x m1, m2, m3 is identical to that of ((x m1) m2) m3. Long cascaded messages are easier to read and write than expressions with many parentheses.

Note that the separating commas are not necessary in the case of unary and binary messages. They are, however, required to concatenate keyword messages, as x m1:y m2:z denotes the message m1:m2: with the arguments y and z, but the form x m1:y, m2:z denotes two separate messages m1: and m2: with the respective arguments y and z. The following example shows a typical use of a cascaded message expression:

Box' method "asString → String":
    -- returns a string with the left, top, right and bottom
    -- coordinates enclosed in parentheses
    ["("+left asString,
        addChar:',',
        add: top asString,
        addChar:',',
        add: right asString,
        addChar:',',
        add: bottom asString,
        addChar:')'   ]

In this method, first an open parenthesis is concatenated with the string representation of the instance variable left. Then successive messages are used to append commas, the string representations of the other instance variables and finally the closing parenthesis to that string.

4.7.3   Precedence of Operations

The EBNF rules listed so far not only describe the correct forms of expressions, but also their precedence. However, this information is hard to extract from the formal description. The precedence rules of Omega are therefore summarized in this section.

Unary messages have the highest, and keyword messages the lowest priority. Successive unary and binary messages are executed from left to right; keyword messages can only be concatenated by means of a cascaded message expression, in which case they also evaluate from left to right. Parentheses can be used to enforce a different precedence of messages. The table in Figure 4-8 shows a few message expressions. In the left column, the expressions are written without parentheses; in the middle column, parentheses are used to specify the same order of evaluation, and the right column lists the messages in the order in which they are executed.

simple message	fully specified form	execution order of messages
x + y * z	(x + y) * z	+ *
x a b + y c d	((x a) b) + ((y c) d)	a b c d +
x + y a − z b	(x + (y a)) − (z b)	a + b −
x a + y m: z	((x a) + y) m: z	a + m:
x m: y + z a	x m: (y + (z a))	a + m:
x m: y + z n: w ~	x m:(y + z) n: (w ~)	+ ~ m:n:

Fig. 4-8: Priorities and evaluation order of messages

Assignments do not quite fit into the priority scheme defined for messages, as they are executed from right to left within the same nesting level of parentheses. When no parentheses are present, an assignment extends until the end of the entire expression. An expression of the form $a+b+c:=d+e+f$ is therefore equivalent to the form $a+b+(c:=d+e+f)$. When two assignments appear within the same expression, the second one is part of the expression assigned by the first one. For example, the expression $a+b:=c+d:=e+f:=g$ has the same meaning as $a+(b:=c+(d:=e+(f:=g)))$.

Note that the right-to-left binding of assignments also applies to conditional assignments and to declarations with explicit initialization.

Whilst assignments within expressions are very handy in some circumstances, they are sometimes hard to understand. It is therefore a good idea to always use parentheses to explicitly delimit the scope of obscure assignments.

4.8 Blocks and Actions

Being a pure object-oriented language, Omega adopts the Smalltalk point of view that even statement sequences (or, rather, expression sequences) should be treated as objects. The following rule shows how such objects can be constructed:

| Block | = "[" [Sequence] "]" .

A bracketed sequence of expressions is called a **block**. It is of the static type Block. When a block is evaluated, its result is the enclosed "dormant" expression sequence. Its evaluation does *not* automatically evaluate the expression sequence.

The expression sequence denoted by a block can be evaluated by sending the message "do" to the block. The result of the message is of type Boolean. Its value depends on the static type of the last expression within the block. When the last expression is of type Boolean, its value is returned, otherwise the value false is returned. The reason for this exceptional rule is that the result of the activation of a block is rarely needed. It would be inconvenient if such a block had to be explicitly terminated with a boolean value (such as [i:=i+1; false]). Note that a block may be empty. The activation of an empty block has no effect and results in the value false.

A block constitutes a separate scope within a method. Variables declared within a block only exist as long as the block is being executed. Hence, they are not visible from outside the block. Inversely, variables known outside the block can be used within the block as well. For this reason, the name of a variable within a block must not conflict with already defined variables. However, two successive blocks within the same method may have a variable with the same name, since the scopes of these variables do not overlap.

The fact that variables belonging to the method containing a block can be accessed from within a block implies that the block cannot be activated when its enclosing method is no longer active. Such a situation could easily occur when a reference to a block was stored in a shared or local variable of an object. In order to avoid this sort of error, a special rule prohibits assignments of blocks to variables. This is also the reason why variables cannot be declared of type Block. The only legitimate use of a block is as an actual argument and as the receiver of a message. Blocks are nevertheless a very powerful concept, as will be shown in Section 4.9 *Flow Control*.

The message return has a special meaning within a block. The expression x return does not just terminate the evaluation of the block itself, but also the entire method containing the block. Such a premature exit from a method is therefore called a **non-local return**. The receiver of return determines the result of the method and must therefore be statically compatible with the method's result type.

The message return can cause other messages not to deliver a result because they simply do not return to their sender. The control flow diagram in Figure 4-9 illustrates how such a situation can arise: The message doSomething is sent to an object x. In the corresponding method, the message perform: with the block [0 return] is sent to yet another object y. In the method perform:, the block passed as argument receives the message do. As the result of this message, the expression 0 return is evaluated, and the value 0 is returned to the sender of doSomething (since doSomething is the method containing the block

[0 return]) and subsequently assigned to the variable v. Note that neither the message perform: in doSomething nor the message do in perform: return to the point from where they were sent. The assignments in which these messages occur are thus never completed.

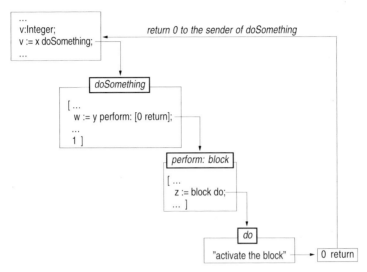

       Other kinds of blocks can have an argument. These sorts of blocks are called **actions** in Omega terminology. The structure of actions is defined by the following EBNF rule:

| Action   = "{" ArgumentDecl "}" Block .

An action is similar to a block in that it consists of an expression sequence enclosed in brackets. The main difference between actions and blocks is that actions begin with an argument declaration within braces. The formal argument of an action is declared in the same way as that of a method with a single argument (see Section 4.6 *Methods*), but in contrast to a method, an action can only have a single argument.

An action with an argument of the static type P is of type Action{P}. It can be activated by means of the message doWith:, which is defined with the following interface in the Action prototype:

doWith: Parameter → Boolean

When an action is activated, its formal argument is assigned a reference to the object passed as argument of the message doWith:. Like blocks, actions always return a boolean value when activated. The last expression determines the result of the activation of the action in the same way as explained above for Block.

The formal argument of an action is considered local to the action; its name must be different from all other names known at the point of the definition of the action. In contrast to temporary variables declared within a block or action, the formal argument is read-only.

Like blocks, actions can only be passed as arguments to messages, and cannot be assigned to variables. Typical uses of actions and blocks are explained in the following section.

4.9   Flow Control

In the previous sections of this chapter, *all* language elements of Omega have been defined. All Omega programs can be expressed with the basic elements summarized in the following:

- literals
- variables
- types and prototypes
- messages and methods
- assignments
- blocks and actions

All other language concepts of Omega are constructed with these basic building blocks. Note in particular that branches and loops are not defined in the language proper, but rather implemented in terms of blocks and actions. In this section, the following topics will be covered:

- predefined flow control elements
- short-circuit evaluation of boolean operations
- iteration over elements of data structures
- exception handling

Some of these operations are implemented by means of so-called **primitive methods**. Primitive methods are methods that for some reason cannot be expressed in Omega. Examples of such methods are the basic operations with elementary data types. The Omega compiler recognizes these methods as special cases and "knows" how to implement them. The same technique is used for some flow control methods. Other methods can be expressed in terms of these basic methods. Wherever possible, the implementation of such "high-level" methods is shown in the following sections.

.9.1   Predefined Flow Control Elements

The basic flow control elements are implemented as methods of the prototypes Boolean and Block. Most of them take an argument of type Block.

Branches

There are four different messages for branches (if statements in conventional programming languages). Only the Boolean method ifTrue: is implemented as a primitive method. It is defined as follows:

   ifTrue: Block → Boolean

If the receiver is true, the block passed as a parameter is evaluated and its result is returned as the result of ifTrue:. If the receiver is false, the block is not evaluated, and false is returned as the result of ifTrue:[18]. For example, the expression
   myWindow==Nil ifTrue: [myWindow := Window copy]
assigns a new window object to the variable myWindow only if myWindow does not yet refer to an object.

All other methods for branches are implemented in terms of ifTrue:. The following methods show their implementations:

Boolean's method "ifFalse: Block → Boolean":
   {aBlock: Block}
   -- *evaluates aBlock and returns its result when the receiver is false.*
   -- *otherwise, true (the value of the receiver) is returned.*
   [self ifTrue: [true return];
      aBlock do   ]

Boolean's method "ifTrue: Block ifFalse: Block → Boolean":
   {trueBlock: Block; falseBlock:Block}
   -- *evaluates trueBlock and returns its result when the receiver is false.*
   -- *otherwise, the result of the evaluation of falseBlock is returned.*
   [self ifTrue: [trueBlock do return];
      falseBlock do   ]

Boolean's method "ifFalse: Block ifTrue: Block → Boolean":
   {falseBlock: Block; trueBlock:Block}
   -- *evaluates falseBlock and returns its result when the receiver is false.*
   -- *otherwise, the result of the evaluation of trueBlock is returned.*
   [self ifTrue: trueBlock ifFalse: falseBlock   ]

---

[18] In Smalltalk, this different behavior of true and false is implemented by means of two classes True and False (see Section 3.3 *One-of-a-kind Prototypes*). Whereas the Smalltalk solution is elegant, the need for two additional prototypes has been avoided in Omega by defining the ifTrue: method as primitive.

Loops

There are several different predefined messages for the implementation of loops. Five of them are implemented in Block. They correspond to while, repeat and loop statements in conventional programming languages. Only the method loop is implemented as a primitive method. It is defined in Block as follows:

    loop → Boolean

The receiver of this message is repeated forever and never returns a result. The only possible way of escaping such an endless loop is by means of a non-local return, as shown in the following implementations of the remaining loop methods of Block:

Block's method "whileTrue: Block → Boolean":
    {whileBlock: Block}
    -- *evaluates whileBlock as long as the receiver evaluates as true.*
    [[self do
                ifTrue: [whileBlock do]
                ifFalse: [false return]
          ] loop
    ]

Block's method "whileFalse: Block → Boolean":
    {whileBlock: Block}
    -- *evaluates whileBlock as long as the receiver evaluates as false.*
    [[self do
                ifFalse: [whileBlock do]
                ifTrue: [true return]
          ] loop
    ]

Block's method "repeatUntilTrue → Boolean":
    -- *evaluates the receiver until it evaluates as true.*
    [self whileFalse: [ ]   ]

Block's method "repeatUntilFalse → Boolean":
    -- *evaluates the receiver until it evaluates as false.*
    [self whileTrue: [ ]   ]

Three more methods for the implementation of loops are implemented in the Integer prototype. Their implementations are listed below.

Integer's method "timesRepeat: Block → Integer":
    {repeatBlock: Block}
    -- evaluates repeatBlock as many times as specified by the receiver.
    [i::=self;
       [(i:=i−1)>=0] whileTrue: repeatBlock;
       self]

Integer's method "to: Integer do: Action{Integer} → Integer":
    {limit: Integer; action: Action{Integer}}
    -- evaluates action for every integer value between the receiver and limit.
    [i::=self;
       [i<=to] whileTrue: [action doWith: i; i:=i+1];
       self]

Integer's method "to: Integer by: Integer do: Action{Integer} → Integer":
    {limit: Integer; step: Integer; action: Action{Integer}}
    -- evaluates action for every integer value between the receiver and limit,
    -- starting with the receiver and incrementing the value by step.
    [i::=self;
       step=0 ifTrue: [self return]; *-- an increment of zero is not allowed*
       step>0 ifTrue:
      [[i<=limit] whileTrue: [action doWith:i; i:=i+step]]
      ifFalse:
      [[i>=limit] whileTrue: [action doWith:i; i:=i+step]]
      self]

The messages to:do: and to:by:do: both iterate over a range of values. For example, the expression

    1 to: arr size do:{i:Integer}[arr at: i put:i*2]

fills all elements of the array arr with the squares of their index. The message semantics of Omega and the special role of the action's argument have two important consequences on the semantics of such "for loops":

- Since the arguments are evaluated before the method is activated, the upper limit of the loop is predetermined before the loop actually starts. The same is true for the increment of the message to:by:do:.
- The argument of the action is *read-only* and local to the block. It is therefore not possible to change its value during execution of the loop. Even if such modifications were possible, they would only affect a single invocation of the action, but not the execution of the loop. The next time through the loop, the argument would again be initialized properly.

Note that no special language rule is necessary to define this behavior of a "for loop". The effects described above are achieved entirely through Omega's message and action semantics.

The methods to:do: and to:by:do: are also implemented in the Real proto-type. Their implementation is almost identical to that of their Integer counter-parts.

4.9.2   Short-Circuit Evaluation of Boolean Operations

The operators "&" and "|" are defined in Boolean as "and" and "or", re-spectively. Both operators take a Boolean argument and return a Boolean result. The trouble with these operators is that they follow the message evaluation rules outlined in Section 4.7.2 *Message Expressions*. That means that in the expression x&y first the receiver x is evaluated, then the argument y, and finally the method "&" is activated. This is unsuitable in some cases, in parti-cular when the evaluation of the argument involves a time-consuming method or when the meaning of y is only defined when the condition x returns true. The expression

(i>=0) & (i<=array size) & ((array at:i)=0)

is an example of such a situation. The expression array at:i is only defined when the value of the index i is between 1 and the size of the array. In the above example, all partial expression would be evaluated in the case i=0, which would lead to a run-time error during execution of the at: method.

Blocks are a very useful concept to help formulate so-called *short-circuit evaluation*. The following methods and: and or: can be used to solve the problem outlined above:

Boolean's method "and: Block → Boolean"[19]:
{aBlock: Block}
-- the same result as self & aBlock value, except that
-- aBlock is not evaluated when the receiver is false.
[self ifTrue: aBlock   ]

Boolean's method "or: Block → Boolean":
{aBlock: Block}
-- the same result as self | aBlock value, except that
-- aBlock is not evaluated when the receiver is true.
[self ifFalse: aBlock   ]

The above problem can be solved by formulating the expression in the following way:

(i>=0) & (i<=array size) and: [(array at:i)=0]

The partial expression (array at:i)=0 is now enclosed in brackets. This means that the *passive* expression is passed as argument to and: instead of its value.

---

[19] Note that the methods and: and or: are implemented in terms of ifTrue: and ifFalse:. In fact, these methods have the same effect. To verify this, refer to the definitions of ifTrue: and ifFalse: in the previous section.

The block is only activated when the receiver (i>=0) & (i<=array size) is true. Otherwise the result false is returned by and: without needing to evaluate the block.

.9.3   Iteration over Elements of Data Structures

Actions are particularly useful for performing certain operations with every element of a data structure. For this purpose, the generic prototype Collection contains the following method:

Collection's method "forAll: Action{Parameter} → Same":
    {elementAction:Action{Parameter}}
    -- executes elementAction for every single element.
    -- ABSTRACT -- must be overridden
    [self abstractMethod]

The method is defined as abstract in Collection. Since Omega does not provide direct support for abstract methods by means of a language element, abstract methods must be simulated by the programmer. For this purpose, Object contains a method abstractMethod that will raise an exception.

    The following method of Array shows a typical real implementation of the forAll: method:

Array's method "forAll: Action{Parameter} → Same":
    {elementAction:Action{Parameter}}
    -- executes elementAction for every single element.
    [1 to: self size do:
        {i:Integer}[elementAction doWith: (self at:i)];
      self   ]

As this method illustrates, the forAll: method is rather easy to implement, but it is even easier to use. The following example shows how the sum of all elements of an array of integers can be computed with the forAll: method:

    sum::=0;
    arr forAll:{value:Integer}[sum:=sum+value];

Note that, since the message forAll: is defined in Collection, the above code fragment would also work if arr were, for example, a set, a list or a binary tree.

    The method forAll: helps to separate clearly the responsibilities for iterating over all elements of a data structure: The data structure defines how and in which order the individual elements are visited, and the client provides the operations to be executed with each element in turn. It is also important to see that the data structure controls the iteration. Whenever an action is to be executed for an element, a *call-back* to the sender (i.e., the method containing the action) is performed.

There are several other useful applications of forAll:. In particular, the message is used in self sends within Collection to implement other iterations over all elements of a data structure. The following five methods are typical examples for advanced iterators:

Collection's method "asString → String":
    -- *returns the receiver's string representation.*
    [self size=0 ifTrue:["()" asString return];
       s::="(" asString;
       self forAll:{elem:Parameter}[s add:elem asString, addChar:','];
       s at:s size put:')']

Collection's method "contains:Parameter → Boolean":
    {testElem:Parameter}
    -- *checks whether the collection contains testElem.*
    [self forAll:{elem:Parameter}[elem==testElem ifTrue:[true return]];
       false]

Collection's method "numberOf:Action{Parameter} → Integer":
    {condition:Action{Parameter}}
    -- *returns the number of elements that satisfy the condition passed as argument.*
    [total::=0;
       self forAll:{elem:Parameter}[(condition doWith:elem)
          ifTrue:[total:=total+1]];
       total]

Collection's method "addAllOf:Collection{Parameter} → Same":
    {other:Collection{Parameter}}
    -- *adds all elements of the argument to the receiver.*
    [other forAll:{elem:Parameter}[self add:elem]; self]

Collection's method "asArray → Array{Parameter}":
    {other:Collection{Parameter}}
    -- *returns an array with the same elements of the receiver.*
    [[Array{Parameter} copy addAllOf:self]]

Note that all these methods are implemented in terms of forAll: without making use of any knowledge regarding the actual implementation of the data structure. The five methods shown above (as well as several others that were not shown here) are therefore completely independent of the receiver's internal organization. Hence, they need not be overridden in other prototypes derived from Collection, except for reasons of efficiency. For example, the method asArray is reimplemented in Array because a simple cloning operation (self clone) is faster than the default implementation of Collection.

    Similar messages are also available in other prototypes that are not derived from Collection. A particularly interesting example is the one-of-a-kind prototype Workspace, whose forAll: method allows iterations over all presently existing objects within the current workspace. Within Workspace, the forAll: method is used to implement a few other methods, two of which are shown below:

Workspace's method "allObjects: Action → IdSet"[20]:
>{condition: Action}
>*-- returns a set containing all elements satisfying*
>*-- the condition passed as argument.*
>[objects::=IdSet clone;
>   self forAll:{obj:Object}[condition doWith:obj, ifTrue:[objects add:obj]];
>   objects   ]

Workspace's method "prototypeNamed: String → Object":
>{typeName: String}
>*-- returns the prototype with the name typeName;*
>*-- Nil if no such prototype exists.*
>[self forAll:{obj:Object}
>   [obj typeName=typeName ifTrue:[obj prototype return]];
>   Nil   ]

The method allObjects: returns a set with all objects satisfying the condition passed as argument. For example, the expression

>Workspace allObjects:{x:Object}[x prototype==Window]

returns a set containing all objects of the class Window. The second message prototypeNamed: can be used to search for a prototype with a given name (see Section 3.7 *Prototypes in Class-Based Languages*). For example, the sequence

>newObj: Object;
>ptName::=fStream nextLine;
>newObj::=(Workspace prototypeNamed:ptName) copy;

first reads the string ptName from the file stream fStream and then looks for a prototype with that name and makes a new copy of the prototype. If no prototype with the requested name had been found, newObj will have the value Nil.

.9.4   Exception Handling

Blocks can also be used for the implementation of exception handlers. The primitive method ifError: is defined in Block with the following interface:

>ifError: Block → Boolean

The method ifError: first attempts to execute the receiver. If the execution of the receiver was successful, its result is returned. If an exception occurred during the execution of the receiver, a string describing the exception is assigned to the

---

[20]   Note that Action and IdSet are both defined with the default parameter type Object. The
         types Action and IdSet therefore have the same meaning as Action{Object} and IdSet{Object}.

shared read-only variable errorMessage (which is defined as of type String in Object), and the block passed as argument is evaluated. The following example shows how the exception that may result from a division by zero can be dealt with by means of the message ifError:.

    [average:=total/count] ifError: [average:=0]

In this example, only one kind of exception can possibly occur. In general, many different errors can cause an exception. The most important predefined exceptions are listed below.

"division by zero"	-- *an integer or real number was divided by zero*
"range check failed"	-- *an array index was outside the valid range*
"numeric overflow"	-- *an integer or real number became too large*
"stack overflow"	-- *the limit of the method stack was exceeded*
"memory overflow"	-- *no more memory available for new objects*
"illegal access to Nil"	-- *an undefined message was sent to Nil*

The above exceptions are raised implicitly when an illegal operation is attempted. For example, an endless recursion of method invocations will eventually lead to a stack overflow, and an attempt to send a message that is not defined in Object to a variable that refers to Nil will result in a Nil access exception. In addition to the exceptions listed above, new ones can be invented by the programmer. To explicitly raise an exception with a particular name, the message error can be sent to a String object. For example, the following code fragment checks whether the String variable ptName refers to a legal prototype name[21].

    ptName size>0 ifFalse:
        ["empty prototype name" error];
    ptName forAll:{ch:Char}
        [ch isLetter | ch isDigit ifFalse:
            ["illegal character in prototype name" error]];
    (ptName at:1) isCapitalLetter ifFalse:
        ["prototype name doesn't begin with a capital letter" error];

The message error is widely used within the Omega system, in particular in prototypes that deal with operating system or external resources (such as files) that may not be available. Immutable objects are also protected against modifications by means of the message error, as illustrated in the following method of StringConstant:

---

[21] It is considered good style to formulate the condition that must be satisfied and then use the message ifFalse: to indicate what is to be done when the condition is not met. Positive conditions are in general easier to understand than negative ones.

StringConstant's method "at: Integer put: Char → Same":
    {index:Integer;ch:Char}
    -- raises an exception, as string constants are immutable.
    ["StringConstants cannot be modified" error; self]

A convenient means for raising exceptions when a condition is not satisfied is provided by the String method assertion:.

String's method "assertion: Boolean → Boolean":
    {condition: Boolean}
    -- raises an exception when the condition passed as argument is not met.
    [condition ifFalse: [self error]]

Using this message, the check for the validity of a prototype name can be reformulated as follows:

    "empty prototype name" assertion: ptName size=0;
    ptName forAll:{ch:Char}
        ["illegal character in prototype name" assertion: ch isLetter | ch isDigit];
    "prototype name doesn't begin with a capital letter" assertion:
        (ptName at:1) isCapitalLetter;

Another example of the assertion: message was given at the end of Section 4.4.2 *Dynamic Compatibility.*
    Exceptions can occur in virtually every expression of an Omega program. It would, however, be rather cumbersome to protect every single expression with an exception handler. In a typical Omega program, exception handlers are employed for the following two purposes:

- Programs should be as robust as possible. Robustness means that the program should not crash when it receives unexpected input. This is particularly important for interactive programs, as the programmer cannot usually predict every possible error a user could make. Exception handling can be used at well-defined points within such programs to catch exceptions caused by illegal user input. The program can then report an error message to the user and continue to accept and process further input.
- Often operations depend on a particular object being in a certain state. In such situations, the state of the object is first transformed, then the desired operations are performed, and finally the object is transformed into its initial state. An example of such a case is a series if input/output operations that are performed with a stream object. In order for the operations to work, the stream must be open. After the operations have been completed, the stream is closed again. An exception handler can be used to make sure that the stream is closed even when an exception (for example, an end-of-file condition) occurs during an input/output operation.

The following examples illustrate these typical uses of exception handlers:

Handling of user errors:

```
[   get user input;
    [   handle user input   ]
        ifError: [ ("Oops, an error occurred: "+errorMessage) ! ]
    user requested termination?
] repeatUntilTrue;
```

State transformation:

```
myStream open;
[   perform input/output operations   ]
    ifError: [ myStream close;  errorMessage error ];
myStream close;  -- the normal case
```

In the first example, the exception is simply reported to the user by means of the message "!". Aside from that, the exception is ignored. In the second example, a corrective action is taken before the exception is re-raised. This gives the next exception handler (which may be one of the first sort) a chance to handle the error.

As indicated by the above example, exception handlers can be nested. in the expression *a* ifError: *b*, the block *b* is executed only if an exception is not protected by another invocation of ifError: within the block *a*. The following simple example illustrates such a case.

```
[ result := x / n;
    [ anotherResult := x / (n–1) ]  ifError: [ "Oops"! ]
] ifError: [ "Sorry"! ]
```

In the presence of nested exception handlers, the innermost exception handler takes control when an exception occurs. In the above example, the message "Sorry" is displayed when n has the value 0, but n=1 will result in the display of the message "Oops".

Omega programs are always executed under control of a default exception handler. When an exception occurs outside the scope of an ifError: message, the default handler will simply display the error message and then abort the program.

4.10 Memory Management

During execution of an Omega program, new objects are constantly created by cloning or copying existing objects. Many of these objects are only needed for a short while and are not used thereafter. In particular, message expressions can lead to many temporary objects that are only used as intermediate results. Consider, for example, the following message expression:

res::=x asString + " + " + y asString + " = " (x+y) asString

When x and y have the values 123 and 321, respectively, the resulting string will contain "123 + 321 = 444". However, this result is achieved in several steps. First, a string object is created by sending the message asString to x. The message "+" is then sent to this object, which results in a new string with the contents "123 + ". The result of the message asString is not referred to by any variable; the object is therefore anonymous and – more importantly – it cannot be accessed any longer. During the evaluation of the above message expression, *seven* string objects are created, but only the last one is finally assigned to the variable res. All previous objects still exist and occupy storage, but they are obsolete.

In most conventional and hybrid languages, data structures that are no longer needed must explicitly be discarded. Special language elements are provided by such languages for this purpose (for example, DISPOSE in Pascal and Object Pascal, and delete in C and C++). These operations are potentially dangerous, as they force the programmer to keep track of all created objects and to decide when they can safely be disposed of. The problem with this strategy is twofold:

- *Objects can be overlooked*. It is rather difficult to find the right moment at which an object should be deleted. There are rare cases in which certain objects are rather short-lived, such that they can be discarded within the same method or procedure in which they were created. More often though, objects are returned as results of messages and passed on to other objects. In these cases, it is easy to "forget" the existence of an object. Such obsolete objects are not a major concern as long as there is only a small number of them. Unfortunately, such objects are often created repeatedly and so eventually occupy so much storage that no new objects can be created any more.
- *Needed objects can be deleted*. As "object variables" do not contain the objects themselves, but rather references to them, several variables can (and actually will) refer to the same object. When the object referred to by the variable $v1$ is deleted, another variable $v2$ may nevertheless still refer to the storage area that once contained the object. When other objects are created, the storage area now available will eventually be assigned to another object. As soon as the non-existent object referred to by $v2$ is accessed, strange things can happen. Since the access to $v2$ can occur quite a long time after the object has been deleted, such errors are particularly hard to track down.

In pure object-oriented languages, explicit disposal of objects is all the more unacceptable, since many objects with varying life-spans are created. Such languages therefore usually provide a mechanism for *automatic storage reclamation* (also called *garbage collection*) and thus relieve the programmer of the
responsibility of object deletion.

In Omega, the entire workspace is occasionally examined by the run-time
system in order to determine which objects can be safely deleted. The remainder
of this section explains which objects are considered obsolete, when they are
deleted, and how the programmer can help in the detection of obsolete objects.

Figure 4-10 shows some objects and two variables which refer to them.
All objects depicted in Figure 4-10 can be reached in some way via the variables
v1 and *v2*. For example, a message could be sent to *v2*, which would result in
the execution of a method of the object *b*. During execution of this method, the
objects *a* and *d* referred to by the instance variables of *b* could be accessed,
and so on. The execution of the assignment *v2*:= *v1* changes this situation
completely. Figure 4-11 shows the resulting object network.

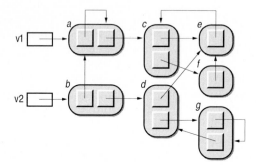

Fig. 4-10: A simple object network

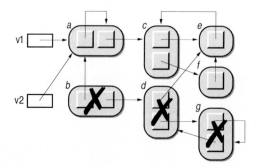

Fig. 4-11: Object network with obsolete objects

Now that *v2* refers to the same object as *v1*, object *b* is no longer accessible
(assuming that no other variables refer to any of the objects shown in Figure

4-11). As the only way to reach the objects *d* and *g* from outside is via the now obsolete object *b*, the objects *d* and *g* have also become obsolete.

As illustrated in Figure 4-11, it is not possible to determine whether an object is obsolete merely by checking whether there is a reference to the object. Cyclic references (such as those between *d* and *g*) require a different strategy to figure out which objects are obsolete. The best way to do that is to see which objects are "alive". The following list defines which objects are considered alive in Omega:

- All prototypes are alive.
- All objects referred to by shared variables are alive.
- All objects referred to by arguments and temporary variables of currently executing methods, blocks and actions are alive.
- All objects referred to by instance variables of alive objects are alive.

All objects that are not alive according to these rules are considered obsolete and can be discarded. The algorithm for detecting obsolete objects closely follows the idea sketched above. First all reachable objects are marked as alive, then all unmarked objects are deleted. Because of this two-step procedure, this algorithm is called *Mark and Sweep*. Of course, the detection and deletion of obsolete objects (called *garbage collection* or *automatic storage reclamation*) can be quite time-consuming. The Omega garbage collector therefore applies some heuristic rules in order to interfere as little as possible with the actual program. This goal is achieved by performing garbage collection only in the following situations:

- When a requested object cannot be allocated because of lack of free space, a garbage collection is performed in order to reclaim enough space to allocate further objects.
- When no user input has been received for a certain period, an intermediate garbage collection is performed. Some heuristics are used to determine the proper moment. For example, no garbage collection will be attempted if only a few objects have been created since the last garbage collection.
- The garbage collector can be invoked explicitly from within an Omega program. The programmer often knows in advance when many objects will be created and can use this knowledge in time-critical situations to avoid delays caused by garbage collections.
- The entire workspace is compacted by the garbage collector just before it is passivated. In this way, obsolete objects do not occupy precious disk space.

Automatic storage reclamation can help to avoid frequent programming errors. The programmer can allocate millions of objects and the garbage collector will remove them again when they are no longer needed. However, the programmer should be aware of the presence of a garbage collector. The following points give some hints about how to use storage efficiently.

- *Reuse existing objects.* The best way to avoid run-time overhead due to excessive garbage collection is to avoid garbage in the first place. In particular, it is a good idea to use a single object during the execution of a loop instead of creating a new one every time the loop body is entered. For example, consider the following code fragment:

```
[   mousePos::=Mouse localPosition;
    button contains:mousePos, ifTrue: [...];
    Mouse buttonDown ]
repeatUntilFalse
```

This code fragment follows the mouse as long as the mouse button is pressed. The mouse coordinates are repeatedly requested by sending the message localPosition to the Mouse prototype. Thousands of point objects can be created in this way every second. It is therefore very likely that the user will experience a noticeable delay when the garbage collector has to dispose of all obsolete points. It is better to reuse the same point object during the entire loop. The method getLocal: of Mouse can be used for this purpose. It places the current mouse coordinates in the x and y components of the existing point object passed as argument. The following code fragment shows how the above loop can be formulated in a more efficient way.

```
    mousePos::=Point clone;
[   Mouse getLocal:mousePos;
    button contains:mousePos, ifTrue: [...];
    Mouse buttonDown]
repeatUntilFalse
```

- *Avoid intermediate objects.* Many operators return dynamically created objects as their result. The following expression (which was already shown at the beginning of this section) is an example of the use of such operators.

```
    res::=x asString + " + " + y asString + " = " (x+y) asString
```

The six obsolete string objects created by this expression are not usually a major concern. But when the expression appears within a loop, it can easily result in thousands of obsolete string objects. Since it is hard to tell in advance whether an expression will be invoked within a loop, it is generally recommended that intermediate results be avoided by assembling an existing string object instead of allowing operators to create new ones all the time. The following example shows how the above sequence of operators can be replaced with a somewhat longer but more efficient expression[22]:

```
    res::=x asString add:" + ", add:y asString, add:" = ", add:(x+y) asString
```

---

[22] Even now, two obsolete string objects are created by the messages y asString and (x+y) asString, but these objects cannot be avoided, whereas the intermediate results created by the successive invocations of "+" can.

- *Remove references to unnecessary objects.* The garbage collector only deletes objects that are *known* to be obsolete. Variables however can exist which refer to objects that were only used for a short time and will never be used again. This is not a major problem with temporary variables within methods and blocks, as these variables generally exist for a relatively short period, but de-facto obsolete objects can also be referenced by instance variables of objects or – even worse – by shared variables. As such an unnecessary object can again refer to other objects that would otherwise be unobtainable, this can seriously affect the operation of the garbage collector. It is therefore recommended that references to temporary objects be removed as soon as they have served their purpose by assigning Nil to variables referring to such objects. This is particularly important for large data structures. Note that an assignment of Nil to a variable is not the same as an explicit deletion of the object referred to by the variable. The object itself is not affected by the assignment; note in particular that it will still remain alive when there are other variables referring to it. An assignment of Nil to a variable can therefore be seen as a simple way of telling the garbage collector that an object will not be accessed through *this* variable any more.

4.11 The Programming Environment

Omega was deliberately designed as an interactive language. There are no language constructs for the creation of new prototypes, variables and methods. In fact, the presence of prototypes requires support from a programming environment, as mechanisms for the modification of existing objects are needed. This section describes the most important features of the Macintosh implementation of the Omega programming environment. Screen snapshots will be used to illustrate some typical situations.

The Omega programming environment operates on a *workspace*, as explained in Section 3.4 *Persistent Prototypes*. The most important parts of an Omega workspace are

- all currently existing objects,
- the symbol table with information about
  - types, their inheritance and genericity,
  - the structure of all classes of objects,
  - the interfaces of all methods,
- the source text of all methods,
- the compiled methods.

In order to ensure integrity among its various parts, a workspace is always processed as a unit. Is is loaded from a disk file at the beginning of an Omega session and saved back to disk at the end of the session. During a session, the user can at any time capture the current state of the workspace in a disk file. In this way, adverse effects of programming errors can be reduced to a minimum.

The Omega programming environment consists of the following parts:

- The *hierarchy browser* allows the inspection of the prototype hierarchy as well as the creation of new and redefinition and deletion of existing prototypes. All other parts of the Omega workspace are accessed through the hierarchy browser.
- An *object editor* allows the interactive definition and modification of an object's structure and contents. It shows the shared and instance variables of an object as well as the interfaces of all its methods.
- A *method editor* facilitates the inspection and modification of the source texts of methods. As soon as changes to a method have been made,
- an *incremental compiler* transforms the source texts into the corresponding machine code.
- An *application generator* can be used to transform certain expressions into stand-alone applications that can subsequently be executed independently of the programming environment.
- A *run-time system* contains all primitive methods, the garbage collector and the default exception handler.
- A *profiler* optionally counts the invocations of all methods and allows the user to inspect the resulting statistics of the interactive execution of an expression.
- A *log window* provides an editable text in which Omega expressions can be entered and executed.

This section is not intended as a user's guide to the Omega programming environment. Its purpose is rather to give an impression of how Omega programs are created. The following subsections will therefore only show some situations that might arise during a typical Omega session.

.11.1   The Hierarchy Browser

Figure 4-12 shows a snapshot of Omega's hierarchy browser.

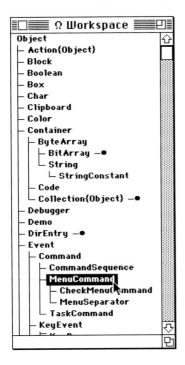

Fig. 4-12: The hierarchy browser

The hierarchy browser shows the type hierarchy in the form of an indented tree. The subtrees starting with BitArray, Collection and DirEntry have been collapsed in order to reduce the size of the tree. Individual nodes can be selected in the hierarchy browser and several menu commands can be applied to them. The following operations, in particular, are performed directly with the hierarchy browser:

- Creation of new types
- Deletion of types
- Renaming of types
- Rearranging the type hierarchy (i.e., changing the inheritance of types)

As types and prototypes always exist in pairs, the hierarchy browser can also be used to access all prototypes. The individual nodes can be regarded as visual representations of the prototypical objects themselves. In Figure 4-12, the MenuCommand prototype has been selected. A menu command can be used to view the object in an object editor, as illustrated in the following section.

4.11.2   The Object Editor

Figure 4-13 shows two snapshots of the MenuCommand object as shown in the object editor.

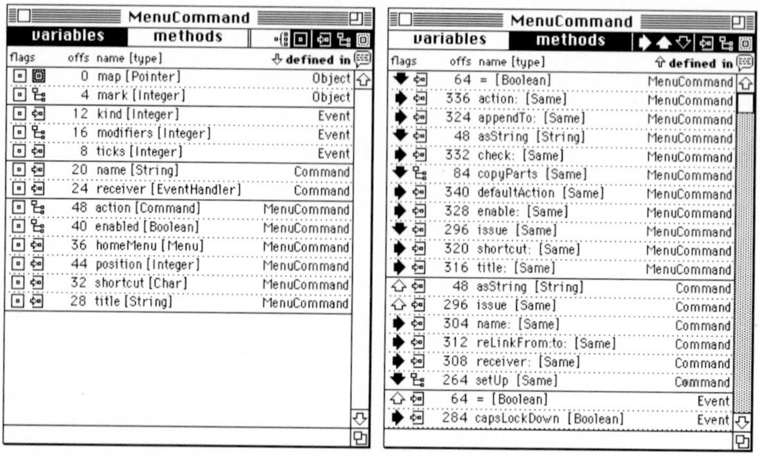

Fig. 4-13: The object editor

The left snapshot shows a view of the prototype's instance variables. The Menu-Command prototype inherits part of its structure from its ancestors Command, Event and, of course, Object. The instance variables map and mark are part of every Omega object. Event adds three more instance variables, kind, modifiers and ticks, and Command defines the instance variables name and receiver. The last six instance variables have been added in the MenuCommand prototype itself[23].

The icons at the left side of each line indicate the location and visibility of an instance variable (see Figure 4-4). The type of an instance variable is shown within brackets after its name.

As the object editor shows a visual representation of a *real* object (here: the MenuCommand prototype), the values of the instance variables can be inspected and edited by means of a menu command. For example, the dialog shown in Figure 4-14 would be used to specify whether the MenuCommand prototype (and with it all objects cloned from it) should be initially enabled or not:

---

[23]   Note that the *entire* contents of an object are visible in the object editor. In contrast, only the *additional* instance variables are visible in a class definition in most other object-oriented languages.

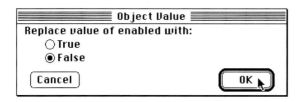

Fig. 4-14: Changing the value of an instance variable

In addition to changes to the contents of an object, the object editor provides operations for the following purposes:

- Addition of instance variables (see Section 4.5)
- Renaming of instance variables
- Redeclaration (with another type) of instance variables
- Removal of instance variables

The right snapshot in Figure 4-13 shows a view of the message interface of the MenuCommand prototype. The names of *all* methods (those implemented in MenuCommand as well as these inherited and overridden messages from ancestors) are displayed in this view. The arrows at the left side of each line indicate which methods override other methods:

▶ A black arrow pointing to the right denotes a method that is neither overridden nor overrides another method.

⬇ A black arrow pointing downward indicates a method that overrides a method with the same name in an ancestor.

⇧ A hollow arrow pointing upward denotes an overridden method in an ancestor.

In the method view, the following operations can be performed with an object:

- New methods can be added (see Section 4.6 *Methods*)
- Methods implemented in ancestors can be overridden
- Methods can be renamed
- The interfaces of methods can be changes
- Methods can be removed

Methods can also be "opened" for editing, as shown in the following section.

4.11.3   The Method Editor

Figure 4-15 shows a method editor with the source text of MenuCommand's method "=".

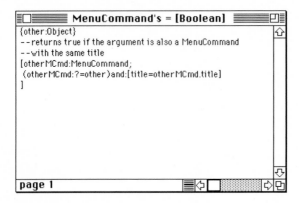

Fig. 4-15: A method, displayed in a method editor

Method editors are regular text editor windows with some additional features. Note in particular that a syntax check of the method being edited can be requested with a single keystroke.

4.11.4   The Log Window

The log window is the Omega programmer's workbench. It contains an editable text that can be used for notes and for the immediate evaluation of Omega expressions. A selected expression can be evaluated by means of a menu command. The result of the evaluation is then again displayed in the log window. The following text shows a typical extract of a log window's contents.

```
...
2^24
»16777216

32769 primeFactors
»(3,3,11,331)

Workspace freeBytes
»527438

Workspace allReferencesTo:Button, size
»0
```

```
FileUtility.toolsMenu
    add:MenuSeparator copy,
    add:(MenuCommand copy name:"Verify..."),
    add:(MenuCommand copy name:"Repair...", shortcut:'R')
...
```

The lines marked with "»" are the results returned from the evaluation of the preceding expressions. As shown here, direct execution in the log window can be used as a means to check the current condition of the workspace and to make certain changes to existing objects that would otherwise be difficult to make interactively.

As its name indicates, the log window also serves as a standard text output medium. The message log (defined in Object) can be used to insert a textual representation of the receiver at the caret position in the log window.

4.11.5 The Profiler

The profiler is a tool that counts activations of methods. After an Omega expression has been evaluated, the profiler displays the collected statistics in a special window, as shown in the snapshots in Figure 4-16.

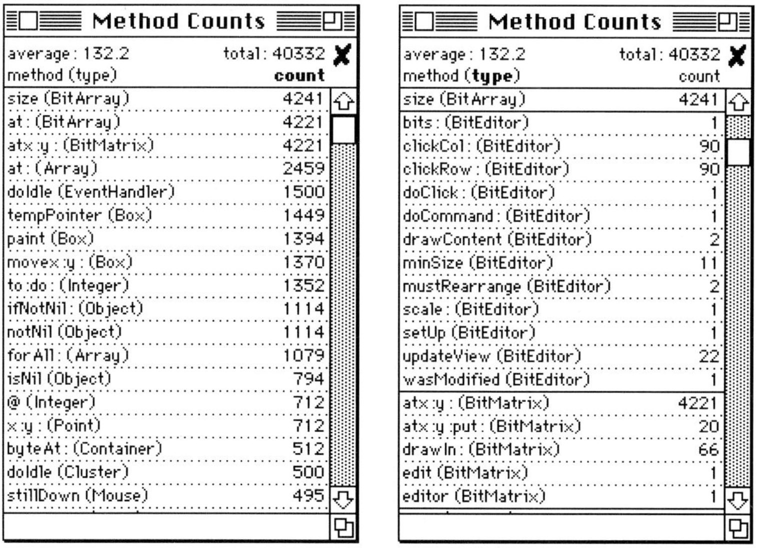

Fig. 4-16: Method counts collected by the profiler

The left snapshot in figure 4-16 shows the method invocations counted during an execution of an icon editor sorted by descending frequency. The right snapshot shows the same numbers, ordered by types. The visible section shows the invocations of all methods of BitEditor and BitMatrix. The information displayed by the profiler can be used for several purposes:

- *Tuning:* When a program turns out to be too slow, the method counts can be used to detect those points that need special attention. Methods which are frequently executed can then be implemented in a more efficient way or – even better – the number of their invocations can be reduced by rewriting those methods that call them.
- *Debugging:* When something doesn't work as expected, the method counts can be used to figure out which methods have actually been executed. Answers to the following questions can be found with the help of the profiler:
  - Has an initialization method been executed more than once?
  - When the method *m2* is supposed to be invoked only from *m1*: Does the count of *m2* match that of *m1*?
  - Is the message *m* to objects of class *C* correctly passed to the overridden method?
  - Does the number of invocations of method *m* correspond to the number of, say, mouse clicks?
  - Are there any other methods that have been invoked the same number of times as *m*?

  Of course, the answers to these questions do not automatically reveal the source of a programming error, but they can at least help to track down the error.
- *Testing:* White box testing requires that every path through a program be executed at least once. A weaker but nevertheless useful criterion is to require that every method be executed at least once. With the help of the profiler one can easily find those methods that so far have not been executed.
- *Learning:* Method counts can provide substantial help for those trying to understand how objects communicate through messages. In particular, the presence of a method in the list and correlations between certain numbers can give important hints about what is going on in a program.

5. Libraries and Frameworks

This chapter explains the importance of libraries for object-oriented software development. The differences between class libraries and conventional libraries, the typical structure and contents of a class library and the common protocol of objects are discussed here. The concepts of class libraries and prototype libraries are very similar. Wherever the term *class library* appears in this chapter, it could therefore equally be replaced by *prototype library*. Particular aspects of *prototype libraries* are dealt with in Section 5.4. The last two sections describe advanced topics such as libraries containing objects and frameworks.

5.1   Conventional and Object-Oriented Libraries

Large programs are hard to implement. The construction of a program with thousands of lines of code would be even harder if every single subproblem had to be solved from scratch. Fortunately, modern programming languages provide mechanisms to reuse existing code.

In order to use an existing piece of code in a new program, a programming language must facilitate separate compilation of parts of a program. With such a mechanism, those code fragments needed frequently can be prefabricated and stored in libraries. Such an instrument was already available in older programming languages. For example, Fortran allows certain functions and procedures to be declared as "external". The compiler assumes the availability of these operations, and the linker finally binds them to the program. This concept is even used for certain language elements, such as mathematical functions. In Fortran, SIN and SQRT are considered part of the language, but they are in fact taken from an external library.

The smaller a language is, the more important is the availability of a library for that language. For example, Modula-2 does not have any language elements for input and output. When such operations are needed (and they are in virtually every program), they have to be imported from a library. In these languages, libraries no longer consist of individual procedures and functions but rather of entire modules containing several related operations. A module might provide a set of mathematical functions or operations on character strings. Moreover, modules can also be used to implement abstract data types and abstract data structures. The advantage of such a module concept is that it facilitates information hiding and division of labor in a comfortable way.

Object-oriented libraries are similar to module libraries, but they comprise classes rather than modules. The most important advantage of a class library over a module library is that modules can only be used as they are, whereas classes can be extended by deriving new classes from them. Figure 5-1 shows the relevant interfaces of modules and classes.

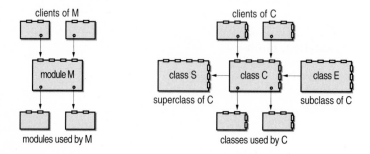

Fig. 5-1: Interfaces of modules and classes

The module *M* has an *import* and an *export* interface. The import interface comprises calls to procedures and functions provided by other modules, and the export interface defines the public operations that may be used by clients. In addition to these interfaces, a class *C* can also have a superclass *S* and other classes can again be derived from *C*.

As shown in Figure 5-1, an existing class can be reused in two different ways. When a class *C* is already suitable for (part of) the solution of a given problem, it can be used as it is, but it is also possible to reuse part of the class's implementation by creating a new class inheriting from *C*. Typical class libraries contain general classes that are destined to be used as they are and other (often incomplete) classes that constitute the basis for future extensions.

Inheritance is not the only way in which an existing class can be extended. Most objects (in particular those for the implementation of user interface elements) contain references to other objects. For example, a window object (of class Window) will typically contain a reference to another object (of class View) that actually determines the appearance of the window's contents and the way in which the user can interact with the window. In such a case, a new class (say, MyView) can be derived from View. Due to polymorphism, objects of this new class are compatible with variables of type View. Consequently, it is possible to fill a window with a new kind of content by embedding a MyView object in a Window object. Dynamic binding makes sure that all messages sent to the view object by the window object are then directed to the new method implementations of class MyView. Objects of library classes can thus cooperate with objects of new classes that were not anticipated when the library was designed. This technique is one of the foundations of object-oriented frameworks (see Section 5.5 *Frameworks*).

Classes can extend the capabilities of programming languages. This is particularly the case with pure object-oriented languages. For example, Smalltalk does not even have basic language elements for arithmetic operations. All elementary data types and all feasible operations pertaining to their objects are provided by library classes. Such extreme examples give some idea of the potential power of class libraries.

However, typical class libraries contain much more than just basic data types. They sometimes contain hundreds of classes for many different purposes. The next section explains what kinds of classes can usually be found in a class library.

5.2   Kinds of Classes

The larger a class library, the greater the chance of finding a suitable class for a given task. In an ideal object-oriented world, programs would be written just by putting the proper classes together. There would be little need to know how to implement, say, an algorithm for storing names in an efficient way, because there would be a class containing the proper data structures and algorithms for storing arbitrary objects and thus also for storing names. The process of solving a problem would therefore not be characterized by the development of new algorithms, but rather by knowing where to find the right class for the task at hand.

Large class libraries can contain hundreds of classes. Some of them will serve very specific purposes, and others will be more general. There will even be many similar classes that only differ in some minor aspect concerning their way of accomplishing a certain task. It can therefore be quite difficult to find one's way through a class library. The goal of this chapter is to identify typical kinds of classes and to show where they would usually be found in a class library [1].

Standard Classes

Standard classes are part of a particular programming language. For example, all elementary data types are implemented by means of standard classes in pure object-oriented languages. In hybrid languages, no standard classes are needed, as elementary data types are already provided by the language. This is particularly the case with object-oriented extensions of conventional programming languages as C++ and Object Pascal. The following list gives some typical standard classes of pure object-oriented languages such as Smalltalk, Self, and Omega.

- Integer, SmallInteger, Real, Float, Fraction
- Boolean, True, False
- Char (or Character)
- String, StringConstant, Symbol
- Block, Action, Behavior
- Object, Class, MetaClass
- Nil

The standard classes can usually be found at a low nesting level (i.e., they are directly derived from Object). In Smalltalk, the numeric classes are located in a separate subtree starting with an abstract class Magnitude, as shown in Figure 5-2. In Smalltalk, there are even several classes for the representation of integer numbers. LargeNegativeInteger and LargePositiveInteger implement integer numbers of arbitrary size, and SmallInteger is optimized specifically for the target machine.

---

[1]   The class browser of the Smalltalk-80 programming environment organizes classes by their category and not by their position in the inheritance hierarchy as in Omega's hierarchy browser.

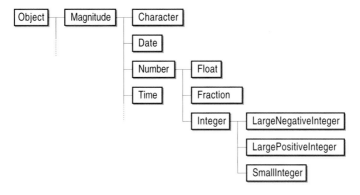

Fig. 5-2: Inheritance diagram of Smalltalk's numeric classes

Collection Classes

The second important category comprises classes whose objects can contain (references to) other objects. As these classes combine numerous objects into a single object, they are usually referred to as *collection classes.*

Although collections are very useful for the flexible construction of object structures, some libraries do not contain collection classes. In particular, the availability of arrays in hybrid languages and the incompatibility of elementary types with objects are used as arguments for the omission of collections[2].

Figure 5-3 shows the inheritance diagram of Smalltalk's collection classes.

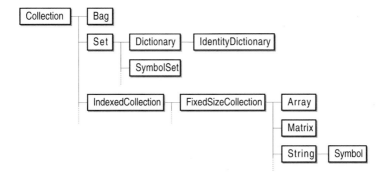

Fig. 5-3: Inheritance diagram of Smalltalk's collection classes

The class Collection is directly derived from Object (which was omitted in Figure 5-3). The classes Bag and Set are rather similar. Both contain objects in an undefined order. Set only holds distinct elements, but Bag also allows dupli-

---

[2]   The Eiffel library is an exception in this respect. Although the language contains elementary data types, compound types such as arrays and records are missing from the language; they are implemented as classes.

cates. A Dictionary is a set of key/value pairs. IndexedCollection represents collections whose elements can be accessed through an integer index. Array is a special case of an indexed collection, as are Matrix and String. Symbol represents a special kind of unique strings (similar to Omega's StringConstants).

Input and Output Classes

In most class libraries, input and output operations are performed with *streams*. A stream is an abstraction of an input/output medium. It can be connected with an arbitrary data structure (including, but not limited to a file). A stream object "knows" how to perform input and output operations on "its" data structure. It has a current position at which all operations take place.

As the actual input and output operations are performed by stream objects, separate stream classes have to be provided for every data structure for which input and output makes sense. Examples of such classes are StringStream, FileStream, PrintStream and TerminalStream. The class Stream defines the common protocol for all these classes. The advantage of this model is that the same input and output operations are available for all sorts of streams. For example, the message printOn: defined in Smalltalk's class Object can be used to output the receiver on the stream passed as argument.

Graphics Classes

Graphics classes are used to draw images on the screen. The way and extent to which graphical operations are supported varies widely from library to library. Typically, the basic classes Point and Rectangle are used to represent items visible on the screen, and classes Font, Color and Pattern are used to describe the appearance of images. In a typical Smalltalk library the actual drawing operations are performed by means of pen objects and bit blocks [Ingalls 1981]. A pen works like a pen in the real world. It can be used to "scribble" on the screen by moving it from one position to the next. Bit blocks are a powerful mechanism for filling screen areas with a pattern in a variety of transfer modes. In libraries for hybrid languages, graphical operations are often not supported at all; the programmer is expected to explicitly call routines of the underlying graphics system.

Some (but not all) libraries also contain classes for real graphical items, such as lines and circles. An object of such a class has all possible visual attributes (for example, position and extent on the screen, line width and color). A common superclass of these classes defines a common protocol for all drawing operations, such as draw, invert and erase. Some examples of such classes are presented in Section 6.5 *Graphical Objects*.

User Interface Classes

Extensive class libraries contain all sorts of classes for various user interface elements, such as windows, menus, buttons, editable text and icons. These classes are often tailored to a specific hardware and operating system, as different user interface mechanisms are generally used on different machines. Section 5.5 *Frameworks* explains some typical user interface classes in more detail.

System Classes

In order to avoid direct access to operations specific for a particular hardware and operating system, many advanced libraries contain mediating classes that provide an abstract interface to low-level features. Examples of such classes are File, Directory, Socket (for network connections), Screen, Memory, Keyboard, and Mouse.

 System classes mimic the behavior of low-level facilities in an object-oriented way and thus deceive the programmer with an intact object-oriented world. Some of these classes are one-of-a-kind classes. For example, there will only be one object of class Mouse, as only one mouse is attached to the computer in the real world.

5.3 Object Protocols

When used by clients, objects should be treated as black boxes; that is, knowledge of their internal structure and the exact implementation of their methods should not be necessary in order to use the objects. To ensure proper usage of objects, the principle of information hiding should be followed as closely as possible. All operations with objects should be performed through a well-defined interface. A set of rules and conventions for the usage of a class of objects is commonly called a **protocol**. Such a protocol ideally consists of

- the interfaces of all publicly available messages,
- the names and data types of all public instance variables,
- descriptions of the purpose of messages,
- pre- and postconditions of messages, and
- an explanation of how objects of different classes cooperate.

The first two points can be extracted directly from the formal description of a class, provided that the implementation language uses static typing. In dynamically typed languages, additional comments are necessary to explain which kinds of objects are expected as arguments of messages and objects of which class are returned by methods.

The last three points require that extra documentation be provided by the implementer of a class[3]. In a prototype-oriented language, the default states of prototypes should also be explained in an abstract manner.

The following example shows an extract of the documentation describing the Omega class Box.

Class:	Box
Superclass:	Object
Purpose:	A box is a mathematical model for a rectangular area. Boxes are typically used to describe the position and extent of graphical items such as windows, panes and images. Boxes also provide a small set of basic drawing operations.
Instance variables:	left, top, bottom, right, all of type Integer. The instance variables are public but read-only for clients. Horizontal coordinates increase from left to right, vertical coordinates increase from top to bottom.
Default state:	The Box prototype is initialized as empty with all instance variables set to zero.
Collaborations:	Point: used as argument type of many Box messages. View and Image: contain boxes that define their location and size. View: The current view is implicitly used for drawing operations.
Messages:	* Box → Same

  returns the intersection of the receiver and the argument in a new object. When the receiver and the argument do not intersect, an empty box (with all instance variables set to zero) is returned.

  asString → String

  returns a textual representation of the receiver in the form "*(left,top,right,bottom)*".

  empty → Boolean

  returns true if the box doesn't contain any points.

  invert → Same

  inverts the area described by the receiver in local coordinates of the current View object. Does nothing when sent to an empty box.

  . . .

---

3   The programming language Eiffel supports the formulation of pre- and postconditions as well as of so-called invariants. These conditions are essential parts of a class interface.

A description of a class in this fashion is sufficient for clients of the class. Implementers of derived classes need more information that has to be provided in a separate document. The following questions, in particular, should be answered in the "extension documentation" of a class *C*:

- Under what circumstances should a new class be derived from *C*? For example:
  - "Application is an abstract class. Create a new subclass of Application when you want to develop a new stand-alone application."
  - "Mouse is a one-of-a-kind class; you should never need to derive a new class from it."
- Which methods should be overridden in which cases? For example:
  - "Override copyParts when your class defines additional instance variables that should also be copied when objects of your class receive the message copy."
  - "The method printOn: prints the receiver's textual representation. Override it when you can provide a better (for example, graphical) representation of your objects."
  - "Object already provides a general implementation of isNil. You should never override this method."
- How can objects of the new subclass be used in place of *C* objects? For example:
  - "Windows and composite views have a Pane object that defines their contents. Install an instance of your new Pane subclass into such an object with the message content: and it will automatically be activated at the proper moments."

 From an academic point of view, such a description of a library class should be sufficient to put the class to work. Unfortunately, a tremendous effort is required to prepare a suitable documentation of a class. The documentation of a class can easily exceed the source text for the class. Furthermore, the documentation must be adapted when changes to the interface of the class are made. For this reason, library implementers often provide only a concise documentation and prefer to distribute the library in source format. As the source text is the only "documentation" that is guaranteed to be up-to-date, such an "open" library is in many situations preferable to a library that is distributed in compiled form only. Furthermore, studies of a library's source text can considerably improve one's understanding of the library's design principles and of object-oriented programming in general.

As inheritance applies to the implementation as well as to the interface of a class, subclasses of a class *C* share the common protocol defined in *C*. Libraries therefore often contain abstract classes that define the interface of an entire sub-tree within the library's hierarchy. Note in particular that most libraries are *single-rooted*; they contain a root class (usually called Object) that defines the common interfaces of *all* objects. However, the number of messages defined in the root class differs widely among libraries. For example, the MacApp Class Library [Schmucker 1986] for Object Pascal defines a root class TObject[4] with the following minimal interface:

```
TYPE TObject = OBJECT
    FUNCTION Clone: TObject;
        (* default method calls ShallowClone *)
    PROCEDURE Free;
        (* default method calls ShallowFree *)
    FUNCTION ShallowClone: TObject;
        (* creates a clone of the receiver with the same instance variables *)
    PROCEDURE ShallowFree;
        (* disposes the receiver only, but not its components *)
END;
```

The minimum interface defined in class **TObject** contains the basic operations for copying and destroying objects. For example, an object **x** that is no longer needed can be discarded with the message x.Free[5].

In contrast to the small general interface of MacApp, the class **Object** of the library distributed with Smalltalk/V [Digitalk 1988] contains more than 70 methods, most of which are applicable to all subclasses and therefore rarely need to be overridden. The following list provides a sample of the most typical methods.

= anObject
    returns true when the receiver and anObject are equal.

~= anObject
    returns true when the receiver and anObject are not equal.

== anObject
    returns true when the receiver and anObject are identical.

~~ anObject
    returns true when the receiver and anObject are not identical.

addDependent: anObject
    registers anObject as dependent on the receiver.

allDependents
    returns a Set containing all dependents of the receiver.

---

[4]   In MacApp, class names always begin with "T" for class.
[5]   Note that Object Pascal follows the spirit of the base language Pascal in that it provides explicit operations for the destruction of objects. Hence, Object Pascal systems do not support automatic storage reclamation.

allReferences

returns a Set containing all objects referring to the receiver.

changed

notifies all objects depending on the receiver of a change
by sending each of them an update message.

class

returns the class of the receiver.

copy

returns a copy of the receiver.
The default implementation returns a shallow copy.

deepCopy

returns a copy of the receiver with shallow copies
of each instance variable.

dependsOn: anObject

registers the receiver as a dependent of anObject.

isKindOf: aClass

returns true if the receiver is an object of aClass or one of its subclasses.

isMemberOf: aClass

returns true if the receiver is an object of aClass.

printOn: aStream

appends the ASCII representation of the receiver to aStream.
The default implementation just "prints" the class name with a
preceding article.

printString

returns a String containing an ASCII representation of the receiver.

release

makes all dependents independent of the receiver.

release: anObject

makes anObject independent of the receiver.

shallowCopy

returns a copy of the receiver that shares the receiver's instance variables.

update: aParameter

reacts to a change of an object on which the receiver depends.
The argument aParameter identifies the kind of change.
The default implementation does nothing.

Smalltalk defines *change propagation* in a general way in class Object. An object x can be registered as dependent on another object y. Whenever the state of y changes significantly, x is informed of the change and can thus update its state such that it reflects the change made to y.

Some Object methods provide similar operations. For example, the messages x dependsOn:y and y addDependent:x have the same effect. In fact, the method dependsOn: is implemented in terms of addDependent:. Similarly, the implementations of "~=" and "~~" contain self sends of the messages "=" and "==". For example, "~=" simply returns the result of the expression (self=anObject) not, where the unary message not means boolean negation. It is important to know which methods are implemented on top of which other messages when a new class is created. For example, only the method "=" needs to be overridden in order to redefine equality for a specific class. Conversely, overriding the method "~=" will not have the desired effect.

Omega's Object prototype provides a similarly large set of methods. The most important parts of Omega's general object protocol are discussed in Section 6.2.

5.4   Prototype Libraries

Classes are static in that they simply describe the structure and behavior of their objects. In the simplest case, a class library is just a collection of text files containing the source texts of all classes. Classes of the library can be used simply by including these files in a new project.

In contrast to classes, prototypes are already objects with prefabricated structure, contents, and behavior. Obviously, different mechanisms are required to include existing prototypes in a new project. The following possibilities exist to achieve this goal:

- Prototypes can be described textually in a class-like manner, but in contrast to class libraries, the textual form of a prototype library must also contain descriptions of the contents of prototypes. For example, a Self prototype can be described textually by the following expression:

```
_AddSlots: ( |
    myPoint = ( |
        - parent = something.
        ^ x <- 0.
        ^ y <- 0.
        ^ print = ( x print. '&' print. y print. ).
    |)
|)
```

When a text file with this expression is "filed in", the expression is evaluated. As a result of this operation, a new prototype is registered in a new slot named myPoint of the global object lobby.

• Prototypes can be passivated and reused by activating them from within another program. The problem with this approach is that activation usually consists of two steps: First a new object of the desired class is created, and then the newly created object is requested to "activate itself", i.e., to initialize its state by interpreting the external representation. In other words, the activating program must already know the prototype in order to generate an object that can read itself. Dynamic linking, as supported by some operating systems, can help in this process.

• A prototype library can be stored in the external image of a workspace. The process of constructing a new program is thus characterized by extending the workspace containing the library. This approach is implemented in the Omega system. Here, parts of a prototype library stored in another workspace can also be imported into the current workspace.

Another important aspect of prototype libraries is that prototypes often refer to other objects that are not prototypes. For example, the prototype for filled rectangles (see Section 2.4 *Inheritance*) could have the structure depicted in Figure 5-4.

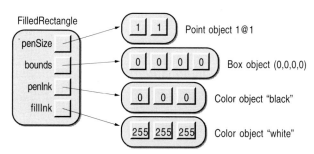

Fig. 5-4: A prototypical object referring to other objects

When such a prototype is stored in a library, not only its own contents but also the contents of the objects referred to by the prototype must be available in the library. This means that a prototype library will typically contain not only prototypes, but other objects as well. For example, a prototype library containing the FilledRectangle prototype depicted in Figure 5-4 will contain at least two Color objects representing the colors black and white. In theory, one of these color objects could be the Color prototype itself. It is, however, better to avoid such direct connections among prototypes, as they could easily lead to prototype corruption. Consequently, every single prototype should have its own "private" data structures that do not coincide with those of other prototypes.

5.5   **Frameworks**

The main purpose of an object-oriented library is to relieve the programmer of routine tasks. A typical library therefore contains at least those classes that can be integrated into almost every program. The parts of a library are the building blocks of which object-oriented programs are made. The construction of a program with a library is a *bottom-up* process. On the basis of fundamental "core" classes, more elaborate classes are constructed. These classes are again used to build application-specific classes, which are finally used in the main program.

Object-oriented techniques can, however, also be used in an entirely different way to facilitate the construction of programs. Note in particular that many programs have similar structures that can, at least in principle, be reused. This is especially true for event-oriented interactive programs. Figure 5-5 shows the typical structure of a conventional event-oriented program.

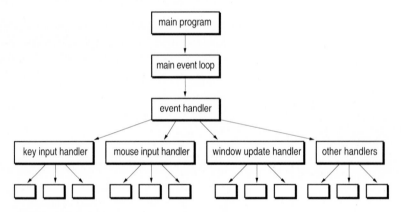

Fig. 5-5: Control flow within an event-oriented program

Event-oriented programming is a common technique used to implement modeless interactive programs. The idea behind event-oriented programming is that *the user and not the program* should control the order of execution. The program should not "ask" the user what to do next, rather the user should provide the program with input which must then be processed correctly. In an event-oriented programming style, all user input (as well as several other things that may influence the execution of a program) are collectively termed "events". Instead of reading a character from the keyboard, an event-oriented program retrieves the next event by calling an operating system routine.

The central part of an event-oriented program is the *main event loop*. This is the place where events are received. The purpose of the main event loop is to repeatedly read events and delegate them to the event handler. An event loop written in Pascal might take the following form:

```
VAR
    done: BOOLEAN;              { true when the user requested }
                               { termination of the program }
PROCEDURE MainEventLoop;
VAR
    eventToProcess: Event;
BEGIN
    done := FALSE;
    REPEAT
        GetEvent(eventToProcess);
        HandleEvent(eventToProcess)
    UNTIL done
END;  {MainEventLoop}
```

HandleEvent is a procedure that determines the kind of the received event and again calls other (more specialized) handlers to process the event. For example, a mouse input handler would usually first determine whether a mouse click occurred in the menu bar and, if so, call the menu handler to actually perform the desired task. This process of distinguishing events continues until a specialized handler finally "knows" the intended meaning of the event and performs the desired operation. After that, control returns to the main event loop and the entire process starts anew.

Investigations of different event-oriented programs show that their event-handling parts are essentially the same. They differ mainly in the actual processing of the events at rather deep levels in the program hierarchy. For example, the meaning of a mouse click will usually become evident in a procedure that handles mouse clicks for a particular window. All that remains to do is to determine which part of the window (e.g., a button, a scroll bar, or an editable text) was hit by the click and to perform the action requested by the user (e.g., perform the action associated with the button, scroll a list of names, place the insertion point in an editable text).

The continued discrimination of events is a process that can be automated to a very high degree. It is possible to construct a universal application that does all event processing until the part responsible for the actual interpretation of the event has been found. Then an appropriate event handling procedure must be called. This is the point where the object-oriented technique of dynamic binding can provide substantial help. For example, a window would "know" all its parts and delegate a mouse click to the mouse click handling method of the part that was hit by the click. The result of this idea is a generic application that can be augmented with application-specific objects – a so-called **application framework**.

In contrast to object-oriented libraries, frameworks make up the *top level* of an application. The main program and the general event handlers are reused, whereas the application-specific functionality is added at the *bottom* of the program hierarchy. Figure 5-6 shows part of the object structure of such an application framework.

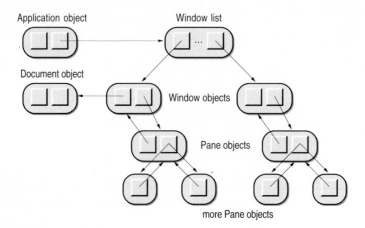

Fig. 5-6: Objects in an application framework

As shown in Figure 5-6, an application "knows" all its currently open windows, each of which is represented by an object. The content of a window is described by a **Pane** object. Panes may be structured and thus contain further panes, until finally the "subpanes" represent elementary user interface objects (see Figure 2-26 in Section 2.10.3 *Is-a and Has-a Relations*).

The **Application** object implements the main event loop (usually in a method called run) and the top-level event handlers. As soon as the destination of an event can be determined, the event is passed to the corresponding object. In the case of a window, a method handleEvent: is invoked with an argument that describes the event. Within this method, the event is further distributed to that part of the window that is responsible for performing the appropriate action. Even though different applications appear to have different window contents, it is rarely necessary to construct a new **Window** type, as the general behavior of windows (i.e., how they are closed, resized and moved around on the screen) does not change from application to application. Only when specialized parts of a window are needed must a new **Pane** subclass be constructed. It is noteworthy that many **Pane** classes can also be reused as they are. For example, editable text fields, buttons and scroll bars are common user interface elements for which classes (or prefabricated prototypes) already exist.

A common characteristic of graphics-oriented applications is that the actual data that are processed by the user are visualized on the screen as graphical images. The programs are constructed such that the user gets the impression that his or her actions directly work upon on the actual data – hence the term *direct manipulation*. Of course, the user's input does not immediately affect the image on screen, but rather influences data structures whose contents are displayed on the screen. This observation led to a programming technique known as the **MVC model** [Goldberg 1983; Krasner 1988], where "M" stands for "model", "V" for "view", and "C" for "controller". Figure 5-7 shows how data are processed with this technique.

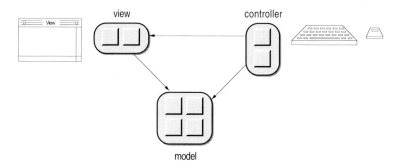

Fig. 5-7: The MVC model; arrows indicate the direction of mutual access

The model is an *internal* representation of the data to be processed. The structure and interface of the model are usually designed such that all operations that the user can perform with the data can be easily applied. The view implements the *external* representation of the model, i.e., how the data are displayed on the screen (typically in a window or part of a window). Note that there is only a single arrow pointing *from the view to the model* in Figure 5-7. The view needs access to the model in order to display the data appropriately, but the model should never know by which views it is represented. The controller is finally responsible for interpreting user input and applying the proper changes to the model. In the case of operations with the mouse, the controller also needs to know which portions of the model are displayed on the screen and at which locations.

The MVC model has the advantage that a single data structure can be displayed in multiple forms at the same time. In this case, multiple view/controller pairs operate on the same model, as depicted in Figure 5-8.

As views and controllers almost always exist in pairs, some application frameworks use a simpler technique in which the view also assumes the task of the controller. Examples of such frameworks are MacApp **[Schmucker 1986]** and ET++ **[Weinand 1988, 1989]**.

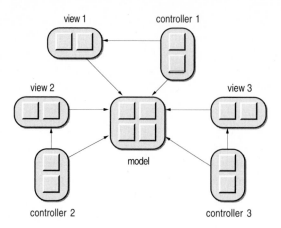

Fig. 5-8: A model with multiple views

In general, frameworks can be used for many problems that appear in different but similar forms. For example, the general structure of database applications can be designed once and provide the basis for the solution of similar problems in the future. Compilers, communications software and CAD programs are other problem domains that can generally be solved with a universal framework. In this respect, an application framework is just a special type of framework, namely one which covers the large category of interactive programs.

 An important property of frameworks is that their general structure has already been designed by object-oriented programming experts. They thus constitute pre-designed solutions to an entire class of problems. For this reason, the term *design reuse* is often heard in conjunction with frameworks. It is much more difficult to construct a framework than just an object-oriented program, as the design of a framework involves the "design of a design", that is, a general design that applies to a large class of problems. Once such a "meta-design" has been made, it is relatively easy to reuse, provided that the framework is accompanied by a description of how to extend the framework in real projects. These aspects of frameworks are covered in the following section.

5.6   Cookbooks and Examples

Libraries with hundreds of classes are sometimes difficult to comprehend. But a firm understanding of what the individual classes are for and how they can be used is absolutely necessary in the design and implementation of new programs. This is particularly so in the case of frameworks, as they consist of many classes which cooperate in a well-defined way. In order to use a library or framework effectively, it is therefore essential to make oneself familiar with it.

It is relatively easy to learn how to use a library, as the programmer is not forced to use a particular class. It is therefore possible to familiarize oneself with the individual classes one by one, as they are needed. A comprehensive documentation of a library together with its source text is usually sufficient for getting acquainted with a library. But even then, it may be quite hard to understand how certain classes work and cooperate with each other. The methods of library classes are usually very short; most of them consist of just a few lines of code. But in these few lines, messages to objects of other classes are sent, which means that several classes must be investigated in order to understand a single class. The process of learning how to use a class library can be simplified by means of examples. For this reason, most commercial class libraries are accompanied with a set of examples that show how the classes can be used effectively.

 An entirely different approach is needed for frameworks. It does not suffice to understand how the individual classes work. Rather, a recipe explaining *how* the framework can be reused in a new project is needed. Such a goal-oriented documentation of a framework is usually called a **cookbook**. The following list shows the typical contents of a cookbook for an application framework.

- *Goal of the framework*. This section explains the goal of the framework and the means with which this goal is achieved. It should also explain what problems are *not* covered by the framework.
- *Structure of the framework*. This section lists the classes of the framework, explains their foundations (in particular, the root class and elementary classes used in many other places) and discusses the connections between objects of different classes.
- *Event flow*. The handling of events is a central point in every application framework. Depending on the target system, different strategies may be used to read events and to pass them to the proper handler. Most application frameworks use references among objects to construct so-called event handler chains. When an object does not know how to handle a particular event, it passes the event to the next object in the chain. This mechanism is usually implemented in a general method of a class EventHandler.
- *"How to" section*. This section addresses several frequently posed questions and lists the steps to be taken in the development of a new application. This is the actual "cookie recipe" part. It usually discusses the following topics:
  - *How do I create a new application?* This is usually done by deriving a new class from Application and by overriding some methods in order to implement the application-specific behavior.

- *How do I represent the data to be processed?* Most application frameworks provide a class Document for this purpose. The class Document serves as an abstract superclass of models to be implemented according to the MVC technique.
- *How do I represent the model on the screen?* This section covers the View classes and the graphics primitives. It also explains how composite views, clipping and scrolling are implemented in the framework. Most application frameworks not only provide an abstract class View, but also a set of generally useful concrete view classes, such as text and list views.
- *How do I handle user input?* This section explains which methods of which classes must be overridden to react on user input in an application-specific manner. A common technique for handling user input is to convert events received from the user into *command objects* which, in turn, are passed to the objects affected by the operation.
- *How can I write to and read from files?* This section explains how activation and passivation are implemented in the framework, in particular, which methods must be overridden in order to determine the external representation of the model.

The cookbook for an application framework is usually accompanied with a set of short examples that show how simple applications can be constructed with the application framework. In order to get acquainted with an application framework, it is a good idea to start with one of these example applications and experiment with it by overriding some methods. In this way, the dynamic aspects of the framework can be explored in a fairly painless way.

6. The Omega Library

This chapter discusses the most important aspects of the Omega library. It does not explain all elements, but just those that are most frequently used in the solution of a problem. The intention of this chapter is to give the reader an idea of what the library contains and how its parts can be reused. As the Omega library closely follows the design principles of other object-oriented libraries, this chapter should also give the reader some insight into object-oriented libraries in general.

6.1   Concepts

The purpose of this section is to give the reader a first impression of the ideas
and principles behind the Omega library. Some properties of the Omega library
have been dictated by the language. Note in particular that the Omega library is
a single-rooted hierarchy without multiple inheritance. This means that the inheritance graph of the Omega library forms a *tree*. Another language-based
property of the library is its self-containment; as Omega is a pure object-
oriented language, the elementary data types must be supported by the library.
An important consequence of this is that the library does not use data types that
are not defined within the library itself.

Genericity is a wonderful concept that allows to customize general objects
in a type-safe manner. It is, however, not that easy to understand all implications
of genericity. It is particularly when a new generic prototype is to be developed.
For this reason, generic prototypes are used in only some places within the
library:

- Action is a generic prototype that is required by the language.
- Collection is a "classic" generic prototype; the parameter type specifies the
  type of the elements that may be stored in a collection. As genericity is an
  inherited feature, the descendants of Collection are also generic.
- Wrapper is a generic prototype that is used internally to make monomorphic objects compatible with variables of type Object. The parameter
  specifies the type of the "wrapped" element.

The default parameter of all generic prototypes is Object. This means that all
types can be used to customize the generic prototypes in the Omega library.

Inheritance is a powerful mechanism for code reuse and for implementing
deviations of existing objects. However, one of the goals in the design of the
Omega library was to avoid overuse of inheritance. Implementation inheritance
is rarely used; in most cases, inheritance serves as a means to describe related
object interfaces. An attempt was made during the design of the library to
implement similar operations with a single prototype instead of creating a new
prototype for every small variant. For example, the prototype Scroller can be
used wherever scrolling is needed, regardless of whether the contents should be
scrolled horizontally, vertically or in both directions[1].

Another design goal was to avoid global state as far as possible. Shared
variables are used primarily for constants (such as true, false and pi). Where
global variables with a long lifetime were inevitable, they were encapsulated in
special-purpose prototypes. An example of such a variable is the list of all
currently open windows (Workspace.openWindows).

---

[1]   An alternative to this design decision would have been to implement an abstract prototype
       Scroller with three children HScroller, VScroller and HVScroller.

The Omega library contains more than 130 prototypes for various purposes. Some of them are general purpose prototypes, and others are part of the Omega application framework. The latter category of prototypes is described in Sections 6.6 *User Interaction*, 6.7 *Views, Windows and Panes* and 6.9 *Applications* of this chapter.

The following sections explain the interfaces of selected parts of the Omega library. For most prototypes only the most important messages are listed with a brief explanation of their purpose. Method implementations are only presented when they may be of specific interest to the reader.

.2   Object Protocol

This section explains most of the interface of the Object prototype. As Object is the root of the Omega library, this section constitutes the foundation for all subsequent sections. The prototype Object serves four purposes:

- It defines the common interface of *all* objects.
- It contains many general methods, most of which can be inherited as they are.
- It provides a set of methods that make the use of objects easier. These methods are actually redundant; they just implement abbreviations of frequently used operations.
- It provides a couple of methods that can be used in self sends to trigger execeptions.

The following subsections list the relevant properties of Object. First the local and shared variables are explained, then the most important messages are listed. In this compilation, the methods of Object are grouped in the following categories:

- *Copying and Cloning:* Basic methods for creating new copies of existing objects.
- *Comparison:* Tests for identity and equality.
- *Meta-Information:* Information *about* objects.
- *External Representation:* Conversion of objects into a legible form and output of objects to external media.
- *Input:* Interactive input and editing of objects as well as retrieval of objects from external media.
- *Exceptions:* Raising common types of exceptions.
- *Workspace Activation and Passivation:* Additional actions that may be required before and after the entire workspace is activated and passivated.
- *Attributes:* General protocol for simple object properties.

- *Change Propagation:* Notification of dependent objects in case of state changes.
- *Miscellaneous:* Other important methods that do not fit into any of the above categories.

The list of methods is incomplete by intention; as the Omega library is described from the client's point of view in this chapter, some internally used methods have been omitted. Each method is presented in the style that was introduced at the end of Section 4.6 *Methods*. The full implementation is shown for most methods. The method bodies were only omitted in the case of primitive methods and methods that would require a thorough understanding of other parts of the library.

6.2.1   Variables of Object

Two *local variables* are defined in Object:

- map (of type Pointer) contains the address of a storage area called "map" that describes the object's structure and behavior (see [Chambers 1989]). All objects of a class share the same map. The map holds all information that is needed for dynamic method lookup and for type tests.
- mark (of type Integer) is exclusively used by the garbage collector. Normally, this instance variable contains the value 0.

Both of these instance variables are defined as *private* and *read-only*. This means that they are inaccessible to methods outside of Object. As the instance variables of Object are automatically included in all other objects, every Omega object has at least these two instance variables. In addition to these local variables, the following *shared variables* are defined in Object:

- false and true (both of type Boolean) are defined as *public* and are *read-only* for all methods. These variables play the role of the boolean constants.
- errorMessage (of type String) is a *public read-only* variable that contains the message associated with the most recent exception (see Section 4.9.4 *Exception Handling*).

These three shared variables have been defined in Object because they are needed throughout the Omega library. Although in principle it is possible to add new shared variables to Object, this is strongly discouraged, as accesses (and modifications) to such global variables can be distributed over the entire inheritance hierarchy. When global variables are needed, they should be bound to specific prototypes.

.2.2   **Copying and Cloning**

Object's method "clone → Same":
    -- primitive method; returns a shallow copy of the receiver.

Object's method "copy → Same":
    -- returns a copy of the receiver by first cloning the receiver and then
    -- sending the message copyParts to that clone. You should never need
    -- to override the message copy. To implement a different copying scheme,
    -- reimplement the method copyParts instead.
    [self clone copyParts]

Object's method "copyParts → Same":
    -- copies the relevant parts of the receiver (in Object:none).
    [self]

clone is an efficient primitive method on which all other copying mechanisms
are based. As the instance variables of the created object will refer to the same
objects as those of the original, this message should be used only when this is
intended. In most cases, the message copy should be used. copy first creates a
clone of the receiver and then orders the thus created copy to make copies of
those instance variables that are unique for every single object. The method
copyParts will typically begin with a parent message and then make copies of
the relevant additional instance variables. For example, a TextPane object has
an instance variable theText that needs to be copied in addition to those already
defined in Pane:

TextPane's method "copyParts → Same":
    [self (Pane) copyParts; theText := theText copy; self]

Although clone is a primitive method, it can be overridden. This is quite useful
in the case of one-of-a-kind prototypes that should never be copied. For
example, the following method shows how clone is reimplemented in Mouse:

Mouse's method "copyParts → Same":
    -- returns self, as there is only one Mouse.
    [self]

It is important to see that the exact meaning of the message copy is not defined
by the Omega library. The developer of a new prototype is free to redefine its
meaning according to special needs. It is, however, a good idea to adhere to the
"principle of the least astonishment" by giving the message copy a "reasonable"
meaning.

6.2.3   Comparison

Object's method "= Object → Boolean":
    -- returns true if the receiver is identical with the argument (PROTECTED).

Object's method "## Object → Boolean":
    {other:Object}
    -- returns true if the receiver is not identical with the argument (PROTECTED).
    [(self==other)~]

Object's method "= Object → Boolean":
    {other:Object}
    -- returns true if the receiver is equal to the argument.
    [self==other]

Object's method "# Object → Boolean":
    {other:Object}
    -- returns true if the receiver is not equal to the argument (PROTECTED).
    [(self=other)~]

Object's method "isNil → Boolean":
    -- returns false unless the receiver is Nil (or something equivalent).
    [false]

Object's method "notNil → Boolean":
    -- returns true unless the receiver is Nil (or something equivalent)
    -- (PROTECTED).
    [self isNil~]

Object's method "ifNil: Block → Boolean":
    {nilBlock:Block}
    -- evaluates the argument if the receiver is nil.
    [self isNil ifTrue:[nilBlock do; true]]

Object's method "ifNotNil: Block → Boolean":
    {notNilBlock:Block}
    -- evaluates the argument if the receiver is not nil.
    [self notNil ifTrue:[notNilBlock do; true]]

This set of methods provides basic comparison of objects or tests against Nil. The identity test methods "==" and "##" are defined as protected for security reasons. Identity is such a central concept that these messages must never be overridden.

"==" is a primitive method, as it would not be possible to implement it in Omega itself. All other methods are implemented in terms of "==". Note that the default implementation of "=" also checks the receiver and the argument for identity. This means that a clone of an object will not be considered as equal to its original. This default behavior must therefore be overridden when equality is to be defined in a different way. The usual technique is to first check whether the argument is at least of the same class as the receiver by means of a conditional assignment and then to test whether "relevant" instance variables are equal or identical, as shown in Section 4.4.2 *Dynamic Compatibility*. As with copying, the definition of equality is up to the implementer of a prototype. Likewise, the definition of what is considered a "nil object" is up to the programmer. Per default, only the Nil prototype and pointers to nonexistent addresses are considered nil objects. The method isNil is thus overridden in Nil and Pointer.

Note that the negated methods "##", "#" and notNil are defined as protected. As they are implemented in terms of their positive counterparts, it is not necessary (and would even be dangerous under some circumstances) to override them.

The methods ifNil: and ifNotNil: have been provided for convenience only. The expression x ifNil: [...] is simply a shortcut for x isNil ifTrue: [...].

6.2.4   Meta-Information

Object's method "prototype → Same":
    -- returns the prototype of the receiver (PROTECTED).

Object's method "parent → Object":
    -- returns the parent prototype of the receiver (PROTECTED).

Object's method "isA: Object → Boolean"[2]:
    {other:Object}
    -- returns true if the receiver is of the same class or
    -- a descendant of the argument (PROTECTED).
    [otherPT::=other prototype; pt:=self prototype;
       [otherPT==pt] whileFalse: [(pt:=pt parent) ifNil: [false return]];
       true]

Object's method "isAn: Object → Boolean":
    {other:Object}
    -- same as isA: (PROTECTED).
    [self isA:other]

Object's method "isPrototype → Boolean":
    -- returns true if the receiver is a prototype (PROTECTED).
    [self==self prototype]

---

[2]   The implementation shown here is only intended to show how the is-a relation *could* be implemented in Omega. In the real Omega library, isA: is implemented as a primitive method for efficiency reasons, as it is, for example, implicitly invoked by the compiler in the case of a conditional assignment.

Object's method "allocatedBytes → Integer":
> -- *returns how many bytes the receiver occupies in memory.*

Object's method "plainTypeName → StringConstant":
> -- *returns the type name of the receiver without taking the*
> -- *parameter of a generic type into account (PROTECTED).*

Object's method "paramTypeName → StringConstant":
> -- *returns the type name of the parameter if the receiver is a generic*
> -- *or generated object, otherwise it returns "" (PROTECTED).*

Object's method "typeName → String":
> -- *returns the full type name of the receiver*
> -- *(including a generic object's parameter type name) (PROTECTED).*
> [(ptn::=self paramTypeName)==""
>   ifTrue: [self plainTypeName return];
>   (self plainTypeName+"{"+ptn+"}") return   ]

Object's method "forAllReferences: Action{Object} → Same":
> -- *evaluates the argument for each object referred to by the receiver*
> -- *(PROTECTED).*

This set of methods provides information about the definition of objects rather than about the objects' state. All these methods (except allocatedBytes) are protected, as they return vital information with a well-defined meaning.

The method isA: is used in expressions like x isA:T to check for dynamic compatibility of x with T. The method isAn: is simply another form of isA: that can be used when the argument's name begins with a vowel (e.g., x isAn:Event).

The messages typeName, plainTypeName and paramTypeName can be used for a variety of purposes. For example, x paramTypeName##"" returns true when x is a generic object, and x plainTypeName==y plainTypeName[3] can be used to check whether x and y are variants of the same generic prototype.

The method forAllReferences: can be used – among other things – for debugging purposes in order to trace the references among objects. It is also used to find out which prototypes are referenced by other objects and to passivate whole object networks (see writeTo: in the next section).

6.2.5   External Representation

Object's method "asString → String":
> -- *returns a string consisting of "a[n]" and the receiver's type name.*
> [self typeName withArticle]

---

[3]   Note the use of "==" instead of "=". The correctness of this expression is guaranteed because plainTypeName and paramTypeName return unique StringConstant objects (see *String Literals* in Section 4.2.2 *Symbols*).

Object's method "log → Same":
   -- writes the receiver's string representation to the log window.
   [self asString log; self]

Object's method "line → Same":
   -- writes the receiver's string representation on a log line.
   [self log; Char.cr log; self]

Object's method "! → Same":
   -- presents the receiver to the user.
   [self asString !; self]

Object's method " asImage → Image":
   -- returns an image representing the receiver; the default
   -- implementation just returns an image of the textual representation.
   [self asString asImage]

Object's method "printOn: Printer → Same":
   {printer:Printer}
   -- prints an image representing the receiver; the default
   -- implementation just prints the result of asImage.
   [self asImage printOn:printer; self]

Object's method "writeTo: Stream → Same":
   -- writes the object network originating in the receiver to the stream
   -- passed as argument in such a form that the object can be
   -- reconstructed from it.

The effect of the method asString is similar to that of Smalltalk's printString; it returns a textual representation of the receiver. The default implementation just returns the object's type name with a leading article (e.g., "an Object" or "a Foo"). Although this default information does not yield especially descriptive strings, it is sufficient in many cases. It is only necessary to override the method asString when more detailed information about objects of a particular type is to be returned.

Note that asString is used in many other methods that deal with external representation of objects. For example, the method log simply converts the receiver into its textual representation and commands the resulting string to write itself to the log window.

By convention, the names of all conversion methods begin with "as" and end with the name of the type of object they return. Since asString and asImage are defined in Object, they are applicable to all objects – even to monomorphic ones. For example, the expression (1<2) asString returns "true".

The message printOn: prints a visual representation of the receiver[4]. The default implementation prints an image of the textual representation. It should

_____
[4] Note to Smalltalk programmers: The Omega method printOn: really *prints* the receiver, whereas the Smalltalk method with the same name writes a textual representation of the receiver to a stream.

be overridden when a more appropriate (for example, a graphical) representation can be provided.

The message writeTo: writes the receiver and all objects directly or indirectly referenced by it to the stream passed as argument. The external representation is similar to the internal representation. writeTo: automatically takes care of recursive data structures and writes the objects in a compact form from which the entire network originating in the receiver can be reconstructed later. The method writeTo: is implemented in a general way that relieves the programmer entirely from activation and passivation; it need never be overridden.

6.2.6   Input

Object's method "fromString: String → Same":
>   {str:String}
>   -- returns an object constructed from a string (ABSTRACT).
>   [self abstractMethod]

Object's method "input: String → Same":
>   {prompt:String}
>   -- asks the user to input an object (the receiver is the default value).
>   [self fromString:(self asString input: prompt)]

Object's method "input → Same":
>   -- asks the user to input an object (the receiver is the default value).
>   [self input: self typeName withArticle + ":"]

Object's method "edit → Same":
>   -- allows the user to interactively edit the receiver (ABSTRACT).

Object's method "readFrom: Stream → Same":
>   -- reconstructs an object network written with writeTo:.

The message fromString: is the counterpart of asString. It is intended to return an object of the same class as the receiver. The contents of the newly created object are determined by the receiver and the string passed as argument. For example, the expression myFont fromString:"Times" (with myFont of the class Font) would return a new font object with the same font size and attributes as the receiver, but in the typeface "Times". Unfortunately, there is no general way to implement this method in Object, so the implementer of a new prototype has to override this method when the conversion from a string into an object of that type is desired.

The message input: is a convenient shorthand that first requests the user to input a string and then converts the string into an object of the same class as the receiver. The string representation of the receiver serves as the default value, and the argument denotes a prompt string. For example, 42 input: "universal number:" will display the dialog depicted in Figure 6-1. The method input is another shorthand that uses the receiver's type name as the prompt string.

The method edit allows the user to interactively modify the receiver. This method is defined as abstract in Object; it must be overridden when such a facility should be provided. Figure 6-2 shows the editing window that is presented when the message edit is sent to a Pattern object.

The method readFrom: reconstructs an object network from an external representation previously stored with the message writeTo:.

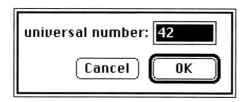

Fig. 6-1: User dialog resulting from the message 42 input: "universal number"

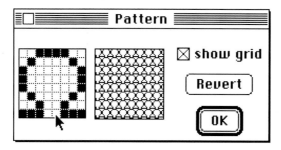

Fig. 6-2: User dialog resulting from sending the message edit to a Pattern object

.2.7   Exceptions

Object's method "abstractMethod → Same":
  -- *raises an "abstract method" exception.*

Object's method "mutationError → Same":
  -- *raises a "mutation error" exception.*
  [("can't modify a "+self typeName+" object") error; self]

Object's method "notImplemented → Same":
  -- *raises a "method not (yet) implemented" exception.*

This set of methods can be invoked under "exceptional" circumstances. For example, abstract methods will typically just contain the expression self abstractMethod (see fromString: in the previous section). The method mutation-Error can be used within methods of objects that are not intended to be modified.

For example, the method edit of Integer is "implemented" in this way. The method notImplemented is handy during incremental software development. Methods that are not yet functional can be marked in this way.

The implementations of abstractMethod and notImplemented are not shown here because they are implemented as primitive methods. They not only raise an exception but also point out which method was being called for which receiver and from where. This detailed information is particularly useful for the developer of an Omega program; the final user should never see the error messages resulting from these methods.

6.2.8   Workspace Activation and Passivation

Object's method "postRead → Boolean":
> *-- performs some postprocessing after reading the workspace*
> *-- should return true if there really was something to do.*
> [false]

Object's method "preWrite → Boolean":
> *-- performs some preprocessing before writing the workspace*
> *-- should return true if there really was something to do.*
> [false]

Object's method "postWrite → Boolean":
> *-- performs some postprocessing after writing the workspace*
> *-- should return true if there really was something to do.*
> [false]

Object's method "preClose → Boolean":
> *-- performs cleanup before closing the workspace*
> *-- should return true if there really was something to do.*
> [false]

This set of methods is automatically called by the programming environment. After a workspace has been loaded into memory, all objects are sent the postRead message. Making a snapshot of a workspace is bracketed with calls to preWrite and postWrite, and the message preClose is sent to all objects immediately before the workspace is discarded from main storage. The main purpose of these messages is to give critical objects a chance to do some house-keeping and to ensure a certain state of passivated objects. For example, Window objects close themselves before the workspace is written and reopen immediately afterwards. They permanently close before the workspace is discarded and make sure they are in a properly initialized state immediately after a workspace has been read. However, most objects will not need to do anything in these situations. They will simply inherit the default implementation and thus report that there was nothing to do.

These messages (in particular postRead, preWrite and postWrite) can be used as a simple means to make sure that prototypes (and other objects as well) are not corrupted (at least initially). For example, Pattern objects reset their size to 8×8 at these opportunities.

.2.9   Attributes

Object's method "attribute: StringConstant → Integer":
    {attr:StringConstant}
    -- returns the value of the attribute with the name attr.
    [Integer.min] *-- represents "unknown attribute"*

Object's method "attribute: StringConstant set: Integer → Same":
    {attr:StringConstant; val:Integer}
    -- gives the attribute with the name attr the value val.
    [self] *-- just ignore the request*

Object's method "allAttributes → Set{StringConstant}":
    -- returns a set containing the names of all attributes.
    [Set{StringConstant} copy] *-- the empty set*

Object's method "hasAttribute: StringConstant → Boolean":
    {attr:StringConstant}
    -- returns true if the receiver has an attribute with the name attr.
    [false]

Object's method "canChangeAttribute: StringConstant → Boolean":
    {attr:StringConstant}
    -- returns true if the attribute with the name attr
    -- can be modified by means of attribute:set:.
    [false]

Attributes are a simple mechanism to handle properties of objects that can be expressed as Integer numbers. Attributes are identified by StringConstants. The following simple examples show how a modifiable attribute "value" representing an instance variable with the same name can be implemented in a prototype P which is assumed to be derived from Q:

P's method "attribute: StringConstant → Integer":
    {attr:StringConstant}
    [attr=="value" ifTrue: [value return];
     self(Q) attribute:attr]

P's method "attribute: StringConstant set: Integer → Same":
    {attr:StringConstant; val:Integer}
    [attr=="value" ifTrue: [value:=val; self return];
      self(Q) attribute:attr set:val]

P's method "allAttributes → Set{StringConstant}":
    [self(Q) allAttributes add:"value"]

P's method "hasAttribute: StringConstant → Boolean":
    {attr:StringConstant}
    [attr=="value" or:[self(Q) hasAttribute:attr]]

P's method "canChangeAttribute: StringConstant → Boolean":
    {attr:StringConstant}
    [attr=="value" or:[self(Q) canChangeAttribute:attr]]

Attributes are a convenient means of determining and changing the properties of unknown objects in a general way. The attribute protocol is, for example, used by scroll bars. A scroll bar can be connected with an arbitrary object and associated with a particular attribute. Whenever the user utilizes the scroll bar, that attribute of the objects connected with the scroll bar is automatically modified (see Section 6.7.3 *Panes*).

It must be emphasized that attributes are merely a means to let user interface objects communicate with each other without knowing their exact protocol. They should *not* be used as the normal way to retrieve and modify properties of objects.

6.2.10 Change Propagation

Object's method "addDependent:Object → Same":
    -- registers the argument as dependent on the receiver.

Object's method "dependsOn:Object → Same":
    {source:Object}
    -- registers the receiver as dependent on the argument.
    [source addDependent:self; self]

Object's method "release:Object → Same":
    -- makes the argument independent of the receiver.

Object's method "independentOf:Object → Same":
    {source:Object}
    -- makes the receiver independent of the argument.
    [source release:self; self]

Object's method "changed:Object → Same":
    -- notifies all objects depending on the receiver of a change.
    -- The argument specifies the kind of change.

Object's method "changed → Same":
    -- notifies all objects depending on the receiver of a general change.
    [self changed: ""]

Object's method "updateTo:Object because:Object → Same":
    {source:Object; reason:Object}
    -- updates the receiver because the source has changed.
    -- reason specifies the kind of change.
    [self]

Omega's change propagation mechanism works in a similar way as that of
Smalltalk (see Section 5.3 *Object Protocols*). When an object announces a
change, it can also supply an object that specifies the kind of change. This
additional parameter is usually a StringConstant. For example, "size" is used by
collections to indicate that one or more elements have been added or removed.
The empty string denotes a general change. This is often sufficient, especially
when an object can only change in *one* significant way or when *any* change
will require appropriate actions by all dependents.

.2.11 Miscellaneous Methods

Object's method "return → Same":
    -- non-local return; terminates execution of the statically
    -- enclosing method and returns the receiver as its result
    -- (PROTECTED).

Object's method "hash → Integer":
    -- returns a numeric representation of the receiver.

Object's method "initialize → Same":
    -- brings the receiver into a well-defined state.
    [self]

The message return was already discussed in Section 4.8 *Blocks and Actions*. It
is not only a primitive method, but also a method that is treated in a special way
by the compiler (hence the attribute "protected").

The method hash returns an Integer number (the "hash value") that
identifies the receiver. As long as an object exists (even across passivation and
activation of the workspace) it will return the same result as response to the
message hash. It is, however, possible that two or more objects return the same
hash value. Hash values are primarily used by some collections to accelerate
search operations.

The method initialize can be used to bring an object into a well-defined state. This method has a specified meaning only for Application and its descendants (see Section 6.9 *Applications*); it can be freely used for other objects. initialize is particularly useful to explicitly restore the state of a prototype that is suspected to be corrupted.

6.3   Basic Types

This section describes the interfaces of the most important standard and system types, in particular, the numeric types Integer and Real, Boolean, Char, Nil and Wrapper. The interfaces of Block and Action have already been explained in Section 4.8 *Blocks and Actions* and are therefore not repeated here. The types Container, Collection, Array, String and StringConstant are described in Section 6.4 *Containers*.

All types discussed here are direct descendants of Object. This means that they are neither statically nor dynamically compatible with each other. No implicit conversions are performed from one type to another, as such hidden conversions often take place in situations that cannot be anticipated by the programmer. Instead, explicit conversion messages are provided by most of these types. This incompatibility is intentional; the programmer should decide which type best fits a particular purpose.

6.3.1   Integer

Integer values are represented as 2's complement 32-bit numbers. As they are monomorphic, the compiler can recognize and optimize most operations with integers. Two shared variables are defined in Integer:

- min contains the lowest possible value of type Integer (–2147483648).
- max contains the largest possible value of type Integer (+2147483647).

Both min and max are defined as *public* and *read-only* for all classes. They can be accessed with the notations Integer.min and Integer.max, respectively.

Arithmetic operations

+ Integer → Integer
    -- returns the sum of the receiver and the argument.
– Integer → Integer
    -- returns the result of subtracting the argument from the receiver.
* Integer → Integer
    -- returns the product of the receiver and the argument.

/ Integer → Integer
>   -- *returns the result of dividing the receiver by the argument.*
>   -- *Fractional digits are truncated.*

\ Integer → Integer
>   -- *returns the remainder of the division of the receiver by the argument.*
>   -- *x\y is defined as x–((x/y)*y).*

^ Integer → Integer
>   -- *raises the receiver to the power of the argument.*

~ → Integer
>   -- *inverts the sign of the receiver.*

abs → Integer
>   -- *returns the absolute value of the receiver.*

sign → Integer
>   -- *returns +1 when the receiver is >0, –1 when it is <0 and 0 when it is =0.*

All arithmetic operations are restricted to the range -2^{31} through to $+2^{31}-1$. An operation whose result exceeded this range would raise a "numeric overflow" exception. Likewise, a "division by zero" exception results when the argument of the messages "/" or "\" happens to be 0.

Comparisons and Tests

== Integer → Boolean
= Integer → Boolean
Integer → Boolean
Integer → Boolean
< Integer → Boolean
<= Integer → Boolean
> Integer → Boolean
>= Integer → Boolean

These messages perform the usual comparisons among integer values. The messages "==" and "=" (and therefore also "##" and "#") have the same meaning for Integer, as Integer objects are *immutable*, that is, it is not possible to change the value of an Integer object by means of a message.

min:Integer → Integer
>   -- *returns the receiver when it is smaller than the argument,*
>   -- *otherwise the argument.*

max:Integer → Integer
>   -- *returns the receiver when it is greater than the argument,*
>   -- *otherwise the argument.*

between:Integer and:Integer → Boolean
>   -- *returns true if the value of the receiver lies in the range*
>   -- *specified by the first and the second argument.*

odd → Boolean
> -- *returns the result of (self \ 2) # 0.*

isPrime → Boolean
> -- *returns true when the receiver is a prime number.*

!>= Integer → Integer
> -- *returns the value of the argument if it is ≥0 and less than or equal*
> -- *to the receiver; otherwise, a "range error" exception is raised.*

This set of messages performs various tests of Integer values. The message
"!>=" is primarily used for range checks during access to array elements.

Conversions

asString → String
> -- *returns a sequence of digits as textual representation of the receiver.*

asChar → Char
> -- *returns the character with the same ordinal number as the receiver.*

asReal → Real
> -- *returns a Real number with the same value as the receiver.*

@ Integer → Point
> -- *returns a Point object with the receiver as x coordinate*
> -- *and the argument as y coordinate.*

Loops (see Section 4.9.1 *Predefined Flow Control Elements*)

timesRepeat:Block → Integer
> -- *evaluates repeatBlock as many times as specified by the receiver.*

to:Integer do:Action{Integer} → Integer
> {limit: Integer; action: Action{Integer}}
> -- *evaluates action for every integer value between the receiver and limit.*

to:Integer by:Integer do:Action{Integer} → Integer
> {limit: Integer; step: Integer; action: Action{Integer}}
> -- *evaluates action for every integer value between the receiver and limit,*
> -- *starting with the receiver and incrementing the value by step.*

6.3.2 Real

Real values are represented as 32-bit numbers in the standard IEEE format. As
they are monomorphic, the compiler "knows" about operations with real numbers and thus can generate efficient code for them. The following shared variables are defined in Real:

- min contains the smallest positive value of type Real ($\approx$ 1.4e-45).
- max contains the largest possible value of type Integer ($\approx$ 3.4e38).

- pi contains the value of π (≈ 3.1416).
- e contains the Euler constant (≈ 2.71828).

All these variables are defined as *public* and *read-only* for all classes. They can be accessed, for example, with the notations Real.min and Real.pi.

The following list gives the most important Real messages. Those which have the same or a similar meaning as those already explained in the previous section on Integer are only listed here with their interface.

Arithmetic operations

```
+ Real → Real
– Real → Real
* Real → Real
/ Real → Real
^ Real → Real
~ → Real
abs → Real
sign → Real

sqrt → Real
        -- returns the square root of the receiver.
ln → Real
        -- returns the natural logarithm of the receiver.
exp → Real
        -- returns Real.e raised to the power of the receiver.
sin → Real
        -- returns the sine of the receiver.
cos → Real
        -- returns the cosine of the receiver.
arcTan → Real
        -- returns the angle whose tangent is the receiver.
```

All these operations raise a "numeric overflow" exception when an operation attempts to produce a result beyond the legal range of type Real. The trigonometric messages sin, cos and arcTan all operate with angles in radians. For example, the expression (Real.pi/2.0) sin returns the value 1.0.

Comparisons and Tests

```
== Real → Boolean
= Real → Boolean
## Real → Boolean
# Real → Boolean
< Real → Boolean
<= Real → Boolean
```

\> Real → Boolean
\>= Real → Boolean
min: Real → Real
max: Real → Real
between: Real and: Real → Boolean
within:Real of:Real → Boolean
     {eps:Real; other:Real}
        -- returns true when the difference between the receiver and the
        -- argument other is less than or equal to eps.

As real values are inaccurate and subject to rounding errors, it is recommended not to test two real numbers for equality, but rather for "similarity". For this purpose, the message within:of: is provided.

Conversions

asString → String
asInteger → Integer
        -- returns an Integer number with the same value as the receiver. Real
        -- values outside the Integer range raise a "numeric overflow" exception.
asString:Integer decimals:Integer → String
     {totalWidth: Integer; decimalDigits: Integer}
        -- returns a string of length totalWidth with
        -- decimalDigits places after the decimal point.
asExpString:Integer → String
     {totalWidth: Integer}
        -- returns a string of length totalWidth in exponential representation.

Loops

to:Real do:Action{Real} → Real
to:Real by:Real do:Action{Real} → Real

6.3.3   Boolean

Boolean values are represented like integer numbers; the value 1 denotes true, and 0 denotes false. Variables of type Boolean can only assume these two values. Note that there are no boolean literals in Omega. The values true and false are available as shared variables of Object.

The following list gives the most important Boolean messages. Those that were already explained in Sections 4.9.1 *Predefined Flow Control Elements* and 4.9.2 *Short-Circuit Evaluation of Boolean Operations* are only listed here with their interface.

Boolean relations

& Boolean → Boolean
   -- "and": returns true when the receiver and the argument are both true,
   -- otherwise false.
| Boolean → Boolean
   -- "or": returns false when the receiver and the argument are both false,
   -- otherwise true.
\ Boolean → Boolean
   -- "exclusive or": returns true when either the receiver or the argument
   -- (but not both) are true.
~ → Boolean
   -- "not": returns the negation of the receiver.
and: Block → Boolean
or: Block → Boolean

Comparisons

== Boolean → Boolean
= Boolean → Boolean
Boolean → Boolean
Boolean → Boolean
< Boolean → Boolean
<= Boolean → Boolean
> Boolean → Boolean
>= Boolean → Boolean

All comparisons are implemented in terms of the internal representation of Boolean. That is, true is considered greater than false. For example, the expression x<y returns true only if x=false and y=true. x#y and x##y are identical to x\y, and x=false is equivalent to x~[5].

Conversions

asString → String
   -- returns "true" when the receiver is true, otherwise "false".
asInteger → Integer
   -- returns 1 for true and 0 for false.

---

[5]   It is considered bad style to test boolean values for equality with true or false. Instead of x=true or x#false, the value of x should be used, and x~ should be used in preference to x=false and x#true.

Flow Control

ifTrue: Block → Boolean
ifFalse: Block → Boolean
ifTrue: Block ifFalse: Block → Boolean
ifFalse: Block ifTrue: Block → Boolean

6.3.4   Char

A Char object is represented as an integer number containing the ASCII value
of the respective character. Variables of type Char can only assume values in
the range 0 through to 255. The following shared variables are defined in Char:
- nul: the "null character" (0 asChar).
- bs: the backspace character (= 8 asChar).
- tab: the horizontal tabulator (= 9 asChar).
- lf: the line feed character (= 10 asChar).
- cr: the carriage return character (= 13 asChar).
- esc: the escape character (= 27 asChar).

All these variables are defined as *public* and *read-only* for all classes. They
can be accessed, for example, with the notations Char.nul and Char.cr.

The following list gives the most important Char messages. Those which
have the same or a similar meaning as those already explained in previous
sections are only listed here with their interface.

Comparisons and Tests

== Char → Boolean
= Char → Boolean
Char → Boolean
Char → Boolean
< Char → Boolean
<= Char → Boolean
> Char → Boolean
>= Char → Boolean

isLetter → Boolean
        -- returns true when the receiver is a letter of the English alphabet.
isDigit → Boolean
        -- returns true when the receiver is a decimal digit.

All comparisons are implemented in terms of the internal representation of
Char. That is, characters are compared according to their ASCII values. For
example, 'a' is considered less than 'b' but greater than 'A'.

Conversions

asString → String

> *-- returns a string of length 1 containing the receiver as the only character.*

ordinalNumber → Integer[6]

> *-- returns the ASCII value of the receiver.*

upperCase → Char

> *-- returns the corresponding capital letter when the receiver is a*
> *-- lower case letter; otherwise, the receiver is returned.*

lowerCase → Char

> *-- returns the corresponding lower-case letter when the receiver is a*
> *-- capital letter; otherwise, the receiver is returned.*

Concatenation

+ String → String

> *-- concatenates the receiver with the argument.*

The concatenation message "+" returns a *new* string object that is one character longer than the argument. For example, the expression 'm'+"ice" will return an object of class String (not StringConstant!) containing "mice".

6.3.5   Nil

Nil is a one-of-a-kind prototype that just serves as a representative for "nothing". It accepts all messages defined in Object and reacts to all other messages by raising a "Nil access" exception. No further messages are defined in Nil beyond those already defined in Object, but some of the inherited messages are overridden:

clone → Same

> *-- always returns self, as Nil is a one-of-a-kind prototype.*

isNil → Boolean

> *-- returns true.*

asString → String

> *-- returns the StringConstant object "Nil".*

addDependent:Object → Same

> *-- does nothing, as no object can depend on Nil.*

dependsOn:Object → Same

> *-- does nothing, as Nil can never depend on another object.*

changed:Object → Same

> *-- does nothing, as Nil can never change.*

---

[6]   The name ordinalNumber was chosen over asInteger in order to avoid ambiguity. The name ordinalNumber makes clear that the ASCII number of the receiver is returned, whereas asInteger could be misinterpreted as a conversion of digits to their corresponding integer values.

No other Object methods are overridden in Nil. Their default behavior is simply inherited. This strategy works because most methods of Object (such as ifNil:) are implemented on top of a small set of elementary methods.

6.3.6   Wrapper

The generic type Wrapper is an auxiliary type that is used by the compiler when an expression *e* of a monomorphic type *T* is assigned to a variable *v* of type Object – either explicitly by *v:=e* or implicitly by passing *e* as an argument to a message where the corresponding formal argument is of type Object.

In such cases, the expression being assigned is "wrapped" in an object of class Wrapper{*T*}. The interface and implementation of Wrapper are designed such that all messages defined in Object are delegated to the monomorphic element that is stored in the Wrapper instance variable content (of type Parameter, and defined as *public*, but *read-only for clients*). For example, the messages asString and "=" are implemented in Wrapper in the following way:

asString → String
     -- *returns the string representation of the wrapped element.*
     [content asString]

= Object → Boolean
     {other:Object}
     -- *returns true if the argument is also a Wrapper with the same content.*
     [otherWrapper:Same;
      (otherWrapper:?=other) and:[content==otherWrapper.content]]

The only additional method implemented in Wrapper creates a new Wrapper with the content instance variable set to the argument:

with:Parameter → Same
     {value:Parameter}
     -- *creates a new Wrapper with a specified content.*
     [new::=self clone; new.content:=value; new]

When the compiler detects an assignment of an expression *e* of a monomorphic type *T* to a (polymorphic) variable *v* of type Object, it automatically wraps the expression in a (polymorphic) Wrapper object and assigns this object to the variable *v*:

     v := Wrapper{ *T* } with:e

When a conditional assignment *v:?=e* of a polymorphic expression *e* to a monomorphic variable *v* of type *T* takes place, the compiler replaces it with the following expression:

```
(   tWrapper:Wrapper{T};
    (tWrapper:?=e) ifTrue:[v:=tWrapper.content; true]
)
```

First the expression is tested to discover whether it denotes a **Wrapper** with an element of the desired destination type T, and, if so, its content is "unwrapped" and assigned to the variable v.

6.4 Containers

This section describes the interfaces of the most important container types, in particular **String**, **StringConstant** and the generic collection types **Array**, **Set** and **IdDictionary**.

The term **container** is used in Omega for objects of *variable size*. A container can be thought of as an elastic bag of unlimited capacity[7]. The term **collection** is used for a generic container type whose parameter type defines which elements it can hold. Figure 6-3 shows the inheritance hierarchy of the most important container types.

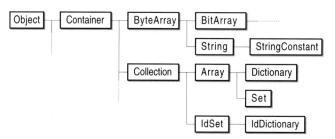

Fig. 6-3: Inheritance hierarchy of Omega's container types

The types shown in Figure 6-3 are used for the following purposes:

- **Container** mainly serves as an abstraction of its descendants and provides the functionality to grow and shrink. The content of a **Container** object is undefined. Pure **Container** objects are used at some points within the library to hold low-level data structures; they should not normally be used otherwise.
- **ByteArray** is a container whose bytes can be accessed individually. The first byte has the index 0. ByteArrays are, for example, used to represent internal images of external data structures (such as files).
- **BitArray** is a variant of a **ByteArray** whose bits can be accessed individually. The most significant bit of the first byte has the index 0. BitArrays are

---

[7]   Of course, there is always a limit to the capacity of containers, as the size of a container cannot exceed the amount of available memory.

mainly used as a compact means of representing sets of integers. BitArray also serves as the basis for several other types not shown in Figure 6.3, for example, Cursor, Icon and Pattern.

- String is a standard type. In contrast to similar classes of other libraries, Omega's strings can arbitrarily grow and shrink, as they are derived from Container.
- StringConstant is an immutable variant of String. The compiler automatically creates StringConstant object when it detects string literals within expressions (see Section 4.2.2 *Symbols*).
- Collection is a generic abstraction of all other types whose objects can hold reference to other objects. It defines the common protocol of all its descendants.
- Array is a collection whose elements can be accessed through integer indexes. The first element of an array always has the index 1.
- Set is a collection that only contains unequal elements (i.e., the relation $x=y$ never reports true for any two elements x and y contained in the same set).
- Dictionary is a collection whose elements can be accessed through key objects. The type of the key is restricted to String in Dictionary.
- IdSet ("identity set") is a collection that only contains different elements (i.e., the relation $x==y$ never reports true for any two elements x and y). IdSet is implemented by means of a hash table and thus facilitates fast lookup of elements in almost constant time.
- IdDictionary ("identity dictionary") is a collection whose elements can be accessed through arbitrary key objects. Such dictionaries are used to implement change propagation.

The following sections show the interfaces of the most important container types. The definitions of BitArray, Dictionary and Set are omitted, as these types are not necessary to understand the rest of the library.

6.4.1 Container

Container defines an additional instance variable size with the attributes *heritage* and *read-only*. The size of a container can only be set implicitly by means of messages.

byteSize → Integer
> -- *returns the number of bytes the receiver can hold (PROTECTED).*
> [size]

changeByteSize:Integer → Same
> -- *resizes the receiver (PROTECTED and HERITAGE).*

size → Integer

-- *returns the "size" of the receiver (default is the byte size).*
[size]

changeSize:Integer → Same

{newSize:integer}

-- *changes the "size" of the receiver (default is changing the byte size).*
[self changeByteSize:newSize]

ofSize:Integer → Same

{newSize:integer}

-- *returns a copy of the receiver with the desired size.*
[self clone changeSize:newSize]

= Object → Boolean

-- *returns true when the receiver is a container of the same*
-- *byte size that is byte-wise equal to the receiver.*

byteSize and changeByteSize: are the basic operations for questioning and manipulating the size of a container. Both methods are protected, and changeByteSize: is also hidden from clients in order to avoid inconsistent states of subtypes that may impose constraints on their size (for example, the byte size of an Array is always a multiple of 4).

The official interface of Container is provided by the methods size and changeSize:. Both methods can be overridden to give a different meaning to the term "size". For examples, arrays and sets will return their number of elements instead of the number of bytes required to hold these elements.

ofSize: is a convenient shortcut that is frequently used when a new container of a specific size is needed. Instead of changing the receiver, ofSize: returns a new object with the same initial contents as the receiver and then re-sizes that object such that it fits the caller's requirements.

4.2 ByteArray

byteAt:Integer → Integer

{index:Integer}

-- *returns the value of the byte at the specified index.*

at:Integer putByte:Integer → Same

{index:Integer; value:Integer}

-- *replaces the byte at index with newValue.*

ByteArray simply extends the interface of Container with two methods for accessing individual bytes. For the client, a byte is represented by an integer number in the range 0 through 255.

Both byteAt: and at:putByte: check for valid indexes. If the condition index between:0 and:size−1 is not satisfied, a "range check failed" exception is raised.

6.4.3   String

A string is a byte array whose elements are characters. The individual characters of a string can be accessed through integer indexes. The first character has the index 1.

String supports more than 120 operations, some of which serve very special purposes. The following summary lists only the most important operations.

Character Access

at: Integer → Char
         -- returns the character at the given index.
at: Integer put:Char → Same
         -- replaces the character at the given index.

Concatenation

add: String → Same
         -- appends the argument to the receiver.
addChar: Char → Same
         -- appends the argument to the receiver.
+ String → Same
       {other:String}
         -- returns the concatenation of the receiver and the argument.
       [self clone add:other]

Comparison

< String → Boolean
<= String → Boolean
> String → Boolean
>= String → Boolean

These operators compare strings lexicographically, i.e., "tiger" is considered smaller than "tiny pussycat" because 'g' is less than 'n' in ASCII. The methods "=" and "#" are inherited from Container.

Insertion and Deletion

before:Integer insert:String → Same
      {index:Integer; str:String}
        -- *inserts str before the character at the position index.*
before:Integer insertChar:Char → Same
      {index:Integer; ch:Char}
        -- *inserts ch before the character at the position index.*
delete:Integer → Same
      {index:Integer}
        -- *deletes the character at the given index.*
deleteFrom:Integer to:Integer → Same
      {first:Integer; last:Integer}
        -- *deletes all characters with the indexes first through last.*
deleteFrom:Integer chars:Integer → Same
      {first:Integer; n:Integer}
        -- *deletes n characters starting at first.*

Searching

indexOf:String → Integer
      {str:String}
        -- *returns the index of the first occurrence of str within the receiver.*
        -- *0 is returned when the receiver doesn't contain str.*
indexOfChar:Char → Integer
      {ch:Char}
        -- *returns the index of the first occurrence of ch within the receiver.*
        -- *0 is returned when the receiver doesn't contain ch.*

Conversion

asString → String
        -- *returns the receiver, as it already is a string.*
      [self]
asInteger → Integer
        -- *returns the integer value denoted by the string.*
        -- *raises an exception when the receiver does not comply with*
        -- *the Omega syntax for integer literals.*
asReal → Real
        -- *returns the real value denoted by the string.*
        -- *raises an exception when the receiver does not comply with*
        -- *the Omega syntax for real literals.*

Exceptions

error → Same

    -- raises an exception; the receiver denotes the error message.

assertion:Boolean → Boolean

    {condition:Boolean}

    -- raises an exception when the condition passed as argument is not met.

    [condition ifFalse:[self error]]

6.4.4   StringConstant

StringConstant objects are immutable and unique strings, but apart from these properties, they behave exactly like String objects. StringConstant is thus derived from String and overrides those few methods that would modify string constants or create identical copies of existing ones[8]. The following methods are overridden in StringConstant to achieve this goal:

- at:put:, add:, addChar: and changeSize: are invalidated by implementations that just contain the message self mutationError (see Section 6.2.7).
- clone is reimplemented such that it returns self.
- asString creates a String object with the same contents as the String-Constant object.
- The concatenation operator "+" is reimplemented such that initially it creates a String object with the same contents instead of cloning the receiver (see the implementation of "+" in the previous section):
        [self asString add:other]

6.4.5   Collection

Collection defines the basic protocol for all operations with containers containing arbitrary objects. It is a generic prototype with the default parameter type Object. Collection supports addition and deletion of elements (or all elements contained in another collection), conversions and iteration over all elements. The following list shows the complete implementations of these methods.

Addition and Deletion

add: Parameter → Same

    {newElement:Parameter}

    -- adds newElement to the receiver (ABSTRACT).

    [self abstractMethod]

---

[8]   In fact, StringConstant is one of the few classes in the Omega library that use implementation inheritance rather than interface inheritance.

addAllOf: Collection{Parameter} → Same
    {other:Collection{Parameter}}
      -- adds all elements of other to the receiver.
    [other forAll:{elem:Parameter}[self add:elem]; self]

remove:Parameter ↦ Same
    {elem:Parameter}
      -- removes elem from the receiver (ABSTRACT).
    [self abstractMethod]

removeAllOf: Collection{Parameter} → Same
    {other:Collection{Parameter}}
      -- removes all elements of other from the receiver.
    [other forAll:{elem:Parameter}[self remove:elem]; self]

+ Collection{Parameter} → Same
    {other:Collection{Parameter}}
      -- returns the union of the receiver and the argument.
    [self clone addAllOf:other]

− Collection{Parameter} → Same
    {other:Collection{Parameter}}
      -- returns a collection containing all elements of the receiver,
      -- but without the elements of the argument.
    [self clone removeAllOf:other]

Conversion

asString → String
      -- returns a string containing the string representations
      -- of all elements of the receiver.
    [self size=0 ifTrue:["()" asString return];
     s::="(" asString;
     self forAll:{elem:Parameter}[s add:elem asString, addChar:','];
     s at:s size put:')']

asArray → Array{Parameter}
      -- returns an Array with the same elements as the receiver.
    [Array{Parameter}copy addAllOf:self]

asIdSet → IdSet{Parameter}
      -- returns an IdSet with the same elements as the receiver.
    [IdSet{Parameter}copy addAllOf:self]

Iteration

forAll: Action{Parameter} → Same
    {act:Collection{Parameter}}
    -- performs act for every element of the receiver (ABSTRACT).
    [self abstractMethod]

forFirst: Action{Parameter} forOthers: Action{Parameter} → Same
    {firstAct:Action{Parameter}; otherAct:Action{Parameter}}
    -- performs firstAct for the first, otherAct for all
    -- subsequent elements of the receiver.
    -- NOTE: This is just a default implementation;
    --   override it if you can do it more efficiently.
    [first::=true;
     self forAll:{elem:Parameter}
      [first
        ifTrue:[firstAct doWith:elem; first:=false]
        ifFalse:[otherAct doWith:elem]
      ]
    ]

numberOf: Action{Parameter} → Integer
    {attribute:Action{Parameter}}
    -- returns the number of elements for which attribute returns true.
    [total::=0;
     self forAll:{elem:Parameter}
      [(attribute doWith:elem) ifTrue:[total:=total+1]];
     total]

contains: Parameter → Boolean
    {testElem:Parameter}
    -- returns true if the receiver contains testElem.
    [self forAll:{elem:Parameter}
      [elem==testElem ifTrue:[true return]];
     false]

allElements: Action{Parameter} → IdSet{Parameter}
    {attribute:Action{Parameter}}
    -- returns a set containing all elements for which attribute returns true.
    [result::=IdSet{Parameter} copy; *-- start with an empty set*
     self forAll:{elem:Parameter}
      [attribute doWith:elem, ifTrue:[result add:elem]];
     result]

It is noteworthy that only three methods (add:, remove: and forAll:) are defined
as abstract in Collection. Only these methods must be overridden in derived

prototypes in order to comply with the Collection protocol. All other methods of Collection are implemented using these basic methods. They can be inherited as they are. It is only necessary to reimplement them when a more efficient implementation can be provided for them (see the comment in forFirst:forOthers:).

.4.6   Array

Array is a Collection whose elements are associated with integer indexes, where the first element has the index 1. The following list shows the complete implementations of the most important methods (except for primitive methods, which are explicitly marked as primitive).

Size Control

changeSize:integer → Same
> {newSize:Integer}
> -- *resizes the array such that it can hold newSize elements.*
> [oldSize::=self size;
>   self changeByteSize:newSize*4;
>   zeroElem:Parameter; -- *initialized to Nil, 0, or whatever is appropriate*
>   oldSize+1 to:newSize do:{i:Integer}[self at:i put:zeroElem];
>   self]

size → Integer
> -- *returns the number of elements in the receiver.*
> [size/4]

Element Access

at:Integer → Parameter
> {index:integer}
> -- *returns the element at the given index.*
> -- *a "range check failed" exception is raised when the index*
> -- *is less than 0 or greater than self size.*
> PRIMITIVE

at:Integer put:Parameter → Same
> {index:Integer; elem:Parameter}
> -- *replaces the element at the given index with elem.*
> -- *a "range check failed" exception is raised when the index*
> -- *is less than 0 or greater than self size.*
> PRIMITIVE

Searching

indexOfFirst: Action{Parameter} → Same
    {attribute:Action{Parameter}}
    -- returns the first index for which attribute returns true; 0 if none.
    [1 to:self size do:{i:Integer}
      [(attribute doWith:(self at:i)) ifTrue:[i return]];
    0]

indexOf: Parameter → Same
    {elem:Parameter}
    -- returns the index of the first occurrence of elem; 0 if none.
    [self indexOfFirst:{x:Parameter}[x==elem]]

Addition, Insertion and Deletion

add: Parameter → Same
    {elem:Parameter}
    -- appends elem to the receiver.
    [self changeSize: (newSize::=self size+1), at:newSize put:elem]

remove: Parameter → Same
    {elem:Parameter}
    -- removes the first occurrence of elem within the receiver.
    [self delete:self indexOf:elem]

delete: Integer → Same
    {index:Integer}
    -- removes the element with the given index.
    -- does nothing when the index is illegal.
    [(index>=1) or: [index<=self size], ifFalse: [self return];
     index+1 to:self size do:{i:Integer}[self at:i-1 put:(self at:i)];
     self changeSize:self size-1]

before: Integer insert: Parameter → Same
    {before:Integer; elem:Parameter}
    -- inserts elem at the index "before".
    [oldSize::=self size;
     self changeSize: self size+1;
     self size-1 to:before by:1~ do:{i:Integer}[self at:i+1 put:(self at:i)];
     self at:before put:elem]

Iteration

forAll: Action{Parameter} → Same
  {act:Action{Parameter}}
    -- *performs act for every element.*
    [1 to: self size do:{i:Integer}[act doWith: (self at:i)]; self]

forFirst: Action{Parameter} forOthers: Action{Parameter} → Same
  {firstAct:Action{Parameter}; otherAct:Action{Parameter}}
    -- *performs firstAct for the first, otherAct for all*
    -- *subsequent elements of the receiver.*
    [self size=0 ifTrue:[self return];
      firstAct doWith: (self at:1);
      2 to: self size do:{i:Integer}[otherAct doWith: (self at:i)];
      self]

Note that only at: and at:put: have been implemented as primitive methods in Array. All other methods are implemented on top of these two basic methods and the methods already inherited from Collection.

.4.7   IdSet

IdSet is an efficient implementation of sets that contain only different elements. A hash table is used to find elements in almost constant time. To achieve this goal, many inherited methods of Collection are overridden, as elements can be found much faster in this way than by iterating over all elements.

IdSet does not extend the interface of Collection. Rather, the message changeSize: is invalidated because shrinking a set would most likely not have the desired result, as the order of elements is undefined. The client would therefore never know in advance which elements would get lost.

There is one important restriction for IdSets: They cannot contain Nil and zero objects. For example, adding Nil to an IdSet{Object} or adding 0 to an IdSet{Integer}[9] would have no effect. This restriction has to do with the implementation of the hash table.

.4.8   IdDictionary

An IdDictionary can be used to keep track of pairs of objects. It is similar to an Array, except that arbitrary objects ("keys") are used to identify the elements instead of integer indexes. The parameter of IdDictionary specifies the possible

---

[9]   Although in principle it is possible to store integers in an IdSet{Integer}, it is usually better to use a BitArray for this purpose.

types of the elements only; the keys can be of any polymorphic type. In addition to IdSet, IdDictionary defines the following messages:

add:Parameter as:Object → Same
  {elem:Parameter; key:Object}
  -- adds elem with the given key. If an element with that key
  -- already exists, it is replaced with elem.

removeKey:Object → Same
  {key:Object}
  -- removes the key/element pair with the given key.

lookup:Object → Parameter
  {key:Object}
  -- returns the element with the given key.
  -- Nil or a zero element is returned when no such key exists.

keyOf:Parameter → Object
  {elem:Parameter}
  -- returns the key of the given element.
  -- Nil is returned when no such element exists.

forAllKeys:Action → Same
  {act:Action}
  -- executes act for every key.

Like an IdSet, an IdDictionary only accepts non-nil and non-zero elements. Similarly, Nil cannot be used as the key of an element.

When an IdDictionary is used, it is important to know that hashing is used for the keys only. All operations for which a key is given (such as add:as: and lookup:) can be executed very quickly, while operations without keys (such as keyOf:) may require a linear search through the entire dictionary. This is similar to a manual search in a phone directory. Whereas the phone number of a given person can be found quite easily, it would be quite laborious to find the person that has a given phone number.

One example of a typical use of an IdDictionary is change propagation, as implemented in the Omega library. Storing the dependents of an object within the object itself would mean that every object would need an instance variable for holding a set of its dependents. To avoid such immense overhead for the multitude of objects that do not have dependents, a global variable Workspace.dependencies of type IdDictionary{IdSet{Object}} is used. The keys within this dictionary are the objects that have dependents. Each key object k has an associated IdSet that contains the objects depending on k. The following example shows how the Object method changed: is implemented by means of this dictionary:

changed:Object ↦ Same
        {reason:Object}
        -- notifies all objects depending on the receiver of a change.
        -- The argument specifies the kind of change.
        [(dependents::=Workspace.dependencies lookup:self) ifNotNil:
            [dependents forAll:{dep:Object}
                [dep updateTo:self because:reason]
            ];
        self]

.5   Graphical Objects

Most object-oriented libraries (especially those for hybrid languages, such as
MacApp and ET++) do not implement graphical output with objects. Instead,
they use conventional procedures as provided by the operating system or a
graphics package. In the Omega library, elementary graphical types (so-called
images) are used for this purpose. Figure 6-4 shows the inheritance hierarchy of
the most important graphical types.

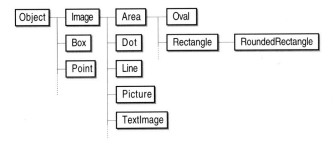

Fig. 6-4: Inheritance hierarchy of Omega's graphical types

Image is the root of the graphics subtree. It defines the general protocol for all
objects that can be displayed on the screen. Area is the root of another group of
graphical objects. It represents objects that have an interior (as opposed to lines
and dots). All types derived from Image and Area adhere to the common
interface defined by their parents. They only add specific methods for the
definition of the layout of the graphical objects and implement those methods
that have been defined as abstract in their parents.

Point and Box represent positions and rectangular areas within views.
They are not displayed on the screen, but are rather used by the actual graphical
objects. Whereas a Rectangle has "visual properties", a Box is a mathematical
concept that can be used for calculations.

In the subsequent sections, first the auxiliary types Point and Box are described. Then the general protocols defined by Image and Area are explained. After that, the elementary graphical objects and their additional interfaces are described. Finally, complex pictures consisting of multiple elementary graphical objects are discussed.

6.5.1 Point

A Point object has two instance variables x and y, where x represents the horizontal and y the vertical coordinate. Both instance variables are *public* and *read-only* for clients. When used in conjunction with graphical objects, the x coordinate increases from left to right and the y coordinate increases from top to bottom. The following list shows the definitions of the most important Point messages.

x:Integer → Same
    -- changes the x coordinate of the receiver.
y:Integer → Same
    -- changes the y coordinate of the receiver.
x:Integer y:Integer → Same
    -- changes the x and y coordinates of the receiver.

= Object → Boolean
    -- returns true when the argument is a point with the same coordinates.

asString → String
    -- returns "x@y".

add:Point → Same
    -- adds the coordinates of the argument to those of the receiver.
sub:Point → Same
    -- subtracts the coordinates of the argument from those of the receiver.
+ Point → Same
    -- returns the vector sum of the receiver and the argument.
− Point → Same
    -- returns the vector difference of the receiver and the argument.
* Integer → Same
    -- multiplies (scales) the receiver's coordinates by the argument.
/ Integer → Same
    -- divides (scales) the receiver's coordinates by the argument.

@ Point → Box
    -- returns the smallest Box containing both the receiver and the argument.

.5.2   Box

A Box object has four instance variables left, top, right and bottom, which define the borders of the box. All these instance variables are *public* and *read-only* for clients. Points along the left and top border are considered within the box, but points along the right and bottom border are not. The box (0@0)@(0@0) is thus considered empty. The following list shows the definitions of the most important Box messages.

left:Integer → Same
    -- *changes the left border of the receiver.*
top:Integer → Same
    -- *changes the top border of the receiver.*
right:Integer → Same
    -- *changes the right border of the receiver.*
bottom:Integer → Same
    -- *changes the bottom border of the receiver.*
left:Integer top:Integer right:Integer bottom:Integer → Same
    -- *changes all borders of the receiver.*

width → Integer
    -- *returns the width of the receiver.*
height → Integer
    -- *returns the height of the receiver.*

leftTop → Point
    -- *returns the left top corner of the receiver.*
rightTop → Point
    -- *returns the right top corner of the receiver.*
leftBottom → Point
    -- *returns the left bottom corner of the receiver.*
rightBottom → Point
    -- *returns the right bottom corner of the receiver.*
center → Point
    -- *returns the center of the receiver.*
size → Point
    -- *returns a point whose coordinates describe the extent of the receiver.*

= Object → Boolean
    -- *returns true when the argument is a box with the same coordinates.*
empty → Boolean
    -- *returns true when the receiver does not include any points.*

asString → Point
    -- *returns "(left,top,right,bottom)".*

contains: Point → Boolean

    -- returns true when the argument is within the receivers boundaries.

moveTo: Point → Same

    -- moves the receiver's top left point to the argument.

    -- The size of the box is retained.

offset: Point → Same

    -- moves the receiver relatively as defined by the argument's coordinates.

    -- The size of the box is retained.

size: Point → Same

    -- resizes the receiver as defined by the argument's coordinates.

    -- the top left corner is retained.

uniteWith: Box → Same

    -- extends the receiver such that it includes the argument.

intersectWith: Box → Same

    -- shrinks the receiver such that it only contains the points enclosed

    -- by the argument; when the receiver and the argument do not

    -- intersect, the receiver is set to the empty box (0@0)@(0@0).

+ Box → Same

    -- returns the union of the receiver and the argument.

* Box → Same

    -- returns the intersection of the receiver and the argument;

    -- when the receiver and the argument do not intersect, the

    -- empty box (0@0)@(0@0) is returned.

6.5.3   Image

Graphical objects are closely related to *views* (see Section 6.7 *Views, Windows and Panes*). A view represents an area in which drawing operations take place. That can be the entire screen, a window, a part of a window, or a sheet of paper. In order to draw something, it would therefore always be necessary to specify the view in which this something should be drawn. In order to avoid an additional parameter for every drawing operation, the desired view is designated as the current view before drawing. This convention is used throughout all image methods. All drawing is automatically performed in the current view; the caller is responsible for making sure that the proper view is being used[10].

An Image object is characterized as a graphical object that can be drawn by "scribbling" with a pen. The size and color of the pen is defined by two instance variables of Image:

---

[10] This is not a problem in the application framework part of the Omega library, as all objects responsible for display and update of windows guarantee that the proper view is being used.

- penSize (of type Point) specifies the thickness of the pen's tip. A pen has a rectangular shape; its width and height are defined by penSize.x and penSize.y, respectively. The Image prototype and all prototypes derived from Image have a pen size of 1@1.
- penInk (of type Ink) specifies the color or pattern with which the pen draws. Ink is an abstraction with several derived types. The most important children of Ink are Color and Pattern. Both prototypes provide some generally useful "inks" by means of public shared variables, for example:
  - Color.black, Color.white, Color.red, Color.blue, ...
  - Pattern.gray, Pattern.hatch, Pattern.chessBoard, ...
  Another useful pattern is Transparent; obviously, nothing is displayed when a transparent pen draws. This sort of ink is nevertheless useful for areas whose borders should not be drawn (see Section 6.5.4 *Area*). The Image prototype and all prototypes derived from Image have Color.black as their pen ink.

Both instance variables of Image are *public* and *read-only*. The objects referred to by these variables are *owned* by an image object. They are thus copied in the copyParts method of Image. For this reason, new graphical objects should always be created with copy instead of clone. The use of clone is only recommended when two or more graphical objects should share these properties. The following list shows the common protocol of all graphical objects, as defined in Image.

Drawing

draw → Same
   -- draws a positive image of the receiver, using drawFrame.
erase → Same
   -- erases the image of the receiver, using drawFrame.
invert → Same
   -- draws a negative image of the receiver, using drawFrame.
drawFrame → Same
   -- elementary drawing method (HERITAGE, ABSTRACT).
! → Same
   -- shows the receiver in a window.

The drawing methods draw, erase and invert constitute the official drawing interface of all graphical objects. All these methods are implemented in terms of drawFrame – an abstract method with the attribute *heritage*. In order to implement a new descendant of Image, only this method needs to be overridden in order to define the graphical object's appearance on the screen.

Pen Properties

penSize: Point → Same
>   -- *changes the pen size of the receiver.*

penInk: Ink → Same
>   -- *changes the pen ink of the receiver.*

Positioning

moveBy: Point → Same
>   -- *offsets the receiver by the relative coordinates of the argument*
>   -- *(ABSTRACT).*

moveTo: Point → Same
>   -- *moves the receiver's reference point to the coordinates*
>   -- *of the argument by sending moveBy: to self.*

bounds → Box
>   -- *returns the smallest Box containing the receiver (ABSTRACT).*

center → Point
>   -- *returns the receiver's center;*
>   -- *the default implementation just returns the center of its bounds.*

refPoint → Point
>   -- *returns the receiver's reference point;*
>   -- *the default implementation just returns its center.*

contains: Point → Boolean
>   -- *returns true if the receiver contains the point passed as argument;*
>   -- *the default implementation returns true if the point is within the*
>   -- *receiver's bounds.*

The internal representation of a graphical object's location and extent depends on its shape. These properties can therefore not be implemented in Image. However, Image already defines that a graphical object should have a reference point. The actual definition of the "central" or "most important" point of a graphical object is up to the implementer of a concrete Image object. Note that moveBy: is the central method for changing a graphical object's position. This method must be overridden in all concrete descendants of Image.

An Image object is an *internal* representation of something that can be drawn. This means that first an object must be created and set up properly. Image cannot provide methods for initializing a graphical object, as these operations depend on the shapes of the objects. It is also important to notice that changing the properties of a graphical object (for example, by sending it the messages moveBy: or penSize:) does not automatically update the object on the screen, as an Image object does not know if and in which view(s) it is being displayed.

Some typical uses of graphical objects are shown in Sections 6.5.5 *Elementary Images* and 6.5.6 *Pictures*.

6.5.4   Area

An area is an image with an interior. The Area prototype specifies two additional instance variables:

- bounds (of type Box) determines the extent (i.e., the enclosing rectangle) of the graphical object. This does not necessarily mean that the graphical object fills the whole area enclosed by bounds. For example, the corners of the enclosing box are not part of a circle. The instance variable bounds has the attribute *heritage*; it can therefore only be accessed through the public methods of Image and Area.
- fillInk (of type Ink) determines the color or pattern with which the area's interior is to be filled. As with penInk, the special ink Transparent can be used to indicate no filling. Like penInk, fillInk is *public* but *read-only* for clients.

An area's shape is assumed to be completely defined by its bounds. The Image methods bounds and moveBy: are therefore overridden in Area. The following list shows the most important methods of Area.

Drawing

draw → Same
        -- *draws a positive image of the receiver, using drawFrame and drawFill.*
erase → Same
        -- *erases the image of the receiver, using drawFrame and drawFill.*
invert → Same
        -- *draws a negative image of the receiver, using drawFrame and drawFill.*
drawFill → Same
        -- *elementary drawing method (HERITAGE, ABSTRACT).*

All drawing methods defined in Image are reimplemented in terms of draw-Frame and drawFill – a new abstract method that determines how the interior of the graphical object is to be drawn. In order to implement a new descendant of Area, both drawFrame and drawFill must be overridden in order to define how the graphical object appears on the screen.

Positioning

bounds → Box
        -- *returns a copy of the receiver's bounds instance variable.*
bounds: Box → Same
        -- *changes the receiver's extent.*

moveBy: Point → Same
     -- offsets the receiver's instance variable bounds as specified by
     -- the coordinates of the argument.
origin → Point
     -- returns the top left corner of the receiver.

6.5.5   Elementary Images

Image and Area already define most of the interface of graphical objects. All that remains for concrete imaging objects is to define the appropriate instance variables that determine the object's shape, to provide additional messages for the specification of the object's shape and to override the abstract methods inherited from Image and Area. The following list shows the interfaces of the most frequently used elementary graphical objects and gives some examples of how they can be used. Only the additional messages that are specific for the respective elementary object are listed here.

Dot

A dot is a small rectangular spot. Its size is determined by penSize. The position of a dot is determined by a *heritage* instance variable pos. The reference point of a dot is its top left corner. There is no additional method for specifying a dot's "layout". The message moveTo: can be used to specify the position of a dot. The Dot prototype has the position 0@0, the pen size 1@1, and the pen ink Color.black. Figure 6-5 shows the result of the following dot operations.

```
d::=Dot copy moveTo:3@3, draw;
10 timesRepeat:[d moveBy:3@2, draw];
d :=Dot copy moveTo:20@10, penSize:5@11, draw;
d:=d copy moveBy:0@12, penInk:Pattern.gray, draw;
```

Fig. 6-5: A sample drawing with dots

Line

A line is specified by a starting point and an end point, represented by two *public read-only* instance variables start and end, respectively. The starting point constitutes the line's reference point. The position of a line can be determined using the following messages:

start: Point → Same
     -- sets the receiver's starting point.

end: Point → Same
    -- sets the receiver's end point.
direction: Point → Same
    -- sets the receiver's end point relatively to its starting point.

The Line prototype has 0@0 as starting and end point, the pen size 1@1 and the pen ink Color.black. Figure 6-6 shows the result of the following line operations.

    Line copy direction:100@0, penSize:2@2 draw;
    line::=Line copy end:10@20, penSize:1@1, draw;
    6 timesRepeat: [line moveBy:6@6, draw]

Fig. 6-6: A sample drawing with lines

TextImage

A text image is determined by a string, a font and a starting point. The starting point is the base line point of the first character of the text, as shown in Figure 6-7.

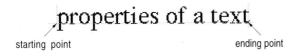

starting point   ending point

Fig. 6-7: Starting and ending points of a text image

The appearance of a text image can be specified using the following messages:

string: String → Same
    -- sets the string to be displayed.
font: Font → Same
    -- determines the font to be used when the text image is drawn.
end → Point
    -- returns the ending point of the text image.

The message moveTo: sets the starting point of a text image, and the message end can be used to determine its ending point.

The TextImage prototype consists of an empty string in the system's default font (Font.default), originates at the position 0@0, and has the pen ink Color.black. The pen size inherited from Image is ignored, as it is not needed to describe a text image. Figure 6-8 shows the result of the following text operations.

```
hello::=TextImage copy
    moveTo:20@20,
    string:"Hello",
    font:(Font copy family:"Helvetica", size:14),
    draw;
world::= hello copy
    moveTo:hello end+10@0,
    string:"World!";
world.font bold:true;
world draw;
Line copy start:hello refPoint, end:world end, draw;
```

Hello **World!**

Fig. 6-8: A sample drawing with text images

Rectangle

Rectangle is derived from Area and thus consists of a border and an interior. The messages inherited from Area suffice for the specification of a rectangle. Only the methods drawFrame and drawFill are overridden in Rectangle to actually draw a rectangle in the current view. The Rectangle prototype has no extension (i.e., the borders of its bounds are all zeros), the pen size 1@1, the pen ink Color.black and the fill ink Color.white. Figure 6-9 shows the result of the following rectangle operations.

```
area::=Rectangle copy;
area
    bounds:(10@10)@(70@35),
    draw;
area
    size:50@40,
    fillInk:Transparent,
    draw;
area
    moveTo:71@35,
    size:25@25,
    fillInk:Pattern.gray,
    penInk:Transparent,
    draw;
5 timesRepeat: [area moveBy:8@8, draw];
```

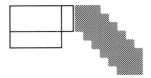

Fig. 6-9: A sample drawing with rectangles

Oval

Oval is about as simple as Rectangle. The only deviation is that the drawing operations are implemented differently. Otherwise, an oval can be drawn with exactly the same operations. Figure 6-10 shows the result of the example shown above for rectangles, where only the first line has been replaced with

    area::=Oval copy;

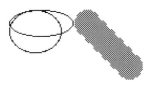

Fig. 6-10: A sample drawing with ovals

6.5.6   Pictures

It is sometimes convenient to compose a complex drawing and store it in a safe place for later use. The prototype Picture provides the functionality needed for this. A picture is simply a graphical object consisting of a series of other graphical objects. It has one additional instance variable elements (of type Array{Image}) that holds the parts of a picture. elements is *public* and *read-only*. This means that all Array messages can be used to manipulate a picture. For example, the first two elements of a picture pict can be swapped with the following sequence:

    temp::=pict.elements at:1;
    pict.elements at:1 put:(pict.elements at:2);
    pict.elements at:2 put:temp;

In order to make the composition of a picture more convenient, Picture provides a shortcut for the addition of a new element. The following list shows the complete implementation of Picture.

asString → String
>   *-- returns the textual representation of all elements.*
> ["Picture"+elements asString]

copyParts → Same
>   *-- copies the elements, as they are owned by the picture.*
> [elements:=elements copy; self]

draw → Same
>   *-- draws all elements.*
> [elements forAll:{elem:Image}[elem draw]; self]

erase → Same
>   *-- erases all elements.*
> [elements forAll:{elem:Image}[elem erase]; self]

invert → Same
>   *-- inverts all elements.*
> [elements forAll:{elem:Image}[elem invert]; self]

moveBy:Point → Same
>   {offset:Point}
>   *-- offsets all elements by the relative coordinates of the argument.*
> [elements forAll:{elem:Image}[elem moveBy:by]; self]

bounds → Box
>   *-- computes the bounds of the entire picture.*
> [bounds:Box:=(0@0)@(0@0);
>   elements
>   forFirst:{im:Image}[bounds:=im bounds]
>   forOthers:{im:Image}[bounds:=bounds uniteWith:im bounds];
>   bounds]

penSize:Point → Same
>   {newPen:Point}
>   *-- changes the pen size of all elements.*
> [elements forAll:{elem:Image}[elem penSize:newPen]; self]

penInk:Point → Same
>   {newInk:Ink}
>   *-- changes the pen ink of all elements.*
> [elements forAll:{elem:Image}[elem penInk:newInk]; self]

add:Image → Same
>   {newElem:Image}
>   *-- appends a new element.*
> [elements add:newElem; self]

The complete implementation of Picture was shown here to demonstrate how easy a composite graphical object can be implemented. All methods except bounds are simple one-liners; The entire implementation (comments and method argument declarations not counted) requires not more than twelve lines. Note that the instance variables penSize and penInk are superfluous in Picture, as each element has its own pen size and ink. These instance variables are therefore ignored and not even copied when a picture receives the message copyParts.

The following example illustrates how the houses shown in Figure 6-11 can be composed and drawn by means of a Picture object.

```
house::=Picture copy;                              -- start with an empty picture
house add:(Rectangle copy bounds:(0@20)@(40@60));     -- the walls
house add:(Rectangle copy bounds:(20@40)@(32@60));    -- the door
roof::=Picture copy;                               -- construct the roof
roof add:(line::=Line copy start:20@0, end:0@20);        -- left part
roof add:(line copy end:40@20);                         -- right part
roof add:(Oval copy bounds:(16@8)@(24@16));              -- skylight
house add:roof, draw;                           -- draw a plain house
house penSize:3@3, moveBy:60@0, draw;           -- draw a thick house
house penInk:Pattern.gray, moveBy:60@0, draw;   -- draw a gray house
```

Fig. 6-11: A sample drawing with pictures

Note that the roof was constructed as a separate picture and then added to the house. This is possible because Picture was derived from Image; Picture objects are therefore compatible with Image variables and method arguments and can thus also be parts of other pictures.

6.6   User Interaction

As already explained in Section 5.5 *Frameworks*, interactive programs are typically implemented in an event-oriented way. The Omega library contains several prototypes which support that style of programming. The first part of this section discusses the kinds of events that may occur; the second part finally shows how these events are handled within Omega programs.

6.6.1   Events

Events are represented by the type Event and its descendants. Figure 6-12 shows the inheritance hierarchy of Omega's event types.

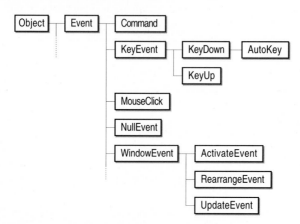

Fig. 6-12: The inheritance hierarchy of Omega's event types

Event defines the common protocol of all event types. In Omega, the following properties are defined for events:

- When did the event occur?
- What was the mouse position in the instant when the event was produced?
- Which modifier keys (such as the shift key) had been pressed at that time?

The Event prototype also provides a method that returns the next outstanding event. Successive invocations of Event next deliver all events in the order in which they occurred. However, the programmer need not normally be concerned with getting events in this way, as the framework automatically takes care of reading and processing events in the proper order.

The different sorts of events have been tailored according to the event hierarchy of Macintosh computers [Apple 1985]. The following are the meanings and properties of the "standard" event types:

- KeyEvent serves as an abstraction of all events resulting from keyboard input of the user. Every key event has two *public read-only* instance variables keyCode (a system-dependent integer code) and keyChar (the character associated with the key) that describe the key that had been pressed or released.
- KeyDown represents "normal" keyboard input. Whenever the user presses a key, a KeyDown object is generated.

- KeyUp objects are generated when the user releases a key. These objects are not normally used, as releasing a key is not usually a significant event requiring an activity.
- AutoKey objects are generated continuously when a key is being held down. It is up to the application whether certain keys should have an "auto repeat" function or not.
- MouseClick events are generated when the user presses the mouse button. MouseClick objects "know" which part of the screen was hit by a click. For example, the message inContent will return true when the content of a window has been hit. In this case, the message window will return the corresponding Window object. When the user releases the mouse button, no event is generated, as clicks normally lead to a state in which the mouse (represented by the one-of-a-kind prototype Mouse; see Section 6.8.1 *Mouse*) is tracked until the button is released.
- NullEvent objects are created when no events are pending. They are usually of no interest. The framework uses these events to give certain objects an opportunity to perform some housekeeping tasks as long as the user does not provide any input.
- WindowEvent is an abstraction of the following two event types. A window event is always associated with a Window object. It returns this object in response to the window message.
- ActivateEvent objects are generated when a window is made active or inactive. When a window becomes the topmost window, an activate event is generated for it and for the previously active window. The message activated returns true when the window has been made active, otherwise false.
- UpdateEvent objects are automatically generated whenever a window or part of a window must be redrawn.

In addition to these usual event types, the Omega library defines two high-level events:

- RearrangeEvent objects are generated when the contents of a window have changed in such a way that the entire window layout must be recalculated.
- Command objects designate operations requested by the user. They are generated internally as soon as the meaning of an event has been determined. Every Command object is identified by a name (usually a StringConstant, such as "Quit" or "OK") that identifies the action that was requested by the user. Command objects are typically created when the user presses a button or selects an item from a menu.

Event objects represent conventional data rather than active entities; they only have a few methods that return specific information about an event, but they have virtually no built-in behavior. The actual handling of events must be done by other objects, as discussed in the following section.

6.6.2   Event Handlers

When an Omega program executes, events are continually read (by means of the message Event next) and passed on to so-called event handlers – special objects that are able to interpret incoming events. Figure 6-13 shows the inheritance hierarchy of Omega's event handler types.

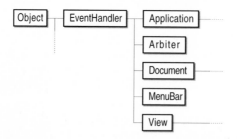

Fig. 6-13: The inheritance hierarchy of Omega's event handlers

EventHandler is an abstraction of all event handling objects. Every event handler has a name (of type String) and an environment (of type Event-Handler). Event handlers are typically nested (as will be shown in the next section). In that case, the instance variable environment refers to the "parent" handler[11].

This section covers the general aspects of event handlers as implemented by EventHandler and Arbiter. Views are discussed in Section 6.7 *Views, Windows and Panes*; applications and documents are explained in Section 6.9 *Applications*. The most important methods of EventHandler are listed below.

handle:Event → Boolean
    {ev:Event}
    -- *attempts to handle an incoming event;*
    -- *true is returned if the event was handled successfully.*
    [key:KeyDown; (key:?=ev) ifTrue:[self doKey:key, return];
      click:MouseClick; (click:?=ev) ifTrue:[self doClick:click, return];
      act:ActivateEvent; (act:?=ev) ifTrue:[self doActivate:act activated];
      ev isA:UpdateEvent, ifTrue:[self doUpdate return];
      ev isA:RearrangeEvent, ifTrue:[self doRearrange return];

---

[11] Note that the event handling hierarchy has nothing to do with the inheritance hierarchy. The "parent" of an event handler object *x* is in this context just that event handler to which an event is passed if *x* cannot handle it.

```
cmd:Command; (cmd:?=ev) ifTrue:[self doCommand:cmd, return];
ev isA:NullEvent, ifTrue:[self doIdle];
false ]
```

doActivate:Boolean → Boolean
doClick:MouseClick → Boolean
doCommand:Command → Boolean
doIdle → Boolean
doKey:KeyDown → Boolean
doRearrange → Boolean
doUpdate → Boolean

The method handle: uses a series of conditional assignments to determine the kind of event and then activates an appropriate method of the receiver. This is one of the few places within the Omega library where it is necessary to determine an object's class in this way.

The Boolean result of the event handling methods tells the caller whether the event has been completely processed. This is important in the case of a "broadcast", where an event (typically a command) is distributed to several handlers until one of them reports back that it was able to handle the event.

The methods whose names begin with "do" are ultimately responsible for handling a specific event. The standard behavior implemented in EventHandler is to do nothing (i.e., to return false).

When the execution of an Omega application starts, control is passed to a special one-of-a-kind prototype Arbiter. This object contains the main event loop. Every received event is passed to Arbiter's handle: method, which determines the primary handler of the event. For example, clicks in a window are passed to that window, keyboard events are passed to the currently active window, and null events are evenly distributed to all open windows, the current menu bar and all active applications.

6.7 Views, Windows and Panes

As already explained in Section 6.5 *Graphical Objects*, all drawing operations take place in *views*. Figure 6-14 shows the position of the view types within the inheritance hierarchy of the Omega library.

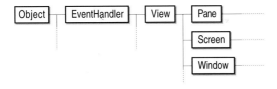

Fig. 6-14: The inheritance hierarchy of Omega's view types

6.7.1   View

View objects serve two purposes. First, they are event handlers, which means that the user can interact with view objects. Second, they are output media for graphical operations. The root prototype View defines the common protocol of all its descendants. It defines the following three variables:

- currentView (of type View) is a *shared* variable with the attribute *heritage*. It always refers to the view that is currently being used as the destination of drawing operations.
- bounds (of type Box) defines the location and extent of the view. In the case of a window, bounds specifies the location of the window on the screen. The bounds rectangle of the one-of-a-kind prototype Screen reflects the size of the physical screen attached to the computer. For panes, the instance variable bounds determines the relative location of the pane within the enclosing window.
- visibleBounds (of type Box) reveals which part of a pane is actually visible within the enclosing window. In most cases, visibleBounds and bounds will be equal; they differ only in the case of a clipped or scrollable pane.

The following extract shows the most important View methods.

use → View
>   *-- designates the receiver as the current view and returns*
>   *-- the previous current view.*

useFor: Block → Same
>   *-- executes the block passed as argument while the receiver*
>   *-- is "current", then reverts the current view to the previous one.*

invalidate → Same
>   *-- marks the receiver's contents as illegal*
>   *-- (the next update event will force the view to be redrawn).*

update → Same
>   *-- restores the view's content.*
>   *-- assertion: the receiver is the current view.*

minSize → Point
>   *-- returns the minimum size beyond which the receiver cannot shrink.*

defaultSize → point
>   *-- returns the desired initial size.*

adjustCursor → Same
>   *-- invoked when the cursor is within the receiver;*
>   *-- default: show the Cursor prototype.*

Before drawing operations can take place in a view v, it must be made the current view by sending it the message use. It is important to restore the previous view after the drawing operations have been performed. The following example shows a typical drawing sequence:

```
previousView::=myView use;
myPicture draw;
previousView use;
```

The message useFor: simplifies this and relieves the programmer from having to keep track of the previous view. The following example shows how useFor: can be used instead of the sequence shown above:

```
myView useFor:[myPicture draw]
```

The main purpose of views is to display a visual representation of an internal data structure (for example, a picture or a text to be edited). Whenever the internal data structure changes, the message invalidate can be used to indicate that the visual image must be updated. This will subsequently lead to an update event for the window containing the view. When that update event is processed, the view is sent the message update. It is generally considered bad style to directly draw into a view; such drawing operations should be performed exclu- sively within update methods.

6.7.2   Windows

Window objects model physical windows of the underlying operating system. Figure 6-15 shows the hierarchy of Omega's window types for the Macintosh operating system:

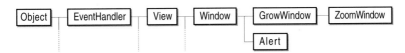

Fig. 6-15: The inheritance hierarchy of Omega's window types

There are only four different window types:
- Window represents a standard window of fixed size.
- GrowWindow represents a window with a grow handle.
- ZoomWindow represents a window with a zoom box.
- Alert represents a modal window with a message and buttons.

Window, GrowWindow and ZoomWindow differ only slightly in their behavior and appearance. Their most important property is that they have an instance variable content of type Pane (see Section 6.7.3 *Panes*). The pane associated with a window defines the interior of the window; the Window object itself only constitutes a frame around the pane. Window contains more than 25 window-specific methods, but only some of them are needed by clients to create a window with a specific content:

content:Pane → Same
> -- *fills the receiver with the given Pane.*

modal: Boolean → Same
> -- *makes the receiver modal when the argument is true.*

moveTo: Point → Same
> -- *moves the window's top left corner to the specified position.*

centerOnScreen → Same
> -- *moves the window to the center of the screen.*

open → Same
> -- *opens the window if it is not already open.*

close → Same
> -- *closes the window if it is not already closed.*

isOpen → Boolean
> -- *returns true when the receiver is visible on the screen.*

The message modal: defines whether the user should be allowed to switch windows arbitrarily. When the argument of modal: is true, the window receiving the message will stick to the foreground as long as it remains open, not allowing the user to interact with other windows.

When a window receives the message open, it uses the messages default-Size and minSize to determine the preferred size of its content. There is usually no need to explicitly set the size of a window. The following example shows a typical sequence for the construction of a window.

```
w::=ZoomWindow copy moveTo:30@30;
w content:myText editor, open;
```

In this example, a zoomable window is created. Before it is opened, it is filled with a text editor. The text editor defines the initial size and the content of the window. As long as the window remains open, all events directed to the window are automatically delegated to the window's content. Only clicks within the window border and commands with the name "Close" are intercepted by the window itself.

Note that there is absolutely no need to construct new window types. To implement a window with a specific content and behavior, a descendant of Pane is created and installed within a standard window.

Alert implements a special kind of modal window that is used primarily for error messages and for questions to the user. An alert has a string and an optional row of buttons. To create and use an alert, only the following three messages are needed:

message:String → Same
  -- *specifies the message to be displayed.*

addButton:String → Same
  -- *adds a button with the specified label.*

reply → String
  -- *displays the alert and returns the label of the button that was pressed.*

The following example illustrates how an alert can be used to ask the user whether or not to delete a certain file. The resulting alert is shown in Figure 6-16.

```
Alert copy
    message:"Delete the file """+myFile name+"""?",
    addButton:"Oh No!", addButton:"Throw it away!",
    reply=="Oh No!" ifFalse: [myFile delete];
```

Fig. 6-16: A sample alert

Note that the buttons are shown in the reverse order in which they have been added and that the first button is outlined as the default button. The Alert prototype also provides some frequently used alert types by means of public shared variables, for example saveChangesAlert and yesNoAlert.

.7.3 Panes

As already explained previously, the actual content and behavior of windows is defined by panes that can be installed in windows. In Omega, panes are equivalent to views with associated controllers in the MVC model (see Section 5.5 *Frameworks*). Whenever a data structure is to be displayed or edited in a window, a pane prototype must be created that "knows" how to display the data structure and how to interpret the user's input. The Omega library already contains a couple of predefined pane types, the most important of which are shown in Figure 6-17.

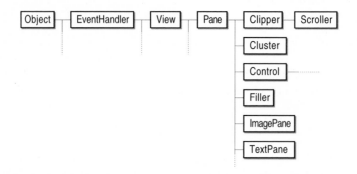

Fig. 6-17: The inheritance hierarchy of Omega's pane types

Panes can only be installed in windows and in other panes. This means that their environment must be a View object. Panes can be nested; the Omega library contains a couple of panes that can be used to structure the contents of a window. A complete explanation of all available pane types would be beyond the scope of this book. Instead, the first part of this section briefly discusses the properties of the predefined pane types and shows their use by means of simple examples. The second part establishes some guidelines for the construction of new panes. The following list explains the purpose of the pane types shown in Figure 6-17:

- Pane defines the general protocol of all pane types. It makes sure that panes are only installed within windows and other panes and provides methods for the iteration over all panes of a given pane hierarchy.
- Clipper contains another pane that can be much larger than the enclosing window or the entire screen. A clipper shows only part of the pane it contains.
- Scroller is similar to Clipper, but contains one or two scroll bars with which the user can control what part of the clipped pane should be visible.
- Cluster contains an array of other panes and arranges them horizontally or vertically. Clusters are a convenient means of implementing an automatic layout of panes within a window. For example, Alert uses a horizontal cluster to line up the buttons.
- Filler is an empty pane. Fillers are typically used within clusters to insert extra space between adjacent panes.
- Control is an abstraction for various user interface elements. The most important concrete descendants of Control are Button, DefaultButton, CheckBox, RadioButton and ScrollBar. These panes are associated with

Command objects; when they are activated by the user, their corresponding command will be received and distributed by the Arbiter the next
time through the main event loop.

- ImagePane is a passive pane that displays an Image object.
- TextPane is a passive pane that displays a string.

Instead of explaining the details of these types of panes, two commented
examples will be give to illustrate the use of panes. The first example demon-
strates how a scrollable picture and a button can be displayed in a window. The
second example is more realistic; it shows how the amplitude, note and duration
of a tone can be edited.

Example 1: A scrollable picture and a button

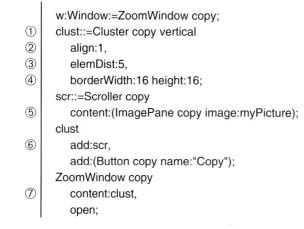

```
      w:Window:=ZoomWindow copy;
①    clust::=Cluster copy vertical
②       align:1,
③       elemDist:5,
④       borderWidth:16 height:16;
      scr::=Scroller copy
⑤       content:(ImagePane copy image:myPicture);
      clust
⑥       add:scr,
         add:(Button copy name:"Copy");
      ZoomWindow copy
⑦       content:clust,
         open;
```

Comments:

① A new vertical cluster is allocated. Cluster is capable of arranging its
   elements both vertically and horizontally. This is a typical example of the
   use of state to modify the behavior of an object. Another solution would
   have been to create separate prototypes for horizontal and vertical groups
   of panes. However, a state variable has the advantage that the appearance
   of the cluster can be changed even while it is being displayed.

② Positive alignment means that the elements will be aligned along the right
   border in a vertical and along the bottom border in a horizontal cluster.

③ The elements of the cluster are to be separated by at least 5 pixels.

④ A border of 16 pixels should be left empty around the entire cluster.

⑤ A new scroller is created and filled with an ImagePane that will display
   the picture object referred to by myPicture. This is all that is to do in order
   to show a scrollable picture.

⑥ The scroller just created and a button with the label "Copy" are added to
   the cluster. Note that the messages ① through ④ only specified the
   properties of the cluster, but not its contents.

⑦ A new zoomable window is filled with the cluster containing the scroller and the "Copy" button.

When the window is opened, it first calculates the preferred size by sending the message defaultSize to its content. The cluster calculates its preferred size by consulting all its parts, which in turn return their preferred sizes. If the resulting size does not exceed the size of the entire screen (which is the case in this example), the window object accepts this suggestion and tells its content (i.e., the Cluster object) to change its size and position such that it appears in the top left corner of the window and fills the entire window by sending it the message bounds: with the dimensions of the window's interior. The cluster reacts to this message by calculating the positions of its elements and sending them the message bounds:. This process continues until all elements have been positioned. Then the window is finally opened, and the update message is sent to its content. Again, the message is distributed to all parts of the window until the whole window content has been displayed. Figure 6-18 shows the result of this process, and Figure 6-19 shows the object structure representing the window and its contents.

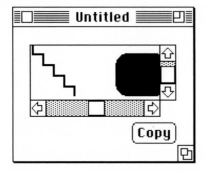

Fig. 6-18: A window with a scrollable picture and a button

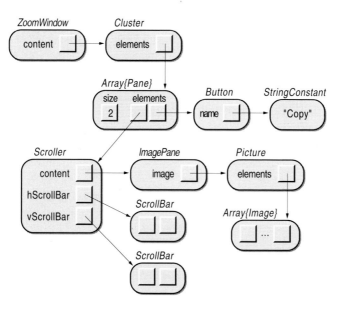

Fig. 6-19: Objects contributing to the window of Figure 6-18

Example 2: A Tone editor

Tone is a child of Sound. It has the following three attributes (see Section 6.2.9 *Attributes*):

- "amplitude", ranging from 0 to 100.
- "note", ranging from 0 to 127, where 60 stands for middle C and 61 for C#.
- "duration", ranging from 0 to 1000 (msec).

A Tone object can be edited by sending it the message edit, as defined in Section 6.2.6 *Input*. The method edit of Tone is shown below:

edit → Same

	-- *pops up a window in which the receiver can be edited.*
①	[w::=Window copy modal:true;
②	w content:self editor, open;
③	Arbiter runUntil:[w isOpen~];
	self]

Comments:

① A simple window is created and defined as modal. This means that the user can do nothing but edit the receiver as long as the window is open.
② The window is filled with a tone editing pane. To create the pane, the receiver is requested to return such a pane. The editor method is shown below.

③ The Arbiter is commanded to start an event loop and to continue processing events as long as the window is open. As soon as the user closes
the window, the Arbiter terminates and returns control to the edit method.
Note that this method can be called from within an event loop. Such a
recursive call to the Arbiter just creates a new temporary event loop. This
is quite usual in the case of modal windows.

The edit method of Tone is relatively simple, as it uses yet another method to
create the editor. This method is shown below.

editor → Pane

```
①    [ c::=Cluster copy align: 1~, elemDist:5, borderWidth:10 height:10;
②      c add:(TextPane copy text:"Amplitude:");
③      sb::=ScrollBar copy maxValue:100, length:200;
④      sb setAttribute:"amplitude", control:self, value:amplitude;
⑤      c add:sb;
⑥      c add:(TextPane copy text:"Note:");
        sb:=sb copy setAttribute:"note", minValue:1, maxValue:127;
        sb value:self note;
        c add:sb;
        c add:(TextPane copy text:"Duration:");
        sb:=sb copy setAttribute:"duration", minValue:0, maxValue:2000,
        sb value:duration;
        c add:sb;
⑦      c ]
```

Comments:
  ① First a cluster is created; the alignment value 1~ specifies left alignment.
  ② A TextPane containing the heading "Amplitude:" is inserted into the
     cluster.
  ③ A scroll bar with the maximum value of 100 and the preferred length of
     200 is created. The default minimum value of the ScrollBar prototype is
     zero; this is alright for the amplitude.
  ④ The scroll bar is configured such that it controls the attribute "amplitude"
     of the receiver. Its initial value is set to the receiver's current amplitude.
  ⑤ The scroll bar is added to the cluster. This completes the editor part that
     controls the receiver's amplitude.
  ⑥ The following lines (up to, but not including the line labelled ⑦) repeat
     the same process for the note and the duration, respectively. The only
     difference is that now the existing scroll bar sb is used as the source of
     subsequent copy operations. This means that properties already defined
     (such as the scroll bar's length and the object that is to be controlled by the
     scroll bar) need not be specified again.

⑦ Finally, the complete cluster containing three text panes and three scroll bars is returned as the result of the message.

Note that only predefined pane types were necessary to construct a tone editor. It was only necessary to make copies of already existing building blocks and to put them together in a suitable way. Figure 6-20 shows the window that appears when the edit message is sent to a Tone object. As soon as one of the scroll bars is utilized, the message attribute:set: is sent to the Tone object being edited.

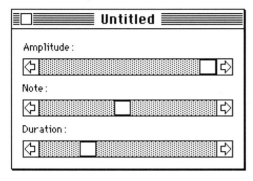

Fig. 6-20: A window with scroll bars controlling a tone's attributes

Creating a New Pane without Pain

Creating a new pane is quite simple, as most of the required functionality can be inherited from EventHandler, View and Pane. The following guidelines show how passive and active panes can be created, where "passive" means that the pane only displays data and does not accept user input.

Creating a Passive Pane

- A pane typically represents some data structure. As windows are moved around and resized, panes will continually need to redraw the image of "their" data structure. They thus need some *instance variables* that refer to the model they represent. It is usually a good idea to protect the model against inadvertent modifications by defining the instance variables with the attribute *heritage* and to provide a small set of methods with which the model and/or its visual representation can be changed.
- If it is very unlikely that the model will be modified while the pane is visible, a Picture can be prepared when the model is attached to the pane. This picture can be stored as an instance variable, which simplifies some methods considerably.
- In order to display an image of the model, the message drawContent must be overridden. This message is guaranteed to be sent when the pane is the current view.

- The message minSize must be overridden to make sure that the pane will have enough space to draw the image. When the pane contains a Picture *p* with a visual representation of its model, the result of *p* size can be returned as response to the message minSize. If that is not possible, the size must be calculated "by hand".
- If the model can change at unexpected times, the pane should make itself dependent on the model and override the updateTo:because: method. If the model announces a change, one must check whether the new image will still fit into the space currently available (i.e., within the area described by the instance variable bounds). If that is not the case, self mustRearrange must be called to force a recalculation of the pane's boundaries, otherwise the message invalidate should be sent to self in order to mark the pane's content as out-of-date.

Creating an Active Pane

In addition to the steps described above for passive panes, the following points should be considered when implementing an active pane:

- If the pane can process mouse clicks, it should override the method do-Click: and perform whatever is appropriate when a click is received. It is not necessary to check whether the mouse location is within the pane, as that is already guaranteed by the sender of doClick:.
- If the pane can process keyboard input, it should override the method doKey:. In order to receive keyboard events, it must also override the message canHandleKey such that it returns true.
- If the pane needs to process commands, it must override the method doCommand:. Within that method, it should check the command's name and return true if it was able to process a command.
- If the pane wants to provide menu commands, it should override the method setUp. This message is sent immediately before the window containing the pane is to be opened. This is the right moment to create a Menu object *m* and add the menu to the window's menu bar with the message

    self window addPaneMenu: *m*

That's all it takes to create a new child of Pane. Most tasks are rather trivial, but, as always, the devil is in the nuts and bolts. The most difficult problems are to determine the size of the area required to display the image within reasonable time and to detect which part of the model is affected by the mouse click.

6.8   One-of-a-Kind Prototypes

The Omega library contains a couple of one-of-a-kind prototypes that serve as links between an Omega program and the underlying hardware. The most

important of these are Mouse, Keyboard and Workspace. These prototypes will
be discussed in the following three sections.

8.1   Mouse

Mouse represents the physical mouse attached to the computer. It provides
methods for accessing the location of the mouse (or, rather, the position of the
mouse pointer on the screen), the state of the mouse button and for tracking
movements of the mouse, as listed below.

globalPosition → Point
  -- returns the mouse position in global (screen) coordinates.
localPosition → Point
  -- returns the mouse position in local coordinates
  -- (i.e., relative to the current pane).
getGlobal:Point → Point
  -- stores the current global mouse position in the point passed
  -- as argument and returns that point.
getLocal:Point → Point
  -- stores the current local mouse position in the point passed
  -- as argument and returns that point.

buttonDown → Boolean
  -- returns true if the mouse button is currently being pressed.
stillDown → Boolean
  -- returns true if the mouse button is still being pressed
  -- after the last MouseClick event.

threshold: Integer trackGlobal: Action{Point} → Boolean
  -- calls the action passed as argument each time the mouse
  -- has moved; the threshold value specifies how far the mouse
  -- must be moved away from the original position in order
  -- to be considered as "moved"; returns true if the mouse
  -- has moved at all.
threshold: Integer trackLocal: Action{Point} → Boolean
  -- same as trackGlobal, but works with local coordinates.

The methods globalPosition and localPosition return a new Point object every
time they are called. To avoid the creation of a multitude of objects during
mouse tracking, getGlobal: and getLocal: reuse an existing Point object (see
Section 4.10 *Memory Management*).

The method buttonDown returns the current state of the mouse. It can be
used, for example, to allow the user to cancel an operation by simply clicking
the mouse button. In contrast to buttonDown, stillDown returns true only if the

mouse button is still being pressed after the last received MouseClick event. The use of stillDown is preferable to that of buttonDown during the processing of click events, as it takes into account that the user may have released and repressed the mouse button since the click event was received. In that case, the state of the button belongs rather to the next click whose event has not yet been received.

The last two methods provide a convenient way to track movements of the mouse after a mouse click has been received. The threshold argument specifies how far the mouse must travel from the point where it was clicked before the actual tracking begins. A threshold value of 0 or 1 indicates that tracking should start immediately. The action passed as second argument is invoked whenever the mouse has moved to a new position. The following example shows the use of a tracking method to let the user scribble on the screen. Whenever the mouse has moved to a new position, a line is drawn from the last position to the now current position.

```
lastPos::=Mouse localPosition;
Mouse threshold:0 trackLocal: {pt:Point}
    [ Line copy start:lastPos, end:pt, draw;
        lastPos:=pt ];
```

6.8.2   Keyboard

Keyboard represents the physical keyboard attached to the computer. It can be used to determine which keys are currently pressed by the user. Keyboard is derived from BitArray. Every key is associated with a bit in this array; the key code can be used as an index into the array to see if the corresponding bit is set or not. The following list shows the relevant methods of Keyboard.

at: Integer → Boolean
    -- *returns true if the key with the given code is being pressed.*
keyDown: Char → Boolean
    -- *returns true if the key corresponding to the given*
    -- *character is being pressed.*

shiftDown → Boolean
    -- *returns true if the shift key is being pressed.*
capsLockDown → Boolean
    -- *returns true if the caps lock key is being pressed.*
controlDown → Boolean
    -- *returns true if the control key is being pressed.*
commandDown → Boolean
    -- *returns true if the command key is being pressed.*

optionDown → Boolean
  -- *returns true if the option key is being pressed.*

The method at: works for all keys, but its use requires knowledge of the hard-ware-specific key numbering scheme. The method keyDown: is more general but only works for printable characters. For example, Keyboard keyDown:' ' returns true when the space bar is being pressed.

The other methods return information about the current state of the so-called *modifier keys.*

6.8.3   Workspace

The Workspace prototype represents that part of the computer's memory that is used for the Omega workspace. It provides statistical information about the current state of memory and facilitates iteration over all currently existing objects. It also keeps track of all windows and streams currently open. Arrays of these objects are referred to by the shared public variables openWindows and openStreams, respectively. The following list shows the most important methods of Workspace.

freeBytes → Integer
  -- *returns the number of bytes available for allocation of new objects.*
objectCount → Integer
  -- *returns the number of currently existing objects (including obsolete ones).*

collectGarbage → Same
  -- *reclaims the space occupied by obsolete objects.*

forAll: Action → Integer
  -- *executes an action for all existing objects (including obsolete ones).*
  -- *returns the number of objects for which the action returned true.*
forAllPrototypes: Action → Integer
  -- *executes an action for all existing prototypes.*
  -- *returns the number of prototypes for which the action returned true.*

allObjects: Action → IdSet
  -- *returns an IdSet containing all objects for which the action returned true.*
allPrototypes → IdSet
  -- *returns an IdSet containing all prototypes.*

allReferencesTo: Object → IdSet
  -- *returns an IdSet of all objects containing references to the argument.*

referencedPTs → IdSet
> *-- returns an IdSet containing all prototypes to which*
> *-- references from other objects exist.*

prototypeNamed: String → Object
> *-- returns the prototype with the given name;*
> *-- Nil is returned if no such prototype exists.*

The methods allReferencesTo: and referencedPTs are particularly useful to prevent prototype corruption, as explained in Section 3.5 *The Prototype Corruption Problem*. When a prototype *P* that should not be referred to by other objects has been found by means of Workspace referencedPTs, the message Workspace allReferencesTo:*P* can be used to find those objects that may cause a corruption of *P*.

6.9   Applications

In contrast to most conventional programming languages, the notion of a *main program* is unknown in Omega. As the programming environment allows the user to execute any expression sequence, every single method can play the role of a main program. It is possible to convert an expression into a stand-alone program by selecting it in the log window of the programming environment and executing the menu command "Make Application". The following example shows a simple "program" that prints the contents of a disk directory specified by the user:

```
dir::=Directory input:"Specify the directory to be printed";
dir ifNotNil: [dir print]
```

While this technique is sufficient for simple applications, the development of complex applications with a graphical user interface requires a different approach. For this purpose, the Omega library provides two prototypes Application and Document. Application is a generic main program that contains the standard menu commands. It can be invoked by executing the expression Application run. The resulting "program" will just present a simple menu bar and continuously read user input until the menu command "Quit" is selected by the user. Of course, this default application is rather useless. Nevertheless, it already contains everything that is needed to construct real programs:

- It contains an instance variable menuBar with all menus that should be available when the program executes.
- It contains a main event loop (using the Arbiter, as described in Section 6.6.2 *Event Handlers*) that executes until the application receives the command with the name "Quit".

- It provides a standard handling method doCommand: for some commonly used commands, in particular "Quit", "New" and "Open".
- It provides "hooks" for application-specific pre- and post-processing.

In order to construct a new application, a new prototype (say, MyApplication) must be derived from Application. The following points illustrate what has to be done to adapt that object to specific needs:

- Create an application-specific menu bar and store a reference to it in the menuBar instance variable of MyApplication. This can be done interactively; it is not necessary to provide a method for this purpose. The menu bar will become a permanent property of the application.
- Override the method initialize if a window should appear when the application is started. The message initialize will be sent to MyApplication immediately before its main event loop is entered. The message self newWindow (see below) can be used as a simple way to construct a new window.
- The method cleanUp of Application is invoked after the event loop has been exited because the user had requested termination of the application. The default implementation closes all windows and files that have not yet been closed. Override cleanUp if your application must tidy up additional data structures, but make sure to call self(Application) cleanUp as the last action within the specific cleanUp method.
- Override doCommand: to react on application-specific commands (in particular, menu commands) that cannot be dealt with by the panes of the active window.
- Override the methods newWindow and openWindow to return new windows. Every window belonging to MyApplication should be set up such that its environment is the application.
- Never use the name MyApplication within methods of your application. Use self instead in order to support the derivation of yet another application from your application prototype.

When the application is started by sending it the message run, it is registered as the current application. the Application prototype provides a shared variable currentApplication that is used be the Arbiter. Figure 6-21 shows the interconnection between the objects of a running application.

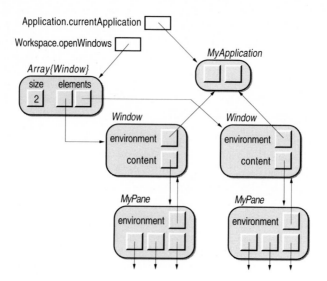

Fig. 6-21: Object references during execution of an application

When the Arbiter receives a command, it delegates that event to the currently active window. If the window cannot handle the command, it passes the command to its environment. All application-specific commands such as "Quit", "New" and "Open" are processed this way.

When a pane represents a complex data structure or when multiple views of the same model are desired, a different approach is required. The Omega library provides a prototype Document that can be used as a representation of a model. Document is derived from EventHandler and can thus process commands. To create an application-specific model, a new prototype (say, MyDocument) must be derived from Document. To ensure correct processing of commands, the document must be registered as the environment of all windows whose panes contain a visual representation of the model implemented by the document. The document object must be set up such that the application object is its environment. Figure 6-22 shows the resulting object network.

As shown in Figure 6-22, commands that cannot be processed by the current window are first passed to the document. Of course, the doCommand: method of MyDocument must be implemented in such a way that the proper changes can be applied to the actual model. When the model has been modified, the document will usually send the message changed or changed: to the affected part of the model. In this way, the panes that depend on the model will be notified that their image of the model must be updated.

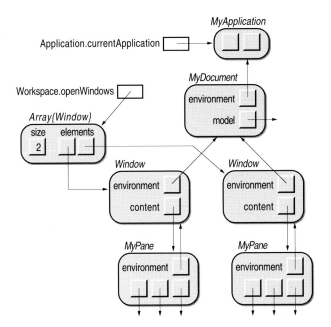

Fig. 6-22: Object references with a Document object

7. Object-Oriented Design

Object-oriented *programming* is only one side of the coin. In order to write object-oriented programs, it does not suffice to have command of an object-oriented programming language, as the development of a program does not start with programming, but rather with the design of the program's structure. This chapter discusses the goals and problems of object-oriented design and gives some hints as to how to design the classes of an object-oriented program. Most of this chapter is independent of the implementation language; only the last section presupposes the existence of prototypes.

7.1   The Goals of Object-Oriented Design

The development of a program always aims at one or more specific goals. There are, however, some general objectives that are valid in every software project:

- *Correctness*. Of course, a program should correctly do the work for which is was developed. This is the most difficult goal to achieve, as it is impossible to develop a large program that does not contain errors. Hence, the goal is to avoid as many errors as possible in order to ensure in most cases trouble-free operation of the program.
- *User-friendliness*. The program should be easy to learn and easy to use. It should fulfill the task in a way that corresponds as closely as possible to the way in which the user thinks.
- *Efficiency*. The program should run fast and require as little memory as possible. In particular, the response times experienced by the user should be kept as short as possible.
- *Maintainability*. The program should be written such that errors can be easily found and corrected and such that extensions can be applied in a simple manner without endangering the already existing functionality of the program.
- *Portability*. The program should not depend on a particular hardware and/or operating system. The system-dependent features should be well encapsulated such that an adaption of the program for a different hardware platform requires as little effort as possible.

Object-oriented techniques can contribute much to achieving the goals listed above. The remainder of this section lists the most prominent properties of "good" object-oriented programs and explains what aspects of object-oriented programs are relevant for these properties.

Flexibility

Polymorphism and *dynamic binding* allow the assignment of various objects with different structure and behavior to variables. A single piece of code can thus operate with objects of many different classes. This feature makes it possible to "plug objects together"[1]. The only requirement is that the different objects must exhibit a common interface. To achieve the same goal with conventional programming techniques, many hard-wired distinctions must be made.

Reusability

Objects of existing classes can be used in new programs. In addition to that, existing classes can be incorporated in programs by deriving new classes from

---

[1]   This is sometimes called the LEGO principle, as putting the pieces of an object-oriented program together is supposed to be as easy as assembling LEGO bricks.

them by means of *inheritance*. *Abstract classes* are particularly helpful in achieving a high degree of reusability, as they not only establish a common interface of different objects, but also provide basic functionality that can simply be inherited by concrete classes derived from them.

Extensibility

Existing programs can operate with new kinds of objects. *Polymorphism* makes sure that objects of new classes are compatible with variables of the corresponding supertypes, and *dynamic binding* guarantees that the proper operations defined for the new kind of object are performed when they receive a message. Furthermore, existing classes can be adapted to new needs by means of *inheritance*. *Application frameworks* are excellent examples of the extensibility of object-oriented programs, as they allow the construction of new programs just by adding a few classes and methods to existing ones.

Simplicity

A well-written class is typically rather small and contains only short methods. These properties are due to the reuse of existing classes by means of *inheritance* and *delegation*. Complex operations can often be provided with just a few lines of code when a powerful *library* is used.

The aforementioned properties are typical of many object-oriented programs, but they are not achieved automatically just by using an object-oriented programming language. Rather, they must be planned very carefully. The following sections will outline some design principles that have proven helpful in the development of object-oriented programs.

7.2   Design Techniques

There is a common consensus that design is a creative process. Like the design of a dress or a house, the design of a program is an *art*. For this reason, it is questionable whether good design can be taught. In fact, the best designers are either especially talented or have gained a lot of experience over years. When confronted with a problem, they seem to grasp the right idea almost at once. It is, of course, not possible to acquire such expertise just by studying a textbook; rather, good design must in most cases be learned the hard way.

Nevertheless, there are some general principles in every design that can be used to avoid the most common mistakes. The purpose of this section is to introduce some techniques that have proven helpful in the initial design of an object-oriented program. In particular, these techniques should help to...

... identify the *classes* that can be used to solve a given problem,

... specify the *responsibilities* of the classes,

... define the class *interfaces*,

... determine the *interactions* among objects,

... work out the *implementations* of methods.

It must, however, be pointed out that the subsequently described techniques are not recipes that guarantee that the resulting design will turn out well. To achieve the goals outlined in Section 7.1 *The Goals of Object-Oriented Design*, a good deal of intuition and experience is still necessary.

Designing a class is similar to designing a conventional module. Note in particular that the criteria for modularization as described in [Parnas 1972; Pomberger 1986; Sommerville 1985] also apply to classes: A class should have a concise and clear interface and strong internal interconnections; it should be responsible for a well-defined task, loosely coupled with other modules and as small as possible. However, the special object-oriented features, polymorphism, dynamic binding, and inheritance, impose additional requirements that are not covered by conventional modularization techniques.

Object-oriented design has been an attractive topic within the "object community" during the past years. One of the first approaches to object-oriented design was *HOOD* (Hierarchical Object-Oriented Design, [Heitz 1988]), a technique for the development of abstract data types. Unfortunately, HOOD was targeted at the design of Ada programs; real object-oriented concepts such as polymorphism, dynamic binding, and inheritance are therefore not covered by this technique. More recent design methods are *RDD* (Responsibility Driven Design, [Wirfs-Brock 1989, 1990]), *OOA* (Object-Oriented Analysis, [Coad 1990]), *OOSD* (Object-Oriented Structured Design, [Wasserman 1990]), *OOD* (Object-Oriented Design, [Booch 1991]) and the technique proposed by Rumbaugh [Rumbaugh 1991][2]. All these design methods have in common that they use special graphical representations to depict the relations among objects and classes. Another visualization technique (that is not related to a particular design method) is presented in [Wilson 1990].

In this chapter, we will refrain from introducing yet another graphical representation and instead present two more fundamental techniques that can help in the design of object-oriented programs. The first technique provides some guidance in the initial design phases to identify classes and methods, and the second technique helps in organizing the classes.

7.2.1   The Vocabulary Approach

The first aim in the design of an object-oriented program is to figure out which classes can be used to solve a given problem. A simple technique for this task was suggested by Russel J. Abbott [Abbott 1983]. The idea described in this

---

[2]   A survey of several design techniques can be found in [Wirfs-Brock 1990a].

article is based on the observation that data types and operations can be described by nouns and verbs, respectively. Abbott therefore proposes that the design process start with an "informal English description" of the problem to be solved. It must, however, be noted that Abbott used his technique to identify abstract data types in Ada programs. That is, the vocabulary approach is actually a conventional modularization method. The following guidelines therefore only summarize the essence of this technique and add some extras that should be taken into account when classes are to be developed.

- The *nouns* within a problem specification are candidates for classes. Whether or not a noun may identify a class depends on the kind of noun and its usage:
  - *Common nouns* (such as *person*, *car*, *window*, *event*) identify classes of things or beings in the real world. They are therefore suitable as classes in an object-oriented program as well. Common nouns can be distinguished by the fact that they can be used with an article (*a*, *an* or *the*) and that they have plural forms (e.g., *persons* and *events*).
  - *Proper nouns* (such as *Fred*, *Austria* and *Omega*) identify unique things or beings in the real world. They can be represented as objects or one-of-a-kind classes/prototypes in programs. Proper nouns can be distinguished by the fact that they denote items that belong to a class that can be identified by a common noun (such as *person*, *country* and *language*).
  - *Direct references* (such as *this car*, *my home town*, *the active window* and *its pane*) are similar to proper nouns. As they only make sense in a specific context, they closely correspond to variables in programs.
  - *Mass nouns* and *units of measure* (such as *gold*, *cattle*, *ton* and *inch*) are not usually candidates for classes. Units of measure can be represented by simple real or integer numbers; in a pure object-oriented language, they may thus be represented as objects of a numeric class[3].
- *Verbs* (such as (to) *move*, *open*, *vanish* and *occur*) denote activities and thus are possible candidates for methods. It is also possible for verbs to appear in a noun form (such as *movement* or *opening*).
- *Adjectives* (such as *red*, *large* and *modal*) indicate properties of objects and therefore are candidates for instance variables.

It must be emphasized that the above rules are merely *guidelines*. There is no way in which the process of finding classes, objects and methods could be automated, as the context of a word must always be considered. For example, the word *fine* can be used as a noun, as a verb and as an adjective. Furthermore, the

---

[3]   In Omega, units of measure could be implemented by means of attributes (see Section 6.2.9 *Attributes*).

specification of a program can easily cover hundreds or even thousands of pages. An attempt to extract all nouns, verbs and adjectives from such a specification in order to find the classes needed to implement the desired program would simply be impractical. It is therefore necessary to find the *relevant* words, and this means that the designer needs a sound understanding of the problem. Nevertheless, this method is quite useful as a starting point. When applied properly, it leads to a set of classes that model the elements of the problem domain. When these classes are then examined more closely, new problems may arise that can again be described informally. This leads to a recursive design (similar to stepwise refinement [Wirth 1971]) during which more and more implementation-specific classes evolve. The advantage of such a successive design process is that it begins with high-level classes and thus reduces the danger of getting lost in irrelevant details.

Once the possible candidates for classes have been found, their details must be specified and the interrelations among them must be defined. This can become rather cumbersome when many classes are involved. The technique introduced in the next section can help to simplify this task or at least to obtain a general view of the classes.

7.2.2   CRC Cards

Before the actual fine-grain design of a class starts, its purpose (the *responsibilities* of the class) must be identified and specified as clearly as possible. Every class should be minimal in that it does just its duty but nothing more. For example, a Window object should only represent a window on the screen, but it should not know anything about its contents. Activities that deal with the image shown within a window should be carried out by Pane objects. This means that objects of different classes must *collaborate* to fulfill a complex task.

Kent Beck and Ward Cunningham [Beck 1989] realized that the responsibilities of and collaborations among classes are crucial to the quality of an object-oriented design. In order to visualize these aspects of classes, they developed a simple, yet surprisingly effective technique. They suggest the use of conventional address index cards, as available at every stationer's shop. One card should be used to identify a single *class*, its *responsibilities* and its *collaborators* (hence the name *CRC* cards). Figure 7-1 shows the proposed layout of such a card.

Class name	
Responsibilities	Collaborators

Fig. 7-1: Layout of a CRC card

A card not only denotes a class but also represents a typical object of that class. When working with CRC cards, the distinction between classes and their objects is irrelevant; Beck and Cunningham even point out explicitly that their method is equally applicable to the design of class-based and prototype-based systems. The sections of a CRC card serve the following purposes (see the sample cards shown in Figure 7-2):

- The *class name* identifies a class and thus defines part of the vocabulary used during discussions about design decisions. It must be pointed out that object-oriented design is very much like language design. The choice of the proper class name can therefore contribute considerably to the readability of an object-oriented program. When it is difficult to find a good name for a class, a different solution should be considered, as inappropriate class names often indicate a misunderstanding during the early stages of the design process.
- The *responsibilities* of a class should be described by "a handful of short verb phrases, each containing an active verb". As the space available on an index card is rather limited, an attempt should be made to express the responsibilities as precisely and concisely as possible. Hours spent during the formulation of the responsibilities of a class are a good investment, as they usually pay off later in the design process, in particular during discussions about the interfaces of classes.
- The *collaborators* of a class are other classes that are needed in order to achieve the goal at hand (i.e., to satisfy the responsibilities of the class). Typically, an object of a class will need to send messages to objects of other classes in order to fulfill its task. The collaborator list of a class indicates the types of instance variables of the class as well as the classes of new objects that will be created in order to fulfill a subtask. The list of collaborators will usually grow as the design proceeds.

As already mentioned above, CRC cards serve as an aid in *discussions* about the design of an object-oriented program. It is expressly recommended that critical design decisions be discussed in small teams, as such an exchange of ideas makes sure that multiple points of view are considered. In this way, hindering or dangerous aspects of a design decision can be detected at an early stage.

The use of *physical* cards proves to be a big advantage during such discussions, as not only the contents but also the *arrangement* of cards play a significant role in the design process. For example, the cards of closely cooperating classes are usually also spatially arranged close to each other, and controlling classes are put above or even on top of the classes they control. Also, part-of relations can easily be expressed by a suitable arrangement of cards. Figure 7-2 shows a typical arrangement of some CRC cards illustrating part of an Omega application.

The arrangement of the cards indicates that there is close cooperation between the Arbiter and Application. Window is located below the Arbiter, as it receives events from the Arbiter; Pane is positioned below and under Window, as a Window object contains a Pane object.

Aside from the conventions indicated above, there is no fixed set of rules regarding how to arrange CRC cards. It appears that this freedom accounts for much of the popularity of CRC cards, as the designers are not constrained by formalisms.

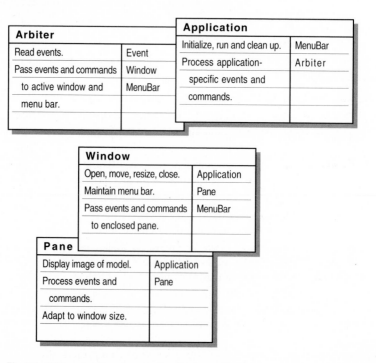

Fig. 7-2: CRC cards of some parts of an Omega application

7.3   Design Guidelines

While informal specifications and CRC cards are most valuable in the process of finding classes and their roles within a program, more specific information is needed to achieve a flexible and reusable solution. This section provides a set of general guidelines that should be heeded during development of an object-oriented program. Some of the hints given here apply only to certain programming languages. They are marked by clarifying footnotes.

7.3.1   Reusability

One of the most attractive properties of object-oriented programming is the ability to reuse existing classes. But whereas it is relatively easy to actually use a class that is already there, it can prove to be quite demanding to construct a reusable class [Meyer 1987; Johnson 1988]. In this respect, two types of reuse can be distinguished:

- **Intra-application reuse** is the multiple use of a class *within a single project*. This sort of reuse results almost automatically when common properties of several classes are implemented in an abstract superclass.
- **Inter-application reuse** is the use of a class in *different projects*. This sort of reuse is achieved by the use of library classes and by explicit development of application-independent classes.

When used without further qualification, the term "reuse" usually means inter-application reuse, as this aspect of object-oriented programming promises a reduction of development effort and time.

Think Ahead

When there is a chance that a class may be helpful in other projects, it is important to consider other uses of the class beyond those required in the currently developed program. The following rules can help in achieving this goal:

- *Provide a broader interface* than needed by the clients of the current project. Use the responsibility list of the class to imagine different ways in which the class could be used.
- *Let others take part in the design of the class*, as people who are not involved in a certain project invent possible other uses of a class more easily.
- *Avoid large methods*. In order to derive a new class with a slightly different behavior, many small methods should be provided that can be overridden separately. Split large methods such that they invoke several smaller method with *self sends*.

- *Make objects adaptable* by providing instance variables that control minor aspects of the objects' behavior. It is easier to change the state of an object than to derive a new class in order to implement a slightly different behavior.
- *Provide documentation* for the class that helps others to decide or figure out whether the class can be used to solve their problems and if so, how.

7.3.2   Safety

Of course, programs should contain as few errors as possible. This requirement is already difficult to fulfill with conventional programming techniques, but object-oriented programming adds new possible sources of errors because polymorphism and dynamic binding allow objects to be used in new contexts that have not been anticipated by their developer. Safety is particularly important in the case of reusable classes, as those who reuse a class should not need to worry about its correctness.

Consider the Worst Case

It is generally a good idea to play the devil's advocate during the development of a program. However, it requires a good deal of imagination and foresight to think of all possible uses (and misuses) of a class. The following checklist should help to avoid at least the most common types of errors.

- *Take a defensive attitude.* Errors can not be avoided altogether, but it is at least possible to detect many of them after they have occurred. The following two points list common techniques for recognizing errors as early as possible, so that they can do no serious harm[4].
    - *Check arguments* of methods to make sure that the client passes proper objects that can really be processed. Don't assume that the clients will use your class as you expect.
    - *Use assertions* at certain critical points within your methods to check whether something has gone wrong.
- *Avoid type casts* of expressions without first checking the class of the expressions against the expected class[5].
- *Use library classes* that can be trusted; otherwise, check whether the classes you use behave as expected.
- *Use exception handling*[6] to minimize the effects of run-time errors while keeping the program structure simple.

---

[4]   The programming language Eiffel provides language elements for checking against such error conditions.

[5]   This is particularly difficult in C++, as the language does not provide meta-information to check the class of an object. More elegant solutions are available in Oberon-2 and Omega.

[6]   Exception handling is available in Eiffel and Omega.

- *Avoid public state*, in particular, public instance variables[7] that may be modified by clients. Instead, provide methods for changing the values of instance variables.
- *Define fool-proof interfaces* by not exporting potentially dangerous methods[7]. This applies especially to auxiliary methods that have been created by splitting large methods into smaller pieces.

7.3.3 Inheritance

Inheritance is often misused as a vehicle for incorporating existing functionality into a new class. If the requirements on a new class *C* are similar to those on an already existing class *B*, the developer may be tempted to derive class *C* from *B*. However, this is not always the best choice. The relation between a superclass and a subclass deserves special attention in the design of an object-oriented program, as a wrong decision can hinder future extensions.

Use Abstractions

A class is similar to an abstract data type and should therefore also be seen primarily as a means to define abstract interfaces to concrete objects. Such an approach can considerably improve the reusability, safety and extensibility of classes. The following are particular guidelines for the development of a class hierarchy.

- *Use is-a relations* wherever possible, that is, select interface inheritance in preference to implementation inheritance when devising a class hierarchy. Try to figure out in which context an object of a new class will typically be used. Derive a class *C1* from another class *C* only when *C1* objects are applicable wherever *C* objects are allowed.
- *Don't inherit too much*. Try to confine the responsibilities of a new class as much as possible, and do not inherit from classes that allow more operations than the new class. Otherwise, you may need to invalidate methods that have been inherited "by accident".
- *Introduce abstract classes* when two classes *C1* and *C2* are similar but no sensible is-a relation exists between them. Isolate the common properties of *C1* and *C2* and construct an abstract class *C* that defines their common interface and provides methods that can be inherited by both classes.
- *Avoid abstraction gaps*. If a new class *C2* deviates from its natural parent *C* in too many aspects (in particular, when it defines a much wider

---

7   Unfortunately, all instance variables and methods are publicly accessible in Object Pascal.
    C++ and Eiffel allow one to specifically hide or export instance variables and methods;
    Oberon and Omega also support the definition of read-only instance variables. In Smalltalk,
    all instance variables are hidden from clients, and all methods are publicly accessible.

interface), create a new abstract class *C1* that defines an important partial aspect of *C2*. Derive *C1* from *C* and then *C2* from *C1*. To find a proper abstraction, try to imagine future "brother classes" of *C2* and devise the abstract class *C1* such that it models their common properties.

- *Promote universal operations.* When an operation is so generally applicable that it not only applies to a class *C1* but also to "brother classes" of *C1*, move the corresponding method into their common superclass *C*. When the actual implementation cannot be shared by all descendants of *C*, implement the method as abstract in *C* and override it in an appropriated way in its children.

7.3.4   Libraries

New classes are rarely developed from scratch. In fact, it is highly recommended to construct an object-oriented program on the basis of an existing class library. A powerful library can contribute much more to the quality of a design than most other object-oriented techniques. Of course, the structure of a library and the relations among its classes must be well understood in order to be used efficiently.

Don't Reinvent the Wheel

Library classes are there to be used. They have been designed and implemented by experienced developers. It is generally advisable to lean on a library in order to help new classes fit into an existing environment. The following list shows a few particularly important points that can increase the quality of a new program.

- *Assemble new objects* from existing ones rather than designing them anew on the drawing board. Use has-a relations and delegation to implement as many aspects of complex objects as possible.
- *Use collaborators* to implement the responsibilities of a class. Break large classes into manageable pieces that can be understood easily. Find library classes that can do part of your work. This "lazy" strategy has the advantage that many methods can be implemented with only a few lines of code, which in turn decreases the probability of errors.
- *Inherit from library classes*. Derive new classes from similar classes of the library. As library classes are often used in many different places, this increases the chance that objects of a new class can be used in many different contexts.
- *Use an application framework* as the starting point for the overall structure of a new program. Many design decisions have already been anticipated in the design of application frameworks. Furthermore, application frameworks make heavy use of collaboration. Following the cook-

book accompanying an application framework therefore helps to achieve a reasonable initial design.

- *Emulate library classes* by designing new classes based on the model of already existing classes. Use the same naming conventions and documentation scheme as already used in the implementation and description of the library. Imitating the typical style of a library class leads to new classes that appear as extensions of the class library and are therefore more readily accepted by other programmers.

- *Study the internals of a library* in order to get acquainted with typical design patterns. Well-designed libraries contain many treasures; invaluable hints can be derived from the inspection of such a library's source code.

7.3.5 Incremental Design

Implementing all classes of a complex system at once is guaranteed to lead to frustration, as it is almost impossible to get everything right from the beginning. It is much better to develop a new program in small steps; object-oriented programming (especially in combination with application frameworks) makes such incremental development possible in quite an effortless way.

Design a Little, Implement a Little, Test a Little

It is recommended to design only as much as necessary and then to try to gain some experience with the results accomplished thus far. Only when the parts developed thus far seem promising, should the remaining parts be designed in the light of the insights gained during the experiments with the present subsystem. The following guidelines give some hints as to how incremental design can be accomplished in real projects.

- *Break the problem into small pieces.* Try to separate the program into pieces that can be designed and implemented as independently of one another as possible. Low-level data structures and operations, graphical objects and application-specific operations are typical examples of separable problem domains.

- *Use an application framework* to implement an "empty program" and then extend that program; that is, start with the overall structure in order to get a feeling of what the program will look like when it is finished, and then add new features step by step.

- *Temporarily use existing classes* as substitutes for classes that will be inserted later. For example, a simple graphical object from the library (such as a rectangle) may serve as a stand-in for a specific view of part of your model.

- *Use abstract classes* to describe varieties of objects. Start with a single descendant of an abstract class to check whether it works correctly and then develop the other variants.
- *Start with simple visual representations* that can be implemented easily. Enhance your application with color and other fancy properties only when the general operation and the user interface of the program have been tested.

7.4   Designing with Prototypes

Until now, only general guidelines have been advanced that can be used in the development of any object-oriented program. The special properties of prototypes add new facets to these guidelines that will be discussed in this section.

The most relevant difference between classes and prototypes is that prototypes are existing objects. This means that a static description does not suffice if a prototype is to be developed. One must also be consider how the prototypical object itself should look. It is important in this respect that a new prototype be viewed as a *black box*. One should first try to investigate the way in which the prototype will be used before trying to define its behavior and content. The following list differentiates prototypes according to their typical use within programs and illustrates these kinds of prototypes by means of examples taken from the Omega library.

- *Template prototypes* are primarily used for the creation of new objects. This kind is the most frequently used sort of prototype. A template prototype is rarely used as it is, but is normally used only as the source of a copying operation. The initial state of such a prototype must be designed such that only small changes must be applied to copies derived from it. For that purpose, special methods must be provided that can be used to adapt the state of copies to particular needs. For example, the Rectangle prototype (see Section 6.5.5 *Elementary Images*) is initialized as an empty rectangle with the line width 1, the pen color black, and the fill color white. A set of methods is provided to change all these properties.
- *Tool prototypes* are one-of-a-kind prototypes that are used as they are. They bear more resemblance to modules than to classes. They normally only provide a set of operations, but do not have a particular state. Examples of such prototypes are Arbiter (Section 6.6.2 *Event Handlers*), Mouse (Section 6.8.1 *Mouse*) and Workspace (Section 6.8.3 *Workspace*).
- *Abstract prototypes* define the properties of their descendants. They are not normally used to create new objects by cloning but rather to create

new prototypes by deriving from them[8]. Abstract prototypes have a *partial state* that is automatically inherited (i.e., copied) to prototypes derived from them. Examples of abstract prototypes are Collection (Section 6.4.5 *Collection*), Image (Section 6.5.3 *Image*) and, of course, Object (Section 6.2 *Object Protocol*).

- *Traits prototypes* are a mixture of tool prototypes and abstract prototypes. In Self, they are used to define the common behavior of a group of objects; delegation is used to inherit from them. In Omega, abstract prototypes (such as Event; Section 6.6.1 *Events*) and tool prototypes (such as Arbiter; Section 6.6.2 *Event Handlers*) take the role of traits prototypes.
- *Pool prototypes* are used as collections of global objects. They provide a set of variables that are of general use throughout an entire system. In Self and Kevo, special objects lobby and Root are used for this purpose. The Omega library does not contain pure pool prototypes; only some prototypes provide global objects in addition to their regular purpose. Examples of such prototypes are Color and Cursor (see below).

Regardless of the kind of prototype, the following activities are part of a prototype's design:

- The *meaning of the prototypical object* itself must be determined. Examples of such specifications are:
  - Font represents the system's default font.
  - Color represents the color *black*.
  - Mouse implements the physical mouse attached to the computer.
  - File is an anonymous empty file.
  - Image is an abstraction; it is not useful by itself.
- The prototype's *typical use* must be specified according to the categories listed above.
- When a prototype constitutes a specific object of the type it represents, other useful *variants* of the prototype should be determined (e.g. FontFamily.times, Color.red, and Real.pi).
- The *default state* of the prototype should be specified in an abstract way, for example:
  - Cluster is an empty vertical collection of left-aligned panes.
  - Dot is a black spot at the position 0@0, 1 pixel wide and tall.
- The *methods* available to modify the state of a prototype must be defined.
- The *semantics of the messages* copy and "=" must be specified. This is particularly important, as copying is the only way in which a client can create a new instance of the prototype.

---

[8]   Nevertheless, some abstract prototypes may be fully functional. For example, Container (Section 6.4.1 *Container*) is used within the Omega library to store untyped low-level data structures.

Of course, all these variants should be documented when the development of the prototype has been finished, as they constitute part of the prototype's protocol. The following example shows how this could look for the prototype Cursor.

1. *Meaning:*
   Cursor represents the default arrow cursor: ➤

2. *Typical uses:*
   Cursor has three different uses:
   – Template: to construct new cursors (Cursor copy, Cursor clone).
   – Tool: to display the default cursor (Cursor use).
   – Pool: to access other cursor forms (e.g., Cursor.cross).

3. *Variants:*
   There are five variants of Cursor, which differ only in their shape. The following variants are available:
   – Cursor.cross: +
   – Cursor.iBeam: ⌶
   – Cursor.plus: ✛
   – Cursor.watch: ⌚

4. *Default state:*
   Cursor is a bit pattern of size 16x16, preset with the default cursor (see 1).

5. *Adaptation messages:*
   The messages atx:y:put:, setx:y:, clearx:y:, invertx:y: can be used to modify the cursor's bit image. The message hotSpot: can be used to define the reference point of the cursor.

6. *Semantics of copy:*
   The message copy has the same meaning as clone; it creates a new cursor with identical shape and the same reference point.

7. *Semantics of "=":*
   The message "=" returns true only when two cursors have the same shapes and reference points.

8. Final Words of Advice

This chapter reviews some of the significant aspects of object-oriented programming. It contains a collection of general hints and warnings that may prove useful in the daily confrontation with objects.

8.1   Object-Oriented Programming – When and How?

Object-oriented programming undoubtedly has a lot of advantages that can considerably reduce the time and effort required to implement software products. But is it a universal technique that can be applied to *all* kinds of problems? Or are there certain problem domains that are better tackled with conventional programming techniques? This question often gives rise to discussions among computer scientists. As there is no general consensus about how widely object-oriented programming should be used to solve problems in the field, it is not possible to give an answer that will please everyone. The purpose of this section is to give an impression of the strengths and the weaknesses of object-oriented programming. It is up to the reader to decide whether and to what extent objects should be used in a particular project.

One of the most popular applications of object-oriented programming is the construction of interactive event-driven programs by means of application frameworks. There is no doubt that programs written in this way are more flexible and extendable and can be developed much faster than equivalent conventional programs. This technique is well understood, and thousands of programs have already been developed in this way. It is therefore quite safe to climb on this sort of object-oriented band-wagon. However, it is not clear whether only the top levels of an application should be constructed with objects. The following points should be considered when objects are to be used in a certain problem domain:

- Objects are great for simulating things in the real world. In fact, object-oriented programming has its roots in the area of simulation. Simula [Dahl 1966] was one of the first object-oriented programming languages.
- Dynamic binding and the memory management required for the allocation and destruction of objects can decrease the efficiency of a program. Objects may therefore not be suited to certain time-critical applications. This aspect is discussed in more detail in the following section.
- A certain memory overhead is involved when many objects are created dynamically. Moreover, method tables and (directly and indirectly) imported library classes require additional memory that may not be available in some environments.
- There are many problem domains for which well-known conventional techniques exist. In such cases, the design of an object-oriented program may turn out to be much harder than a simple "reuse" of an already established method.
- Some problems are so simple that an object-oriented solution would mean cracking a nut with a sledge-hammer.

- The contents of a class library can greatly influence what parts of a program are best implemented by means of objects. For example, a library supporting complex numbers may lead to an object-oriented solution of certain technical applications, whereas the presence of classes for data base access can ease the modelling of real-world data in commercial areas.
- Classes do not only reduce complexity; they also add a certain amount of new complexity to a program. The abstraction has to be understood, and the names, parameters and effects of messages must be learned.

Objects are definitely a good choice when different yet similar "things" are to be managed by a program or when flexibility and extensibility are important criteria. Change propagation is another feature of object-oriented systems that can be a determining factor in the decision about whether objects should be used.

Hybrid languages allow conventional and object-oriented techniques to be mixed. They make it possible to use objects within procedures and to use conventional data structures and procedures within objects. It is, however, difficult to decide which parts should be implemented conventionally and which parts should be designed in a purely object-oriented fashion.

In the author's opinion, there is almost no area where objects cannot improve the quality of software. Objects constitute abstractions of otherwise complex data, they provide a clear interface to clients and can be extended and used in many different contexts. It should therefore be attempted to use objects in as many places as possible.

.2 Efficiency Considerations

One of the reasons why conventional programming is proposed in some areas is that object-oriented programs are often considered inefficient. The following points, in particular, are often used as arguments against object-oriented programming:

- *Dynamic binding* takes place at run time. More instructions are needed to find the proper method than in a simple procedure call.

    This is correct, but the effects of dynamic binding on the performance of a program are negligible. Compilers for object-oriented languages use very efficient techniques to determine the method for a message. Normally, only three or four additional instructions are needed to implement a message send. Other factors (such as parameter passing and the setup of the call chain) cost much more.

- *Objects are dynamic data structures*. The allocation of memory takes time, and access to objects always requires an indirection via a pointer.

This is true. The allocation of many objects and indirect access to objects can indeed decrease the efficiency of a program. Although the same effect is encountered in conventional programs using dynamic data structures, object-oriented programs use dynamic data more intensely.

- *Garbage collection* costs more than explicit deallocation of obsolete data structures.

  This is also true, but automatic garbage collectors are much better than programmers at determining which objects are obsolete and which are not. Systems with garbage collectors are therefore much more reliable than those with explicit deallocation of data structures.

- *Instance variables are accessed via messages*. The execution of a method is needed to retrieve or change the value of an instance variable.

  This is only true for languages that do not support the specification of public instance variables, such as Smalltalk. And even then, the time required to access an instance variable via a message is a small price for the safety and abstraction gained by information hiding. By the way, this indirect access is not specific to object-oriented programming; the same effect is encountered in conventional programs that use modules and abstract data structures to encapsulate private data.

- *Pure object-oriented languages* are less efficient than hybrid or conventional languages.

  This is wrong. It is in general incorrect to speak of an inefficient *language*, as it is usually the *compiler* that determines the quality of the generated code. It is, however, possible that a language contains elements that are inherently inefficient. For example, Smalltalk requires dynamic binding even with elementary data types, thus forcing the compiler to generate message sends. This is the reason why elementary data types were defined as monomorphic in Omega.

- *The use of library classes* leads to more indirection than necessary. Many methods send several messages to other objects. It is much more efficient to directly include the necessary code within the respective method.

  It is true that class libraries are used more intensely in object-oriented programs than procedure or module libraries in conventional programs. However, the classes of a library are normally highly optimized. Delegation of an operation to an object of a library class is therefore often cheaper than a "hand-made" implementation.

The conclusion of these arguments is that object-oriented programs can in fact be slower than equivalent conventional programs. However, the loss in speed can often only be measured in milliseconds. In an interactive program, the user will scarcely notice excessive response times. On the other hand, the gain in flexibility and extensibility by far outweighs the loss in efficiency.

Is is recommended to disregard efficiency considerations as far as possible during the design of an object-oriented program. The first concern should be to construct a well-structured and reliable program. If the program turns out to be too slow, it is best to initially isolate those parts that are responsible for the inefficiency. A profiler (see Section 4.11.5 *The Profiler*) can provide invaluable hints in this process. When the culprit has been found, it should first be attempted to find a better algorithm without abandoning the object-oriented overall design. Only when that fails should a conventional solution of the relevant part be considered.

8.3   The Influence of the Programming Language

Programming languages are not just vehicles to transform a design into a running program. They also have an immense influence on the way in which a programmer thinks [Rechenberg 1990]. As the programming language is normally known before the design of a program starts, certain features of the language (or the absence thereof) naturally have an impact on the design. This is particularly the case with object-oriented languages, as they differ in many important aspects from each other. The following list illustrates some typical influences of selected languages.

- *Smalltalk* is mainly distinguished by pure object-orientedness and the lack of static type information. Variable names are often chosen such that they express the class of the object they are supposed to refer to (such as aView). Implementation inheritance is used in the design of a class hierarchy, as there are no static compatibility rules that need to be observed in assignments of object references to variables. Class objects are used for object creation and class variables represent global state. Block objects are sometimes used to modify the behavior of objects. Objects are not deallocated explicitly, as they are automatically cleaned up by a garbage collector.
- *C++* is primarily seen as an extension of C. C constructs are therefore often dominant in C++ programs. Non-virtual methods and inline methods are used to avoid dynamic binding where efficiency is deemed crucial. Static objects are used where dynamic allocation and deallocation of objects is not desired. Operator and function overloading are used to simplify the formulation of frequently needed operations. The absence of garbage collection is partially compensated for by means of constructors and destructors. Visibility attributes and friend classes are used to govern the access rights to variables and methods.
- *Eiffel* is characterized by the presence of multiple inheritance, genericity, assertions, exception handling and garbage collection. Multiple inheritance is frequently used in order to reuse as much code as possible, and

genericity is used to create variants of classes. "Features" are redefined and renamed in subclasses in order to avoid clashes resulting from multiple inheritance. Pre- and post-conditions, assertions and invariants are used to specify the protocol of classes, and exception handling is used to deal with violations of such conditions.

- *Self* is distinguished by pure object-orientedness with prototypes and delegation and by the lack of dynamic type information. No distinction is made between methods and instance variables. Parent slots are used for sharing properties, and special traits objects are devised in order to define the common behavior of groups of objects. Assignable slots are used to dynamically change the inheritance of objects. New "classes" are created either by constructing new prototypes from scratch or by cloning an object and applying individual modifications to it.
- *Omega* is characterized by pure object-orientedness with prototypes, static typing, genericity and monomorphic types. Prototypes are created interactively and then used for the generation of new objects. Abstract prototypes describe common protocols. Genericity is used for defining the elements of collections. Visibility attributes and write-protection are used to specify access rights to variables. Shared variables are used to implement global state. Objects are not deallocated explicitly, as they are automatically cleaned up by a garbage collector.

The only thing the programming languages listed above have in common is that all of them meet the basic requirements for object-oriented programming by supporting polymorphism, dynamic binding and inheritance, but they differ notably in *how* these requirements are fulfilled. As exemplified by the above list, developers that use different languages will take a significantly different attitude in solving the same problem.

The different properties of programming languages give rise to the question whether there is such a thing as an ideal universal language that …
… is easy to learn and comprehend,
… covers as many aspects of object-oriented programming as possible,
… allows the construction of reliable software, and
… does not prohibit the generation of efficient code.
There is no easy answer to this question, as the adequateness of a programming language cannot be measured. It is primarily a matter of taste which language is considered best. However, the following points should prove useful in the selection of an object-oriented language:

- *Pureness:* The language should be purely object-oriented. This is particularly important for beginners, as pure languages enable the developer to concentrate on the essentials of object-oriented programming. In fact, they virtually enforce a plain object-oriented style, as they provide no other mechanisms for the construction of programs. A pure object-oriented language thus makes it easier to get acquainted with "object-oriented thinking".

- *Simplicity:* Program development is already hard enough; the language should not complicate it more than necessary. Languages suffering from "featurism" are hard to comprehend in all their details; the more elements a language provides, the harder it is for the developer to decide which one to use in a particular situation. Another advantage of simplicity is that languages with only a few basic concepts are normally accompanied by a library that enhances the language. The use of such a language thus encourages the developer to explore the library, which in turn leads to a better object-oriented programming style.
- *Static typing:* Programming errors should be detected as early as possible. A statically typed language forces the developer to explicitly declare the intended purpose of variables and messages and thus enables the compiler to check their correct usage. This is particularly important for applications that must meet high standards of quality. Another aspect of static typing is that it provides additional information for the compiler that can be used to generate more efficient code.
- *Garbage collection:* Object-oriented programs generate a lot of objects at run time. Many of them are only used temporarily, others are used throughout the entire execution of a program, and some even survive the programs that created them. As objects may be referred to from many different places, it is extremely hard to determine when an object can be safely deleted. Automatic storage reclamation by a garbage collector is therefore a must for a programming language that conforms to the state of the art.

8.4 Possible Pitfalls

Object-oriented programming provides useful features for the construction of flexible and extensible programs, but it is exactly these features that can make object-oriented programs hard to understand. This is already true for the basic properties of object-oriented languages:

- *Polymorphism* allows the association of objects of many different classes with a single variable. It is therefore not possible to determine the dynamic type of a variable by a mere static inspection of the source text [Ponder 1992].
- *Dynamic binding* determines the method to be executed at run time. In conjunction with polymorphism, dynamic binding makes it impossible to statically tell which operations will be executed in response to a message.

- *Inheritance* distributes the functionality of a class over several classes, as part (generally, even most) of a class' methods are inherited from its ancestors. In order to understand a class, it is first necessary to understand its superclass.

In addition to these general aspects, a typical object-oriented programming style is readily distinguishable by its collaboration of objects and excessive reuse of existing classes. Many methods are very short but nevertheless hard to understand, as they make use of delegation to accomplish their task. Understanding an object-oriented program is therefore about grasping the interconnections among objects rather than just understanding the workings of individual classes.

As if that weren't enough, some programming languages contribute considerably to the complexity of object-oriented programs by providing a vast variety of ways in which classes can be constructed and objects can be used. The following list shows some typical problems of object-oriented programming in general and some languages in particular. This list is by no means complete, but it should at least provide some general hints on how common errors can be avoided.

- *Cloning and copying:* Cloning creates an object with exactly the same contents as the original it was derived from. Note that the instance variables of both the original and the copy refer to the same objects (see the next point). Copying creates an object that is "similar" to its original. There is, however, no definition of "similarity" in this context. The copy and the original may be independent of each other and they may share certain properties. In order to avoid surprising results, copy operations should always be defined such that all objects owned by an object are copied as well. Consequently, clients should always copy objects rather than cloning them.

- *References and identity:* Objects do not contain other objects, but rather refer to other objects. This means that changes to on object via a variable *x* can have an influence on several other objects as well. This is intentional in some circumstances but can also lead to inadvertent modification of the semantics of objects.

- *Equality:* It is sometimes difficult to decide whether or not two objects are to be considered equal. For example, arrays of objects may be treated as equal when they refer to the same (i.e., identical) objects or when they refer to "equal" objects. Things get even more complicated when an array contains a reference to yet another array. In such a case, the definition of equality may become recursive. During the design of a class one should consider carefully under which circumstances two objects of that class shall be treated as equal or not. In many cases, intuition and the simulation of typical scenarios can provide a proper definition of equality.

- *The desire to know everything:* Humans tend to be curious. Programmers are no exception in this respect; it is only natural to want to know how exactly a certain part of a program works. However, polymorphism and dynamic binding hamper the understanding of certain details as once acquired knowledge may not be true under different circumstances. Instead of digging into the details of used objects, it is therefore recommended to stick to interface specifications as far as possible. This is particularly important when certain operations are delegated to other objects. The client should rely on the abstract protocol of the class, and the "server" must make sure to satisfy this protocol. Of course, static typing is very useful to define a protocol and let the compiler check the proper use of objects.

- *Self sends and infinite recursion:* It is a common technique to split large methods into smaller pieces and to use self sends to other methods in order to accomplish a given task. It is, however, important to define which methods are considered basic and which others are constructed on this basis, as self sends can otherwise easily result in endless indirect recursion. This is particularly critical when methods are overridden. For example, the Image message drawFrame is sent to self within the method draw (see Section 6.5.3 *Image*). When a descendant overrides drawFrame such that it uses self draw, the methods draw and drawFrame will repeatedly call each other until a "stack overflow" exception is raised.

- *Non-virtual methods:* C++ allows the definition of statically bound ("non-virtual") methods. The effect of the corresponding message is predetermined statically; although it is possible to override such a method, the *static* type of the receiver will be used to determine the operation to be performed. It is therefore advisable to renounce this questionable optimization technique and instead declare all messages as virtual[1].

- *Unexpected objects:* In languages without static typing (in particular, Smalltalk and Self) methods are always dynamically searched for when a message is sent. It is therefore possible to send a message to an object that will not be understood at run time. This can be particularly nasty in the case of method arguments, as the clients of a class cannot generally be trusted to pass only arguments of the proper class. It is therefore a good idea to check the expected class of objects in critical situations.

- *Static objects:* C++ and Oberon-2 allow the declaration of static objects. This means that the compiler already reserves memory space for static object variables. A consequence of this is that such variables cannot be assigned objects of other classes, as they may require more memory space

---

[1]   Unfortunately, non-virtual methods are the default in C++. It would have been less error-prone to define methods as virtual per default and to let the programmer explicitly declare a method as non-virtual in the unlikely case that the costs of dynamic binding are unacceptable.

than is provided by the variable[2]. Accordingly, polymorphism is not possible with statically declared variables. Even though static objects have some useful applications, dynamically allocated objects should be the normal case in object-oriented programs.

- *Type casts:* It is sometimes necessary to widen the view of objects by "assuring" the compiler that a variable actually refers to an object of a more specific class than determined by the variable's static type. Such type casts are extremely dangerous, as messages to objects of the wrong class can have disastrous effects. It is therefore absolutely essential to make sure that the variable will in fact refer to an object of the indicated class. Unfortunately, C++ does not provide any mechanisms to check the class of an object at run time. Utmost care on the side of the programmer is therefore required in order to avoid unpredictable behavior of a program. By the way, it is generally a sign of bad style when a program contains many type casts, as the use of such explicit conversions to specific types can severely hamper the reusability of a class.

- *Independent classes:* Some programming languages support the construction of new classes without inheriting from existing classes (see Section 2.10.1 *Single-Rooted and Multi-Rooted Class Hierarchies*). When using this facility, the developer should be aware that objects of such an independent class are inherently incompatible with variables of other types and that they do not conform to a common protocol. It is therefore suggested that a common root class be always used even when the programming language does not prescribe it.

- *Prototype corruption:* Carelessness can easily lead to prototypes whose contents are inadequate for the construction of new objects. It is therefore important to avoid references to prototypes and to use template prototypes (see Section 7.4 *Designing with Prototypes*) only for the creation of new objects. It is generally a good idea to provide an initialization method that can be used to restore the state of corrupted prototypes.

Some of the errors described above can be avoided by using programming conventions. It is also a good idea to record all kinds of errors ever made. Such notes can provide substantial help in the development of future projects.

It is also generally recommended to use a programming environment to organize the classes of a project and to keep track of the various relations among objects. Examples of such environments are ET++PE [Gamma 1989], Dogma [Sametinger 1991], Sniff [Bischofberger 1992a] and, of course, the Smalltalk environment [Goldberg 1984].

---

[2] In Oberon, such assignments are allowed, but the additional instance variables that do not fit into the space provided by the variable are truncated. Such assignments are therefore not truly polymorphic, but rather involve a mutation of objects. One exception is the passing of static objects as reference parameters, where no truncation takes place.

8.5 The Spirit of Object-Oriented Programming

Object-orientedness is intruding more and more often into other areas of computer science. The unique properties of objects make them ideal for many different purposes. Current research focuses on distributed and concurrent systems as well as on object-oriented databases, but objects are also being used successfully in special application domains, such as process automation and compiler construction.

But what actually makes object-oriented programming so attractive? Object-orientedness has certainly become a mark of quality – if it's object-oriented, it must be good. This attitude though had almost brought object-oriented programming into disrepute, as all sorts of software products were marked object-oriented in order to profit from the reputation of objects. Fortunately, more and more people are becoming aware of what object-orientedness really means. Many respectable software companies now use object-oriented techniques in order to improve the quality and rationalize the development process of their products. But there is also a more emotional reason for using object-oriented programming: it's simply the appeal of doing something different and – *it's fun*.

Object-oriented programming is not a mystery. As repeatedly emphasized in the previous chapters, its essence can be summarized with the key words *abstraction*, *polymorphism*, *dynamic binding* and *inheritance*. Yet, it takes more to develop good object-oriented programs than just to know about these basic concepts. Rather, it is essential to develop an object-oriented way of *thinking*. Whereas conventional programming is characterized by thinking in operations on passive data, object-oriented programming focuses on the data and breathes life into them. Object-oriented thinking is determined by the following capabilities:

- Find the classes needed to solve a problem.
- Identify the responsibilities of classes.
- Determine collaborations among classes.
- Specify the interfaces of classes.
- Think ahead.
- Find abstractions.
- Reuse things that are already there.

You will definitely know you have become a *real* object-oriented programmer when you find yourself murmuring "Everything is an object", or – as an anonymous Smalltalk programmer expressed it –

"The World is an Object."

References

[Abbott 1983]   Abbott R. J.: *Program Design by Informal English Descriptions*; Comm. of the ACM, Vol 26, Nr 11, 1983

[Anderson 1992]   Anderson B.: *Ellie: a general, fine-grained, first-class, object-based language*; Journal of Object-oriented Programming, Vol. 5, Nr 2, 1992

[Apple 1985]   Apple Computer Inc.: *Inside Macintosh, Vol I*, Addison-Wesley, 1985

[Beck 1989]   Beck K., Cunningham W.: *A Laboratory for Teaching Object-Oriented Thinking*; Proc. of OOPSLA '89, 1989

[Bernat 1987]   Bernat A. P.: *ACTOR*; AI Expert, March 1987

[Bischofberger 1992] Bischofberger W., Pomberger G.: *Prototyping-oriented Software Development*; Springer, 1992

[Bischofberger 1992a] Bischofberger W.: *Sniff — A Pragmatic Approach to a C++ Programming Environment*; Proc. of USENIX C++ Conference, 1992

[Blaschek 1991]   Blaschek G.: *Type-Safe Object-Oriented Programming with Prototypes – The Concepts of Omega*; Structured Programming, Vol. 12/4, Springer, 1991

[Boar 1984]   Boar B.: *Application Prototyping*; John Wiley & Sons, 1984

[Booch 1991]   Booch G.: *Object-Oriented Design with Applications*; Benjamin/Cummings, 1991

[Borning 1981]   Borning A. H.: *The Programming Language Aspects of ThingLab, a Constraint-oriented Simulation Laboratory*; ACM Transactions on Programming Languages and Systems, Vol. 3, Nr 4, 1981

[Borning 1986]   Borning A. H.: *Classes versus Prototypes in Object-oriented Languages*; Proc. of ACM/IEEE Fall Joint Computer Conference, Nov. 1986

[Chambers 1989]   Chambers C., Ungar D., Lee E.: *An Efficient Implementation of SELF, a Dynamically-Typed Object-Oriented Language Based on Prototypes*; Proc. of OOPSLA '89, 1989

[Chambers 1991]   Chambers C., Ungar D.: *Making Pure Object-oriented Languages Practical*; Proc. of OOPSLA '91, 1991

[Connell 1989]   Connell J. L., Shafer L. B.: *Structured Rapid Prototyping*; Yourdon Press, Prentice Hall, 1989

[Coad 1990]   Coad P., Yourdon E.: *Object-Oriented Analysis*; Prentice Hall, 1990

[Cox 1986]   Cox B.: *Object-Oriented Programming: An Evolutionary Approach*; Addison-Wesley, 1986

[Dahl 1966]   Dahl O., Nygaard K.: *Simula – An Algol-based Simulation Language*; Comm. of the ACM, Vol. 9, Nr 9, 1966

[Digitalk 1988]   Digitalk Inc.: *Smalltalk/V Mac — Object-Oriented Programming System Tutorial and Programming Handbook*; Digitalk Inc., Los Angeles, CA, 1988

[Ellis 1990]   Ellis M. A., Stroustrup B.: *The Annotated C++ Reference Manual*; Addison-Wesley, 1990

[Floyd 1984]   Floyd C.: *A Systematic Look at Prototyping*; in: *Approaches to Prototyping*; Springer, 1984

[Gamma 1989]   Gamma E., Weinand A., Marty R.: *Integration of a Programming Environment into ET++ – A Case Study*; Proc. of ECOOP '91, Cambridge University Press, 1989.

[Goldberg 1983]   Goldberg A.: *Smalltalk-80: The Interactive Programming Environment*; Addison-Wesley, 1984

[Goldberg 1984]   Goldberg A. and Robson D.: *Smalltalk-80: The Language and its Implementation*; Addison-Wesley, 1983

[Halbert 1988]   Halbert D.: *Types vs. Prototypes*; Proc. of OOPSLA '88, 1988

[Heitz 1988]   Heitz M.: *HOOD: A Hierarchical Object-Oriented Design Method*; Proc. of the Third German Ada Users Congress, Gesellschaft für Software Engineering, 1988

[Hölzle 1991]   Hölzle U., Chambers C.: Ungar D.: *Optimizing Dynamically-typed Object-oriented Languages with Polymorphic Inline Caches*; Proc. of ECOOP '91, Springer 1991

[Ingalls 1981]   Ingalls D. H. H.: *The Smalltalk Graphics Kernel*;
                      BYTE Vol. 6, Nr 8, 1981

[Johnson 1988]   Johnson R. E., Foote B.: *Designing Reusable Classes*;
                      Journal of Object-Oriented Programming, Vol. 1, Nr 2,
                      1988

[Krasner 1988]   Krasner G. E., Pope S. T.: *A Cookbook for Using the
                      Model-View-Controller Interface Paradigm in
                      Smalltalk-80*; Journal of Object-Oriented Programming,
                      Vol. 1, Nr 3, 1988

[Kristensen 1987]   Kristensen B. B. et al.: *The Beta Programming
                      Language*; in: Shriver B., Wegner P. (ed.): *Research
                      Directions in Object-oriented Programming*; MIT Press
                      1987

[LaLonde 1986]   LaLonde W. R., Thomas D. A., Pugh J. R.: *An
                      Exemplar Based Smalltalk*; Proc. of OOPSLA '86, 1986

[LaLonde 1989]   LaLonde W. R.: *Designing Families of Data Types
                      using Exemplars*; ACM Transactions on Programming
                      Languages and Systems, Vol. 11, Nr 2, 1989

[Lieberman 1986]   Lieberman H.: *Using Prototypical Objects to Implement
                      Shared Behavior in Object-oriented Systems*; Proc. of
                      OOPSLA '86, 1986

[Meyer 1987]   Meyer B.: *Reusability: The Case for object-Oriented
                      Design*; IEEE Software, Vol. 4, Nr 2, 1987

[Meyer 1988]   Meyer B.: *Object-oriented Software Construction*;
                      Prentice Hall, 1988

[Mössenböck 1991]   Mössenböck H., Wirth N.: *The Programming Language
                      Oberon-2*; Structured Programming, Vol. 12, Nr 4,
                      1991

[Mössenböck 1993]   Mössenböck H.: *Object-Oriented Programming in
                      Oberon-2*; Springer, 1993

[Parnas 1972]   Parnas D. L.: *On the Criteria to be Used in
                      Decompositing Systems into Modules*; Comm. of the
                      ACM Vol. 15, Nr 12, 1972

[Pomberger 1986]   Pomberger G.: *Software Engineering and Modula-2*;
                      Prentice Hall, 1986

[Pomberger 1991]   Pomberger G. et al.: *Prototyping-Oriented Software
                      Development – Concepts and Tools*; Structured
                      Programming, Vol. 12, Nr 1, 1991

[Ponder 1992]   Ponder C., Bush B.: *Polymorphism Considered
                      Harmful*; Sigplan Notices, Vol. 27, Nr 6, 1992

[Pree 1990]   Pree W.: *DICE – An Object-Oriented Tool for Rapid
                      Prototyping*; Proc. of TOOLS Pacific '90, Sydney, 1990

[Rechenberg 1990]   Rechenberg P.: *Programming Languages as Thought
                      Models*; Structured Programming, Vol. 11, Nr 3, 1990

[Reiser 1992]   Reiser M., Wirth N.: *Programming in Oberon – Steps
                      Beyond Pascal and Modula*; Addison-Wesley, 1992

[Rumbaugh 1991]   Rumbaugh J., et al.: *Object-Oriented Modeling and
                      Design*; Prentice Hall, 1991

[Sametinger 1991]   Sametinger J.: *DOgMA: A Tool for the Documentation
                      and Maintenance of Software Systems*; Report, Dept. of
                      Software Engineering, Johannes-Kepler-Universität
                      Linz, 1991

[Saunders 1989]   Saunders J. H.: *A Survey of Object-Oriented
                      programming Languages*; Journal of Object-Oriented
                      programming, Vol. 1, Nr 6, 1989

[Schmucker 1986]   Schmucker K. J.: *Object-Oriented Programming for the
                      Macintosh*; Hayden, 1986

[Sommerville 1985]   Sommerville I.: *Software Engineering*; Addison-
                      Wesley, 2nd edition, 1985

[Stein 1987]   Stein L. A.: *Delegation is Inheritance*; Proc. of
                      OOPSLA '87, 1987

[Stein 1988]   Stein L. A., Lieberman H., Ungar D.: *A Shared View of
                      Sharing: The Treaty of Orlando*; In Kim W.,
                      Lochowsky F. (ed.): *Object-oriented Concepts,
                      Applications and Databases*; Addison-Wesley, 1988

[Stroustrup 1986]   Stroustrup B.: *The C++ Programming Language*;
                      Addison-Wesley, 1986

[Taivalsaari 1992]   Taivalsaari A.: *Kevo – a prototype-based object-
                      oriented language based on concatenation and module
                      operations*; Technical Report LACIR 92–02; University
                      of Victoria, B.C., Canada, 1992

[Ungar 1987]   Ungar D., Smith R. B.: *Self: The Power of Simplicity*;
                    Proc. of OOPSLA '87, 1987

[Ungar 1991]   Ungar D., Chambers C., Chang B-W., Hölzle U.:
                    Organizing Programs Without Classes; Lisp and
                    Symbolic Computation, Vol. 4, Nr 3, 1991

[Wasserman 1990]   Wasserman A. I. et al.: *The Object-Oriented Structured
                    Design Notation for Software Design Representation*;
                    IEEE Computer, Vol. 23, Nr 3, 1990

[Wegner 1990]   Wegner P.: *Concepts and Paradigms of Object-oriented
                    Programming*; ACM OOPS Messenger, Vol. 1, Nr 1,
                    1990

[Weinand 1988]   Weinand A., Gamma E. Marty R.: *ET++ – An Object-
                    oriented Application Framework in C++*; Proc. of
                    OOPSLA '88, 1988

[Weinand 1989]   Weinand A., Gamma E., Marty R.: *Design and
                    Implementation of ET++, a Seamless Object-oriented
                    Application Framework*; Structured Programming Vol.
                    10, Nr 2, 1989

[Wharton 1983]   Wharton R. M.: *A Note on Types and Prototypes*; ACM
                    SIGPLAN Notices, Vol. 18, Nr 12, 1983

[Wilson 1990]   Wilson D.A.: *Class Diagrams: A Tool for Design,
                    Documentation, and Testing*; Journal of Object-
                    Oriented Programming, Vol. 2, Nr 5, 1990

[Wirfs-Brock 1989] Wirfs-Brock R., Wilkerson B.: *Object-Oriented
                    Design: A Responsibility-Driven Approach*; Proc. of
                    OOPSLA '89, 1989

[Wirfs-Brock 1990] Wirfs-Brock R., Wilkerson B., Wiener L.: *Designing
                    Object-Oriented Software*; Prentice Hall, 1990

[Wirfs-Brock 1990a] Wirfs-Brock R., Johnson R. E.: *Surveying Current
                    Research in Object-Oriented Design*; Comm of the
                    ACM, Vol. 23, Nr 9, 1990

[Wirth 1971]   Wirth N.: *Program Development by Stepwise
                    Refinement*; Comm. of the ACM, Vol. 14, Nr 4, 1971

[Wirth 1985]   Wirth N.: *Programming in Modula-2*; Springer, 1985

Figures

3 Prototypes

4 The Programming Language Omega

5 Libraries and Frameworks

6   The Omega Library

7   Object-Oriented Design

A The Syntax of Omega

Character Set

decimalDigit	=	"0"	"1"	"2"	"3"	"4"	"5"	"6"	"7"	"8"	"9" .
hexDigit	=	decimalDigit	"a"	"b"	"c"	"d"	"e"	"f" .
letter	=	"a"	"b"	"c"	"d"	"e"	"f"	"g"	"h"	"i"
			"j"	"k"	"l"	"m"	"n"	"o"	"p"	"q"	"r"
			"s"	"t"	"u"	"v"	"w"	"x"	"y"	"z" .
capitalLetter	=	"A"	"B"	"C"	"D"	"E"	"F"	"G"	"H"	"I"
			"J"	"K"	"L"	"M"	"N"	"O"	"P"	"Q"	"R"
			"S"	"T"	"U"	"V"	"W"	"X"	"Y"	"Z" .
separatorChar	=	"'"	"\""	"(" | ")"	"["	"]"	"{"	"}"	";"	","	"." .
opChar	=	"+"	"–"	"*"	"/"	"\\"	"="	"<"	">"	"&"	"|"
			"#"	"@"	"$"	"%"	"~"	"^"	":"	"?"	"!" .

Syntactic Symbols

assignmentOp	=	":="	":?=" .
parenthesis	=	"(" | ")" .
bracket	=	"["	"]" .
brace	=	"{"	"}" .
separator	=	";"	","	"." .

Identifiers and Keywords

identifier	=	letter { letter	capitalLetter	digit } .
ptIdentifier	=	capitalLetter { letter	capitalLetter	digit } .
declaredIdent	=	identifier ":" .
initIdent	=	identifier "::=" .

Literals

integer	=	decimalInteger
			base hexDigit { hexDigit } .
decimalInteger	=	decimalDigit { decimalDigit } .
base	=	decimalInteger "r" .
real	=	decimalInteger "." decimalDigit { decimalDigit }
			[exponent] .

exponent	=	"e" ["+"	"–"] digit { digit } .
character	=	"'" (printableChar1	"'" "'") "'" .
printableChar1	=	*any printable character except* "'" .
string	=	""" { printableChar2	""" """ } """ .
printableChar2	=	*any printable character except* """ .
Literal	=	integer	real	character	string .

Operators

operator	=	opChar { opChar } .
opChar	=	"+"	"–"	"*"	"/"	"\"	"="	"<"	">"	"&"	"|"
		"#"	"@"	"$"	"%"	"~"	"^"	":"	"?"	"!" .

Types and Prototypes

Type	=	ptIdentifier ["{" Type "}"]
		"Same"
		"Parameter" .
Prototype	=	Type .

Message Definitions

MessageDef	=	UnaryDef
		BinaryDef
		KeywordDef .
UnaryDef	=	identifier	operator .
BinaryDef	=	operator Type .
KeywordDef	=	keyword Type { keyword Type } .

Methods

Method	=	[MethArguments] "[" Sequence "]" .
MethArguments	=	"{" ArgumentDecl { ";" ArgumentDecl } "}" .
ArgumentDecl	=	declaredIdent Type .
Sequence	=	Expression { ";" Expression } .

Expressions

Expression	=	ElementaryExpr
		MessageExpr
		CascadedExpr .

ElementaryExpr	=	Literal
	I	Prototype
	I	"self"
	I	Declaration
	I	Variable
	I	Assignment
	I	"(" Sequence ")"
	I	Block
	I	Action .
Declaration	=	declaredIdent Type [":=" Expression]
	I	initIdent Expression .
Variable	=	[ElementaryExpr "."] identifier .
Assignment	=	Variable (":=" I ":?=") Expression .
MessageExpr	=	UnaryExpr
	I	BinaryExpr
	I	KeywordExpr .
UnaryExpr	=	ElementaryExpr UnaryMsg
	I	UnaryExpr UnaryMsg .
UnaryMsg	=	[Parent] (identifier I operator) .
BinaryExpr	=	BinaryOperand BinaryMsg
	I	BinaryExpr BinaryMsg .
BinaryOperand	=	ElementaryExpr I UnaryExpr .
BinaryMsg	=	[Parent] operator BinaryOperand .
KeywordExpr	=	KeywordOperand KeywordMsg .
KeywordOperand	=	ElementaryExpr I UnaryExpr I BinaryExpr .
KeywordMsg	=	[Parent] keyword KeywordOperand { keyword KeywordOperand } .
Parent	=	"(" ptIdentifier ")" .
CascadedExpr	=	MessageExpr { "," Message }.
Message	=	UnaryMsg I BinaryMsg I KeywordMsg .
Block	=	"[" [Sequence] "]" .
Action	=	"{" ArgumentDecl "}" Block .

B The Omega Type Hierarchy

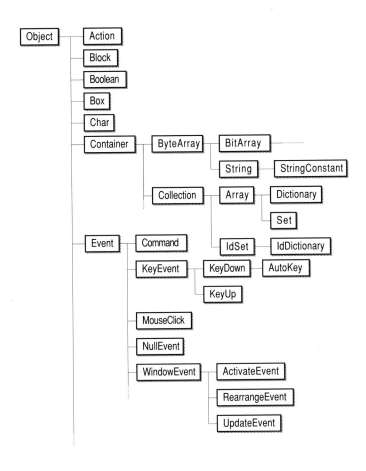

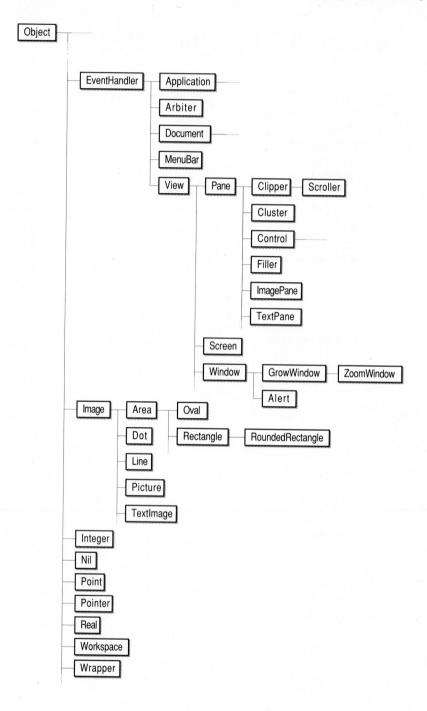

Index

Omega Demo Version

If you want to try programming in Omega yourself, you may want to check out the publicly available demo version of the Omega programming environment. The Omega system is currently available *only for Macintosh computers*. If you have access to Internet, you can use anonymous FTP to download the Omega system:

host name:	ftp.swe.uni-linz.ac.at
login name:	anonymous
password:	*any password*
directory:	/pub/omega

If you cannot use FTP, you can order a demo disk directly from the author. The contact address is:

Günther Blaschek
Johannes Kepler University Linz
Informatik / Software
Altenbergerstr. 69
A–4040 Linz
Austria

The author can also be reached via electronic mail at the following addresses:

gue@soft.uni-linz.ac.at
blaschek@jk.uni-linz.ac.at

Springer-Verlag
and the Environment

W̲e at Springer-Verlag firmly believe that an international science publisher has a special obligation to the environment, and our corporate policies consistently reflect this conviction.

W̲e also expect our business partners – paper mills, printers, packaging manufacturers, etc. – to commit themselves to using environmentally friendly materials and production processes.

T̲he paper in this book is made from low- or no-chlorine pulp and is acid free, in conformance with international standards for paper permanency.

Printing: Mercedesdruck, Berlin
Binding: Buchbinderei Lüderitz & Bauer, Berlin

REC